Evergreen Ash

UNDER THE SIGN OF NATURE: EXPLORATIONS IN ECOCRITICISM

Serenella Iovino, Kate Rigby, John Tallmadge, Editors

Michael P. Branch and SueEllen Campbell, Senior Advisory Editors

Evergreen Ash

ECOLOGY AND CATASTROPHE IN
OLD NORSE MYTH AND LITERATURE

Christopher Abram

University of Virginia Press
Charlottesville and London

University of Virginia Press
© 2019 by the Rector and Visitors of the University of Virginia
All rights reserved
Printed in the United States of America on acid-free paper

First published 2019

9 8 7 6 5 4 3 2 1

Library of Congress Cataloging-in-Publication Data
Names: Abram, Christopher, author.
Title: Evergreen ash : ecology and catastrophe in Old Norse myth
    and literature / Christopher Abram.
Description: Charlottesville : University of Virginia Press, [2019] |
    Series: Under the sign of nature : explorations in ecocriticism |
    Includes bibliographical references and index.
Identifiers: LCCN 2018041484 | ISBN 9780813942261 (cloth :
    alk. paper) | ISBN 9780813942278 (paperback : alk. paper) |
    ISBN 9780813942285 (e-book)
Subjects: LCSH: Old Norse literature—History and criticism. |
    Mythology, Norse. | Disasters in literature. | Apocalypse in
    literature. | Environmental disasters.
Classification: LCC PT7154 .A227 2019 | DDC 839/.609—dc23
LC record available at https://lccn.loc.gov/2018041484

Cover art: Skútustaðir, Northeastern Region, Iceland.
(imageBROKER/Alamy Stock Photo)

Contents

Acknowledgments

The seed that grew into this book was planted when Annika Lindskog invited me to contribute to a team-taught course on Nordic landscapes at University College London. I'm grateful to her for believing that Old Norse trees might be something our students might benefit from learning about and for starting me on the path that led me to ecocriticism. Another colleague at UCL, Claire Thomson, invited me to write up my thoughts on trees for a volume on Nordic naturecultures that she was planning. Although in the end I didn't manage to get my piece together for that book, some of the first words of what became *Evergreen Ash* were written for Claire, and I'm grateful to her for giving me that opportunity. I should also like to record with the utmost fondness my gratitude to the Department of Scandinavian Studies at UCL and my colleagues there: Margrethe Alexandroni, Michael Barnes, Karin Charles, the late Helena Forsås-Scott, Haki Antonsson, Helga Hlaðgerður Lúthersdóttir, Mary Hilson, Tom Lundskær-Nielsen, the late Thomas Munch-Petersen, Daisy Neijmann, Richard Perkins, Jakob Skougaard-Nielsen, and Marie Wells. Working with them was a privilege, and my time at UCL changed me and my work irrevocably and, I think, for the better.

When I moved to Notre Dame, I found to my delight another community of scholars whose support of both medieval studies and ecocriticism is wholehearted and sustaining. Special thanks for many, many acts of kindness go to Thomas Burman, Michelle Karnes, Kathryn Kerby-Fulton, Jesse Lander, Tim Machan, Kate Marshall, Valerie Sayers, John Sitter, and John Van Engen. I have been fortunate to have been able to think through some of this book's ideas with two groups of brilliant Notre Dame PhD students in a class called The (Un)Natural World in Medieval Literature, to whose curiosity, critical acumen, and openness to exploring new ways of thinking and reading I am much indebted: Mimi Ensley, Richard Fahey, Maj-Britt Frenze, Alexandra Hernandez, Emily Hirschmann, Leanne MacDonald, Angel Matos, Dan Murphy, Katie Osborn, Brian Santin, Becky West, and Jill Wharton in 2013; Patricia Bredar, Julian Dean, Margie Housley, Emily Mahan, Jake McGinnis,

Emily McLemore, Laura Ortiz Mercado, Carlos Arenas Pachecho, Logan Quigley, and Stacy Stavinski in 2017.

Above all the debts I owe to my colleagues at Notre Dame, however, looms my obligation to the peerless Interlibrary Loan and Document Delivery Department of the Hesburgh Library. Our library staff are a treasure, and I'm not sure whether I'd have managed to write this book without their help.

For assistance, friendship, and moral support during the period I was working on *Evergreen Ash* I am also grateful to Eleanor Barraclough, Michael Bintley, Lindy Brady, Richard Cole, Alison Finlay, Shaun Hughes, Mae Kilker, Rosalind Love, Robyn Malo, Mathias Nordvig, Heather O'Donoghue, Carl Phelpstead, Chris Scheirer, and Elaine Treharne. Charlotte Parkin and Alice Tyrrell looked after me while I spent a semester at Notre Dame's global gateway in London. I was lucky enough to be able to present work in progress from this book at seminars at Harvard, Oxford, and UCL, and I am grateful to Stephen Mitchell, Carolyne Larrington, and Richard North for their gracious invitations to those events.

I could not have been happier with the enthusiasm and care with which the University of Virginia Press has undertaken to publish this book. To the editors of the Under the Sign of Nature series, and especially to Boyd Zenner, I send my undying appreciation. Ruth Melville copyedited this book, brilliantly, and I'm grateful to her, too. Enid Zafran did a wonderful job with the index, and I am pleased to acknowledge the support of Notre Dame's Institute for Scholarship in the Liberal Arts in funding her work.

Very special thanks and much love go to my parents, Carl and Valerie Abram, and to my in-laws, Steve and Martha Mulligan. They could not have been more generous or kind.

But above all I am grateful to Amy Mulligan and our son, Henry. In the midst of her own book-writing travails, Amy has never been anything less than amazingly supportive of this project, and that support has been more important to me than I can adequately express here. She is a brilliant scholar, a wonderful mother, and a partner whose patience, care, and love I can hardly repay but only hope to emulate. As for Henry? He's just an awesome kid. This book is for both of them, with love.

Note on Texts, Translations, Spelling, and Pronunciation

I hope that *Evergreen Ash* will be of interest to readers beyond the community of Old Norse specialists. Accordingly, I have cited primary sources in English translation in the main body of this book, with the original-language texts presented in the endnotes.

The two most important sources for this investigation are the thirteenth-century Icelandic mythological compendia known as the Eddas. I cite the *Poetic Edda* from *Eddukvæði*, edited by Jónas Kristjánsson and Vésteinn Ólason and published in the Íslenzk fornrit series. My preferred translation of the *Poetic Edda* is Carolyne Larrington's, published by Oxford University Press. I refer throughout to the second edition of that work. Larrington's translation does not always accord with the Íslenzk fornrit edition, and I have at times found it necessary to alter her translation to follow more closely the base text I have been using. Such alterations are noted where they occur.

All citations from Snorri Sturluson's prose *Edda* are taken from Anthony Faulkes's three-volume edition, published by the Viking Society for Northern Research. Faulkes has also produced a single-volume translation of Snorri's work, which I cite here.

One of the challenges that face the writer of a book about Old Norse texts intended for an Anglophone audience is the lack of a standard protocol for rendering Norse names into English orthography. Old Norse uses several characters that are not employed in contemporary English, and translators have never been able to agree whether these letters should be transliterated by their closest phonetic equivalents or with letters that most closely resemble them visually. Thus one tends to see the name Óðinn, the chief of the gods, given as either Othin or Odin in English translations. For the sake of accuracy and consistency I have chosen to retain the original Old Norse spelling of place- and personal names, given in the nominative case, throughout this book. While this approach to names has distinct advantages, it does run the risk of making them less easily pronounceable for readers unfamiliar with Old Norse. A rough-and-ready guide to the pronunciation of these characters—based closely on the way Modern Icelandic is spoken today—follows.

Consonants are pronounced much as in English with important exceptions of the characters *eth* <ð> and *thorn* <þ>: both of these letters represent sounds that are rendered in English as <th>. *Eth* <ð> occurs in the middle and at the ends of words, and is pronounced as in English "breathe." There is a subtle difference between this sound and the unvoiced *thorn* <þ>, which resembles the *th* sound at the start of "think." In the normalized orthography of the Old Norse editions used in this book, *thorn* only occurs at the beginning of words.

The Old Norse vowel system is more complex, with each vowel possessing a short and long variant—long vowels are indicated by an acute accent. There are also several characters that we do not normally use in English that are deployed to represent diphthongs. Nobody knows exactly how Old Norse was pronounced: the following guide is based upon modern Icelandic phonology.

á	Like English n*ow*
é	Like English *yes*
í	Like English *ea*t
ó	Like English r*oa*m
ú	Like French b*ou*che
ý	Like English *ea*t
æ/œ	Like English m*y*
ø/ǫ	Like French p*eu*r (this sound may also be represented by ö)
au	Like French *œi*l
ei/ey	Like English b*ay*

Evergreen Ash

Prologue

Ash

THE ANGLICAN BURIAL SERVICE, as laid out in the Book of Common Prayer, commits the body of the departed to the ground with the words "earth to earth, ashes to ashes, dust to dust." This phrase, present in Thomas Cranmer's original prayer book of 1549,[1] draws on Genesis 3:19: "In the sweat of thy face shalt thou eat bread, till thou return unto the ground; for out of it wast thou taken: for dust thou art, and unto dust shalt thou return." There are no ashes in God's prescription for the fallen Adam's fate, but at some point the phrase must have been expanded, possibly in order to take account of those few Christians whose bodies were (in exceptional circumstances) cremated—or who might have died in an accidental fire, leaving no conventional remains for burial.[2] Cremation was perceived as a distinctively pagan practice in medieval Europe; early Christians were much concerned that burning the corpse would prevent bodily resurrection on the Last Day. But this addition to the liturgy predates Cranmer: it translates a Latin formula—*terram terrae, cinerem cineri, pulverem pulveri*—found in a late medieval liturgical manual from Salisbury.[3] It is a peculiarly English phrase, even in Latin: it is found in no other church's burial rite, although it is related to the ritual bestowal of ashes upon supplicants on the first day of Lent, a practice that is almost universal across Western churches. It is also a rather curious idea, though little remarked upon: the Bible tells us clearly that Adam was made of dust, and to dust he will return. But how can a man be made out of *ash?* Of course, *cinerem cineri* could simply be intended as a euphonious but redundant complement to *terram terrae* and *pulverem pulveri*. Ash, however, is not quite like "earth" or "dust," both of which terms relate to the ground that supports life and receives the dead. Ash is lighter than either of the other substances, and more ethereal. It simply blows away. It is always a by-product of a destructive force. It is what is left after the substance of a thing has been through the flames. Although it has its uses in various situations—wood ash can be a beneficial soil additive because it lowers acidity—it has no nutritive value. Ash is not really part of the life cycle: it is a product of death. We can easily imagine ending up as ashes, but nothing comes from ash. Nothing *returns* to being ash.

Well—almost nothing. The power of the story of the Phoenix comes precisely from the bird's somehow achieving life out of the sterility—the utter deadness—of its previous incarnation's ashes. The Phoenix became an admirable symbol for Christ resurrected for precisely this reason: Christ's earthly incarnation was utterly annihilated; but he rose again, the same being reborn in the same form. The Phoenix burns almost to atoms; nothing of it is left but ash, in which nothing will grow. Nonetheless, out of nothing the Phoenix flames back into being.[4] Its triumph over death is the more complete for being figured as a fiery holocaust. To rise from the ashes is therefore to cheat death and to overturn the natural order of the world. But Christ and the Phoenix are exceptional. On this earth, life does not normally come out of ashes. Ash is an ending, not a beginning.

In thirteenth-century Iceland, Snorri Sturluson made this point in a passage describing the deeds of Alfǫðr (All-father), a deity of Snorri's own invention that combines a name and certain functions of the Norse god Óðinn with the nature and achievements of the Christian God: "But [Alfǫðr's] greatest work is that he made man and gave him a soul that shall live and never perish though the body decay to dust or burn to ashes."[5] With its anticipatory echo of the wording that would find its way into the Book of Common Prayer, Snorri's contrasting of the soul's eternal life with the transitory existence of the body is a conventional Christian move. At the same time, it confirms that ash could represent the end of physical existence, an ultimate finality, in medieval Iceland—a place with more experience of ash than many.[6]

This book is mostly concerned with Iceland. Iceland is moderately icy, certainly, although its climate is remarkably temperate for its latitude, thanks to the ameliorating effects of the Gulf Stream. But there are many environmental features that are more specifically Icelandic than ice. For obvious reasons, early settlers wished to give their new, essentially uninhabited homeland a more inviting and glamorous name than Volcano Land, Boiling River Land, Barren Treeless Desert Land, Nothing-to-Eat Land, Biting Wind and Midge Land, or the like. They did not go so far as the frankly deceitful first European settlers of Greenland, whose branding of the new country was as cynical as it was audacious, but nor did they focus on one of Iceland's more unusual characteristics when choosing a name for it. The settlers could, for example, have called their nation Ashland and nobody would have blinked—unless they had a speck of ash in their eye. Iceland, after all, is a by-product of conflagration, born of fire.

Iceland—land of ash. The eruption of the volcano under Eyjafjallajökull in April 2010 sent 250 million cubic meters of tephra—ash and larger particles of volcanic effluvium—nine kilometers into the sky. Although the effect of this eruption on Iceland itself was surprisingly small and localized, the rest of Europe experienced a sort of mock apocalypse. Air travel was suspended for a full week. For some twenty-first-century Europeans, this felt like the end of the world.

The idea of the apocalypse just around the corner seems to hold the human imagination in perpetual sway, but we have no definitive knowledge of how the end will come, what it will feel like, how we are supposed to react. In April 2010, we gained a partial insight into these matters: the cause of the apocalypse was a "natural" disaster. The apocalyptic effects that we felt were all cultural: it was not life, but our way of life—our right to be in a place of our choosing at a time of our choosing—that collapsed. There was a collective feeling of loss and disorientation and above all of inconvenience. The apocalypse, when it happens, will indeed be an inconvenient truth. Perhaps the degree of inconvenience one is experiencing could even be a viable diagnostic of whether the apocalypse has happened or not.

This book is much concerned with the end of the world: Iceland, Ashland, this land that teeters always on the edge of catastrophe, is a useful entry point to thinking about apocalypses. Iceland is an island-sized doomsday device: its weapon of mass destruction is ash (and lava and poisonous gases, especially sulfur dioxide). When another Icelandic volcano, Laki, erupted for eight months in 1783–84, almost a quarter of the Icelandic population died as a result. The millions of tons of sulfur dioxide that Laki emitted had global climatic effects: a sixth of the population of Egypt died in an ensuing famine, for example.[7] Summers became hotter, while the winter of 1784 was the longest winter ever recorded in North America, and there was frost in Suffolk, England, two days after midsummer.[8] The English diarist and naturalist Gilbert White described the effects on his native Hampshire in doomy prose:

> The summer of the year 1783 was an amazing and portentous one, and full of horrible phaenomena; for besides the alarming meteors and tremendous thunder-storms that affrighted and distressed the different counties of this kingdom, the peculiar haze, or smokey fog, that prevailed for many weeks in this island, and in every part of Europe, and even beyond its limits, was a most extraordinary appearance, unlike anything known within the memory

of man. By my journal I find that I had noticed this strange occurrence from June 23 to July 20 inclusive, during which period the wind varied to every quarter without making any alteration in the air. The sun, at noon, looked as blank as a clouded moon, and shed a rust-coloured ferruginous light on the ground, and floors of rooms; but was particularly lurid and blood-coloured at rising and setting. All the time the heat was so intense that butchers' meat could hardly be eaten on the day after it was killed; and the flies swarmed so in the lanes and hedges that they rendered the horses half frantic, and riding irksome. The country people began to look, with a superstitious awe, at the red, louring aspect of the sun.[9]

Was this the end of the world? Yes and no. In the most literal sense, many thousands of people worldwide experienced their own private apocalypse as they died from the direct or, mostly, indirect effects of Laki's explosions.[10] Eschatology works on both microcosmic and macrocosmic levels: the fate of the individual and the fate of the world run parallel—and entwine—in many apocalyptic traditions. To think about the world's death is to think about one's own death, and vice versa. The Laki eruption was also apocalyptic in its bundling of natural and cultural causes and effects. Although White describes perfectly natural phenomena, he describes the unnaturalness of the effects they produce using heightened, clearly apocalyptic imagery.[11] He hints that his less educated neighbors, with their "superstitious awe," were inclined to place these happenings in the realm of the "supernatural"—of imputing some numinous significance to physical processes they did not understand. It is not surprising that White also dwells on the inconvenience of meat spoiling too quickly in the uncommon heat. The apocalypse, for him, means an interruption in his food supply, a slight diminution of his living standards—an inconvenience. But others in England were less fortunate: some thirty thousand deaths above the prevailing mortality rate can be attributed to Laki's effect on the English climate. The mortality rate in France increased by at least the same amount, and possibly much more.[12]

The first Norse inhabitants of Iceland arrived in the 870s. In 870 or 871—at precisely the time that a few Vikings first thought it a good idea to move, lock, stock and barrel, to the newly discovered outpost to the north—the Bárðarbunga volcanic system, which runs beneath Iceland's largest glacier, Vatnajökull, erupted along the Vatnaöldur fissure. Between 934 and 938—four years after the founding of the Alþingi, Iceland's national parliament—Eldgjá, part of the Katla volcanic system that neighbors Eyjafjallajökull, erupted. Eldgjá spewed magma—perhaps as much as eighteen cubic kilometers of lava—over eight hundred square kilometers of southern Iceland. It became the largest deposition of flood basalt in the historical era.[13] In 1104, by which time the Icelanders had converted to Christianity, Hekla, Iceland's biggest and most notorious volcano, erupted for the first time in 250 years. Tephra from this eruption covered half the island. Farms were simply buried in this ash, as far as seventy kilometers from the fissure. Around this time, Iceland's status as a motor of environmental devastation—and a strange and hostile otherworld— began to impinge on the European consciousness.

As early as the 1120s there is an apparent reference to a volcanic island in the North Atlantic in an Anglo-Norman version of the popular *Navigatio sancti Brendani.* In *Le voyage de saint Brendan,* Brendan and his companions see several infernal visions of foul-smelling, sulfur-emitting fiery islands in response to the saint's prayer that he should be allowed to see what hell is like:

A dark land appeared before them,
Of black fog and cloud;
It was smoking with putrid fumes,
Stinking more than putrefying flesh;
It was surrounded by a great blackness.
The monks do not desire to take rest.
And from far away have now heard
That there they would not be very welcome.
They make great efforts to direct their course elsewhere;
But they must take their course hither;
For the wind led them there;
And the abbot instructed them well,
And has said to them: "Gentlemen, be aware
That you are compelled to go to hell."[14]

It is impossible to identify the hellscape of *Le voyage de saint Brendan* precisely with Iceland, but this North Atlantic inferno is clearly imagined as a volcanic landscape. Brendan's vision could well be the first iteration of the idea of Hekla as the actual entrance to hell, an idea that had considerable traction in medieval Europe.[15] The Norwegian *Konungs skuggsjá,* a thirteenth-century Old Norse treatise in the widespread *speculum regale* (mirror of princes) tradition, for example, gives no reason to doubt Iceland's infernal reputation: "now no one may deny it who can see it with his own eyes; because such things are told us concerning the torments of hell as one may now see on that island which is called Iceland: for there are vast and boundless fire, overpowering frost and glaciers, boiling springs, and violent ice-cold streams."[16]

The idea that Iceland was the location—the actual physical location—of the entrance to hell meets with no resistance in medieval literature. Indeed, the notion persisted beyond the Reformation: a seventeenth-century French traveler, Pierre Martin de La Martinière, reports his Icelandic guide as attributing Hekla's unearthly noises to damned souls from all over Europe being flown into the volcano's mouth by a force of demons. La Martinière also suggests that Lucifer used Iceland's natural advantages to make hell's torments especially piquant: between roastings in the volcano, sinners could be plunged into the icy waters of the North Atlantic—a punishment in itself, perhaps, or a malicious respite from the burning that would only serve to intensify the agony when it resumed.[17]

In Sigurður Þórarinsson's popular history of this "notorious volcano," the superstition linking hell and Hekla is identified as a specifically *Catholic* one—and I think Sigurður's choice of words is careful: it distances Lutheran Icelanders from a credulous nonsense that marks out their nation as the epicenter of the devil's activities.[18] Nobody wants to have hell on their doorstep, presumably.[19] In more credulous times, the Icelanders were a little more credulous. Following the eruption of 1341—which came hard on the heels of a particularly devastating previous eruption in 1300 that had covered about thirty thousand square kilometers of the country in ash and killed five hundred or so—the author of the *Flateyjarbók Annals'* entry for the year states that "people went to the mountain where the lava was being thrown up, and it sounded to them as if a great boulder were being flung back and forth inside the mountain. It seemed to them that they saw birds, both large and small, flying in the fire with large cries. These they took to be souls."[20] But as Oren Falk notes, references to volcanic activity in Old Norse–Icelandic literature are remarkably sparse, considering that Hekla alone erupted eight times between 1104 and 1440, a period to which almost the whole extant literary corpus could reasonably be ascribed.[21] The fourteenth century was particularly turbulent, with significant eruptions of Grímsvötn in 1332, 1344, and 1354; Hekla in 1300–1301, 1341, and 1389; and Öræfajökull in 1362. But what seems so ever present in our imaginings of Iceland, so typical of the nation, hardly figures at all in medieval sagas, for all their renowned realism.

Aside from the entry in *Flateyjarbók*, there is a description of the Icelandic landscape that lingers for a moment on its volcanic features in *Guðmundar saga byskups*, which was composed in the middle of the eruptive fourteenth century. In this piece of religious propaganda there are distinctly hellish undertones to the natural phenomena that the text reports:

> There are other mountains in this land, which emit awful fire with the most violent hurling of stones, so that the crack and crash are heard throughout the country, as far in every direction, people say, as fourteen dozen [miles] straight sailing out from every headland. Such great darkness can follow downwind from this terror that, on midsummer at midday, one cannot make out one's [own] hand. Following such portents it has happened that, a league of sea to the south of the land, a huge mountain has come up on account of the fire-flowing in the very ocean, and another has sunk down in the same place, which had first come up through the same cause. There are plenty of gushing hot springs and sulphur there.[22]

This ominous account reads as though written for outsiders—and indeed it probably was: *Guðmundar saga* was produced as part of a concerted effort to have Bishop Guðmundr Arason consecrated as a saint, and overseas ecclesiasts were an important part of its intended audience. There is a sort of ghoulish fascination, a sense of exoticism, in *Guðmundar saga*'s description of volcanic phenomena that they do not seem to have aroused elsewhere in the sagas.

Perhaps Iceland's diabolical landscape is also being figured as somehow unchristian. In *Kristni saga,* a vernacular history of the island's conversion that dates from the thirteenth century, an eruption is supposed to have taken place at the moment the Icelanders decided to convert en masse to Christianity in 999. Icelanders in the pagan camp—those who had opposed the Alþingi's decision—suggest that the old gods were venting their anger seismically. The Christians respond, however, by noting that there were plenty of lava fields around that must have flowed down from the mountains when the pagan deities still held sway—what had they been angry about back then?[23] As far as I can tell, this eruption of 999 is the saga author's invention. Following a great deal of volcanic activity in the first half of the century, Iceland enjoyed a relatively quiet period between the eruptions of Hveravellir in 950 and Grímsvötn in 1060.[24] But one can understand the usefulness of an eruption to an author writing about the conversion: volcanoes are apocalyptic; volcanoes are unchristian by their association with the landscape of hell. They make a good symbol of epochal change, destroying all existing structures in their path and providing a tabula rasa for the creation of new worlds. As both *Guðmundar saga* and *Kristni saga* reveal, the Icelanders were conscious of both the destructive and the creative power of lava: the landmass and their fledgling nation would not exist without peri-odic catastrophic effusions of magma. *Kristni saga* also uses the trope of an eruption to make a sardonic point about the credulousness of the pagans or the fickleness of the idols they worship. Geological phenomena are endowed with ethical meanings.

As the Eyjafjallajökull eruption of 2010 reminded us—that little foretaste of one possible apocalypse—we are all living under the volcano. The Iceland-ers have always lived a more deeply shadowed life than many communities: for a civilized, European society, their existence has always been marginal and imperiled. The Icelandic experience, to date, has been bookended by the Bárðarbunga eruption of 870—the source of the so-called settlement ash layer, so useful to archaeologists—and the twin catastrophes of Eyjafjallajökull and the country's disastrous flirtation with financial speculation that ended in the crash of 2008. We no longer believe that Hekla is the mouth to hell, but sometimes Iceland still seems a land accursed.

How does one live in hell on earth? How does one deal with the constant imminence of environmental catastrophe? We spend enough time wondering *when* the end of the world will happen—but what will it be like, how should we respond to it? These are some of the ideas that I wish to explore in this book and some of the questions I should like to answer. They are ecological ideas and questions: they relate to the interrelatedness and interdependence of people and not-people; of organisms and the media (earth, air, water, fire) in which they are born, live, and die. Because Iceland is, by its nature, per-petually on the brink of one disaster or another, Iceland provides us with an unusually compelling environment in which to think through some of these ideas, which are of pressing concern to all of us.

The Ash

Ash is a by-product, a waste product, an end product. It will be what is left of us when there is nothing of us left. Ash is dead. But ashes live: "ash" is the name is given to a wide variety of trees and shrubs found all over the world, first among them *Fraxinus excelsior,* the common or European ash. *Fraxinus excelsior* is a large, deciduous tree that flourishes across most of Europe and the British Isles. The northern extremity of its range is found around Trond-heim in Norway. In Latin, *fraxinus* means "spear," and the common English name derives from Old English *æsc,* which also denotes this type of weapon.[25] It is a natural thing that gains its name from its cultural function. Although the common ash does not resonate quite as strongly (in Britain, at least) as the oak, that symbol of tradition, steadfastness, stoutheartedness, and (by appropriation) the British Conservative Party, the ash is a tree that has been important in Europe for millennia, and not merely for the production of weapons.[26] The ash is connected with acts of creation and the origins of humankind: according to Hesiod's *Works and Days*, the Bronze race of mortals descended from ash trees (or the Melian [i.e., "ash-tree"] nymphs):

> Zeus the father made a third age of mortals,
> this time of bronze, not at all like the silver one.
> Fashioned from ash trees, they were dreadful and mighty
> and bent on the harsh deeds of war and violence;
> they ate no bread and their hearts were strong as adamant.[27]

In pagan Norse mythology, the Indo-European significance of the ash manifests itself in two ways. Just like Hesiod's mortals, the first two humans in the world, man and woman, were thought to have been made—although, as we shall see, "made" is not quite the right word—out of tree trunks. The first man is called *Askr*—"Ash." (The first woman is called *Embla*, which may be another tree name, though its etymology is disputed; she undoubtedly shares Askr's arboreal origins, however.)[28] The first people's bodies are created out of another substance, just as Adam is made from clay in the Hebrew Bible. The human is a microcosm of the world—which is a macrocosm of the human. Norse cosmology strengthens this connection by structuring the whole universe around the roots, trunk, and branches of the great tree Yggdrasill. Its limbs limn the full extent of everything. Yggdrasill is an ash. This ash is humanity's point of origin and its home in the universe, its *oikos*. All life depends on the ash.

Yggdrasill is not any old ash, however: it is, according to the Old Norse Eddic poem *Vǫluspá* ("The Seeress's Prophecy"), verdantly eternal (and possibly eternally verdant). It may even be an impossible thing, an evergreen ash.

> An ash I know that stands, Yggdrasill it's called,
> a tall tree, drenched with shining loam;
> from there come the dews which fall in the valley,
> it stands ever green over the well of fate. (*Vǫluspá* [K] 19)[29]

All European members of the genus *Fraxinus* lose their leaves in winter. (*Fraxinus uhdei* is sometimes called the evergreen ash, but it is native to Mexico and presumably has nothing to do with Yggdrasill. *Fraxinus uhdei* is not a "true" evergreen—at the extremities of its range, it will drop leaves if the winter becomes cold enough.) *Vǫluspá*'s description of the tree, if we take it to imply that Yggdrasill is evergreen in the sense we normally use this term, renders the symbolic and actual center of the natural cosmos *unnatural*. It should not exist. Critics who dislike inconsistencies in their mythology have tried to resolve this contradiction: perhaps Yggdrasill was actually a yew, another tree with considerable numinous significance in ancient Germanic culture.[30] *Askr* becomes, by this reckoning, simply a metonym for any sort of tree.[31] We might explain the confusion by remembering that *Vǫluspá* is, in its present form, an Icelandic poem. The European ash did not grow in medieval Iceland—not very many trees grew there, then as now.[32] The Icelandic poet may have let his ignorance of real trees make a mess of his description of a mythical tree.

But to say that Yggdrasill *stendr æ yfir grœnn* is not quite the same as mislabeling the ash as a conifer. The important point about the tree is its permanence, the stability that it represents and offers. Anglophone readers of the poem can't help but hear "ever green" when they read *yfir grœnn,* but it is *æ* that means "always," with the preposition *yfir* anticipating the final line of the stanza. It's a small change, but it at once makes Yggdrasill less chimerical: ashes are green, after all, even if they aren't green all the time. And, as Lotte Motz points out, the name Yggdrasill is always collocated with the noun *askr* in both the *Poetic Edda* and *Snorra Edda,* while *askr* can be used to refer to the world tree on its own.[33]

Yggdrasill is an iteration of the tree of life, familiar from so many world mythologies. Its greenness represents the life force that sustains it and with which it sustains the rest of the universe. Yggdrasill demarcates the boundaries of space—nothing in the Norse cosmos exists beyond it—and time: whether or not the ash is evergreen, it is greenly immortal. As we shall see, Yggdrasill survives the apocalypse of Ragnarǫk. While very nearly everything else in all the nine worlds of creation—from Hel down beneath the roots to the gods' home Ásgarðr high in the branches—crumbles into dust or burns to ashes in Ragnarǫk's cataclysm, Yggdrasill shudders, and groans, and bends, but never breaks. This ash never dies because it is capable of continual rebirth.

In our world, meanwhile, ashes are dying. In February 2012 a nursery in Buckinghamshire reported the first instance of ash dieback in the UK. Caused by the fungus *Hymenoscyphus fraxineus* (also known as *Chalara fraxinea* and *Hymenoscyphus pseudoalbidus*),[34] ash dieback represents another small apocalypse in the history of ash and ashes. Known since 1992 on the European continent, *Hymenoscyphus fraxineus* is generally fatal to trees. Its spores spread promiscuously: by July 2014 the disease had been found at 666 sites across the country.[35] This ash Ragnarǫk is still in progress as I write, but we British immediately began processing it as a potential apocalypse, trying to imagine a landscape without the "noble ash" and trying to find someone to blame.[36] An article of 14 May 2013 in the London *Daily Mail* gives us a flavor of contemporary woodland apocalypticism:

> Rudyard Kipling once wrote that the graceful ash would stand proud in our woodlands and hedgerows "till judgement tide."
>
> For anyone who loves Britain's patchwork countryside, it has been impossible to recall Kipling's paean to England's trees this spring without feeling a pang of sadness.
>
> For if the predictions from scientists are right, the magnificent ash, a tree that has been part of our landscape and culture for thousands of years, will be gone within a decade, a victim of the deadly ash dieback fungus.[37]

If the *Daily Mail* were not notoriously beyond parody, one would think that any article in that newspaper that quoted Kipling in its first paragraph had self-parodic intent. But perhaps it takes Kipling to get this newspaper interested in tree diseases: the *Mail* is not aligned, by and large, with "Green" causes. A front-page splash on 3 June 2013, for example, came down strongly against a recent report by British MPs that made the suggestion, uncontroversial in ecological circles, that eating less meat would be a good idea if we wish to ensure food supplies for a growing global population. The *Mail* called this "nannying."[38]

It is gratifyingly easy to unpick the *Mail*'s sudden concern for the natural environment in the case of the ash, however. In fact, David Derbyshire's article makes it quite clear that the ash, this "magnificent," "noble," "great native tree," is a thing of culture. The ash is important above all because it is British; it has a long pedigree in our landscape. Romans, Anglo-Saxons, Vikings are all invoked, and Yggdrasill is conjured up. Derbyshire notes that some British military aircraft of the Second World War had wings made of ash. *Hymenoscyphus fraxineus*, meanwhile, is a dastardly import from—yes, inevitably—Europe. The *Daily Mail*, for readers unfamiliar with British newspaper politics, is uneasy about the UK's relations with its European neighbors and played a leading role in the campaign that led to Britain voting to leave the European Union in 2016. The ash and its nemesis are transfigured—as if in an unfunny and heavy-handed editorial cartoon—into John Bull of Old England and Johnny Foreigner, respectively. For, in this instance, the Dutch are to blame, with their graspingly amoral capitalistic approach to tree propagation:

Most frustrating is the fact that the UK doesn't need to import ash saplings: our soils and climate are perfect for them. Anyone with an ash tree in their vicinity knows that ash saplings quickly spring up if winged nuts are allowed to settle in the soil.

Yet in recent years, UK nurseries have been unable to meet the demand for broad-leaved native trees at a price that British landowners were willing to pay.

Our oaks, ashes and beech trees have increasingly been imported from countries such as Holland—home to the world's most skilled horticultural industry.

With their cheap running costs, Dutch growers have cleaned up. Last year, they were able to supply a year-old-ash sapling to a British nursery for just 10p.[39]

Ironically, many of these saplings were grown from seeds collected in Britain and shipped overseas, then returned to these shores. I almost expect an exposé of how naive young British ashes are kidnapped and groomed for a life in some sort of hellish Dutch tree brothel to follow. (The Dutch, of course, have form in this field, giving their name to the elm disease that up to now has been the worst tree pathogen in British history.)

For the *Daily Mail*, "nature" is a stick with which to beat the targets of its indignation as it feels appropriate: it discusses trees in resolutely cultural terms, with cultural aims in mind. It laments the loss of the ash from Britain's "countryside" and "landscape," both of which are entirely cultural (nonnatural) constructs. The *Daily Mail* does not care what dieback is like for the trees; it pays no attention to the multitude of nonhuman species that rely on ashes for their habitat or food supply; still less is it interested in the point of view of *Hymenoscyphus fraxineus*. As it happens, and unfortunately for this jingoistic appropriation of the nonhuman for all too human purposes, ash dieback is an entirely natural disease: it has no discernible cultural causes. Even its transmission across the English Channel may have been haphazard, rather than a product of diabolical Dutch agribusiness. Studies quickly established that the fungus's spores can travel relatively long distances on the wind, though the movement of infected plants is probably the vector most likely to account for the disease's rapid spread around Europe.[40]

Ash dieback is another example of a natural catastrophe defined by its cultural effects: it is not caused by human agency, but it becomes important to (some) people because of the ash's constructed ideological significance. It threatens to be an apocalypse *of* trees, but it is an apocalypse *for* people: as the

Daily Mail figures the catastrophe, a particularly British apocalypse. North American ashes, meanwhile, are afflicted by a similarly apocalyptic antagonist, *Agrilus planipennis,* the emerald ash borer. This native of China has wreaked havoc on indigenous ash species since the early 2000s. After an initial infestation, the emerald ash borer can kill all specimens in a given location within about ten years, and the insect is now found in all states east of the Rockies, as well as in three Canadian provinces.[41] It is conceivable that the main species of *Fraxinus* in both Europe and North America will collapse utterly under these attacks, becoming extinct in the current century.

Since there are few specimens of *Fraxinus excelsior* or any other ashes in Iceland, ash dieback will impinge little on the Icelandic imagination, one would think. At the same time, the loss of trees resonates with the Icelandic environmental experience. As we will see in chapters 4 and 5, deforestation was one of the most immediate and most significant environmental consequences of the settlement of the island. Deforestation took place quickly and completely—perhaps within the lifespan of the first generation of settlers. Iceland's much remarked upon barrenness has (partly) cultural causes: people chopped down the country's tree stock—such as it was—in order to build houses and ships and to burn for warmth and cooking. They cleared woodland for grazing animals. And then Iceland was effectively treeless until efforts at reforestation began in the twentieth century. The effects of Iceland's arboreal apocalypse have been significant: soil erosion is a constant problem even in the more fertile coastal areas of the country. But deforestation has also had cultural effects, primarily in contributing to the idea of Iceland as an unworldly or otherworldly landscape. To European observers, the absence of trees is, together with the presence of volcanoes and their products, one of the clearest markers of Iceland's otherness. Much of Iceland seems like a desert, with all the cultural baggage that that term carries.[42] In the latter part of the twentieth century it became conventional to use the moon—that paragon of wastelands, the *non plus ultra* of inhospitable environments—as a frame of reference for Iceland's terrain. Who could live in such a place? And how?

These questions are easily answered: the "who" are the Icelanders, obviously. As to the "how," I should say *imaginatively.* Migration is an imaginative act. The first settlers of Iceland had to imagine its entirely new, bizarre, decidedly undomestic topography as their home, both prospectively, in order to motivate their migration, and retrospectively, to make the new country theirs, to make sense of their new environment, and to reconcile themselves to new ways of life. They had to live imaginatively—resourcefully, by their wits, confronted with a previously scarcely imaginable environment. But their change of scenery required the colonizers of Iceland to reconfigure their imaginations according to their experiences, to imagine livingly. This they did in remarkable ways. The great efflorescence of Old Norse–Icelandic literature—sagas and poetry, history and myth, religious texts and romances—is the legacy of this ecological imagining.

Mythologies of Ash

Volcanoes and trees—ash and the ash—provide us with two puzzling points of entry into the ecological imagination of medieval Iceland. To us, volcanoes signify Iceland; the *want* (in the sense of both "lack" and "desiring") of trees signifies Iceland. In most medieval Icelandic texts, however, volcanoes are conspicuous by not being there.[43] They were a fact of life, a powerfully destructive and creative force, a threat constantly looming on the horizon, but they did not capture the Icelanders' imagination. Trees, on the other hand, were physically absent from the landscape from an early period but retained their actual and symbolic importance in Icelandic cultural life.

There are several ways of explaining these apparent contradictions. The Icelanders' interest in trees may simply be part of their Norse inheritance. Trees were of cultic significance to Scandinavian pagans, and knowledge of the world tree Yggdrasill traveled overseas with the settlers. The imaginative associations made between people and trees are generally manifest in skaldic and Eddic poetry, which are pan-Scandinavian rather than uniquely Icelandic traditions. The mythico-religious significance of trees adhered to the Norse colonists on their journey to the new land, to implant itself in the incipient Icelandic consciousness. Ironically, trees' centrality to Norse cosmology and poetics did nothing to prevent the Icelanders taking their axes to the island's sparse and fragile woodlands almost as soon as they arrived.

Volcanoes, meanwhile, are found largely, though not solely, in Iceland's uninhabitable center. They did not impinge upon the space that the Norwegians wished to settle, their occasional eruptions apart. They can be figured as belonging to an otherworld in opposition to the world people actually inhabit. The new Icelanders were already accustomed to thinking of their own, conceptually central cultural space as geographically peripheral.[44] Norway's most hospitable regions also lie along its coasts, a narrow ribbon of farmable land trapped between a fertile sea and a barren interior of mountains and glaciers. From a psychogeographic perspective, Iceland could be experienced, with relative ease, as a second Norway—so long as you ignored the igneous, which the Icelanders tried their best to do in their literature.

But not all their literature. The "realistic" sagas of Icelanders certainly find volcanoes inimical or uninteresting for some reason—presumably because their plots invariably take place in Iceland's social sphere, which rarely overlaps with the volcanic. This type of prose narrative, with very few exceptions, avoids descriptions of nature (or even landscape) except when topographical features impinge directly upon the protagonists' experiences or have specific social or historical resonances. The sagas and their characters show little interest in admiring the view. Elsewhere in the Old Norse–Icelandic literary corpus, however, we find different and deeper engagements with the physical world. In another apparent irony, it is in those genres which are less invested in "social realism," further removed from a direct representation of Iceland itself, which may bring us closer to the lived experience of this bizarre, unearthly, beautiful, marginal, terrifying homeland. Poetry and myth, always so closely entwined in Norse culture, may reveal much more about the Icelanders' relationship with the world around them than the sagas that tell the story of Iceland's discovery and settlement and the people's apparent (if tenuous) mastery of the land.

Myth is not merely a repository of inherited cultural values. It also changes over time to reflect the changing realities that face a community and to assimilate ancient beliefs into the necessities of living in the here and now. The presence of volcanoes and the relative scarcity of trees were two natural phenomena with which the Norse settlers of Iceland had to reach a speedy accommodation. They needed to incorporate them into their worldview. This they did not through verbal description of the land but through the sublimation of these specifically Icelandic landscape features into mythopoetic otherworlds. According to this reading, the importance of trees in Old Norse–Icelandic mythologies is not only a reflection of their general importance to Germanic pagans. It is also a locus for feelings of loss, nostalgia, and anxiety that deforestation had engendered among the Icelanders in their new, very specific naturecultural situation. We will explore these tree feelings thoroughly later in this book. But for now, let us return to the other sort of ash: ashes to ashes.

The idea of the volcano and the idea of apocalypse, as we have seen, go well together. An eruption is one of the few cataclysms that can threaten a community with instant oblivion. It cannot be prevented; its course cannot be altered. Poisonous gases and abrasive grit kill people and livestock; lava flows and tephra deposits obliterate buildings and render fields unfit for farming. But volcanoes are also a metamorphic, creative force, albeit a profoundly disorienting one. Even if there are survivors of an eruption, even if structures are left standing and sheep continue to graze in nearby fields, the volcano's effects are sufficiently transformative to reshape the world; to bring one world to an end and replace it with another, different from the last in ways more or less subtle, more or less devastating to life and disruptive of one's worldview.

The whole landscape changes: new hills appear where formerly there were none. The fissure that Iceland sits on regularly coughs up whole new islands out of the ocean—Iceland itself is merely the biggest of these basalt outcrops. Between 1963 and 1965, an eruption under the ocean south of Iceland led to the creation of Surtsey, an island of solidified lava and tephra large enough to withstand the waves' erosion. Surtsey has become an ecological laboratory: human access is significantly restricted so that biologists can study the process of allochthonous biocolonization—what happens to an ecosystem that starts with a clean slate—on a pristine, virgin landmass. In 1998 the first tree—a tea-leaved willow, capable of growing to four meters in good conditions—was found on Surtsey.[45] Along with the gulls, guillemots, mosses and lichen, starfish, seals, and orcas, the presence of a new tree on Surtsey makes an ironic counterpoint to the human colonization of the Icelandic mainland, which resulted in the wholesale destruction of native ecosystems.

Surtsey is "Surtr's Island." Surtr is the great fire-giant of Norse mythology, one of the agents of the world's destruction at Ragnarǫk. He comes from the hot southlands that he inhabits to the last battle "with harm of branches" (*með sviga lævi*)—a kenning for the fire that shines from his sword.[46] As Simon Halink notes, "By linking the new island toponymically to Iceland's ancient literary tradition (in this case: the Eddas), this new geographical feature became encapsulated in the old framework of mythological thought, embedded in an imagined Icelandic mythscape."[47] But Surtr is hardly a propitious mascot for a new landmass. At Ragnarǫk, Surtr kills Freyr, the god of fertility, of good weather and prosperity, of hearth and homefield.[48] Fire overruns the Earth. A moment later, *Vǫluspá* describes this effect in a verse that marks the very end of the world, the precise moment of apocalypse:

> The sun turns black, land sinks into the sea,
> the bright stars vanish from the sky;
> steam rises up in the conflagration,
> a high flame plays against heaven itself. (*Vǫluspá* [K] 55; 54 in Larrington)[49]

This vision of the world's fiery death has struck many of *Vǫluspá*'s readers as a distinctively Icelandic—and distinctively volcanic—end. An ash cloud has the capacity to hide the sun and stars from our vision. Molten lava can slide down a mountainside and into the sea; steam and flame are everywhere; all is confusion. The elements do not seem to be in their proper places; they mutate; matter is in flux. Although this Ragnarǫk does not take place on Iceland—this myth offers no geographical bearings, there is no Norse Mount Olympus to provide a tangible gateway to the gods' domain—*Vǫluspá*'s evocation of a burning landscape suggests familiarity with volcanic activity that, in the Norse world, would have been most readily available to people who knew (or knew of) Iceland. Clive Oppenheimer and his coauthors go so far as to propose that there is a direct historical correlative to *Vǫluspá*'s volcanism in the terrible Eldgjá eruption, which they are able to date categorically to 939–40 CE. They suggest that the poem was composed within a generation or two of this eruption and preserves firsthand memories of an event that was likely to have had dire effects upon the Icelandic population.[50] While this argument implies an earlier date for *Vǫluspá*'s composition than is conventional—other critics have seen the eruption of Katla in 1014 as providing a more proximate source of volcanic anxiety for the poem's conversion-era audiences, for example—it seems as though *Vǫluspá* gives us our first hint of what may have happened to the absent volcanoes of the Old Norse–Icelandic literary imagination.[51] They have been displaced—or *de-placed*. They have been denatured (de-*natured*). They have been sublimated. The immense destructive potential of Iceland's volcanoes is deferred (and thereby diffused) by their dislocation, from the everyday world of Icelanders' experience, into the nowhere-and-everywhere cosmos where the pagan gods are to be found. The doomed gods will be the ones to bear the brunt of the earth's anger, not the actual Icelanders. And the temporal dislocation is important, too. Apocalypses are constantly being deferred; every prediction of the world's end has so far proven to be false—to those who were still alive to see the clock tick around to the date designated for doomsday, at any rate. By making such a catastrophe part of a general, inevitable schema of cosmological history, it may become less of a specific threat to one's psyche in the here and now. The end of the world keeps on not happening, right until it does happen—and by then it's too late to worry about it.

Vǫluspá thus can be read as mythologizing volcanic activity. It renders strange and significant what is a very quotidian part of the Icelandic experience. (To this day, the hot water in one's Reykjavik apartment carries the eggy smell of geothermal activity.) It provides a mental space in which thoughts and feelings about Iceland's environment can be processed at a remove from their place in everyday life. Myths can be very good at explaining phenomena, at helping us to work out how to deal with them. And Norse mythology, so I will argue, is full of mythologized ecological concerns like this. It is a product of a new mythopoetic culture, deeply rooted in the pagan traditions of mainland Scandinavia but conditioned by the radically new physical and social landscape that the settlers of Iceland had to contend with. Volcanoes are a unique natural feature of this new landscape; apocalypticism is a cultural phenomenon common to many mythologies of this period (and others). In *Vǫluspá*, the two things are entwined (or enmeshed): the natural and cultural spheres of the Icelandic experience are symbiotically related to one another. They are part of the same ecology.

1   Ecocriticism and Old Norse

THIS BOOK LOOKS at Scandinavian myths and Old Norse–Icelandic literature through an ecocritical lens, which is to say that it is concerned with relationships between texts, humans, and the nonhuman world. It places texts in the physical contexts that provide the conditions in which all cultural life on earth takes place. It asserts the possibility of extending the critic's realm of inquiry into existences beyond human control and perhaps even beyond human experience. As Cheryll Glotfelty famously defined it, ecocriticism "takes an earth-centred approach to literary studies."[1] Or, as Serpil Oppermann states, as a loose and amorphous movement, ecocriticism can be identified by "its interest in environmental literature, its aim in promoting ecological awareness and bringing ecological consciousness to the practice of literary criticism."[2] By these standards, all literature may be considered potentially open to "environmental" criticism, though in practice certain genres have proven much more congenial to ecocritics than others.

All cultural production takes place within particular ecological contexts in which both human and nonhuman actors are enmeshed, and the whole business of human life takes place in a biosphere shared with countless other actants: there is no pristine "cultural" realm into which we can retreat to escape the influence of the world-beyond-us. To think otherwise runs the risk, in the light of the ecological crises that have been unfolding around us for decades, of leading us into what Gillen D'Arcy Wood has called a "dangerous determinism": "Historical materialism without ecological awareness [is liable to produce] a grand narrative of class, government, empire, and trade whose anthropocentric terms are no less a product of imperialism and the Enlightenment than the current ecological crisis itself."[3] Nature abhors a vacuum, so the saying goes, yet prevailing humanistic critiques have been guilty of attempting to vacuum seal Society away from Nature, either by ignoring the nonhuman world altogether or by backgrounding it as merely the stage on which the drama of human history takes place. Ecocriticism asserts that nothing—not class, race, gender, or any other form of hegemonic or counterhegemonic power structure—operates beyond or apart from the *oikos*. Everything is ecology.

And since nothing exists outside ecology, there is a growing feeling in the twenty-first-century academy that all scholarship has to be engaged with, or at least informed by, ecological concerns. The burgeoning field of the environmental humanities encourages humanists to look beyond the human, and indeed beyond the humanities, in an attempt to confront a crisis in the world-beyond-us that we believe may be unparalleled in history. The catastrophe that is unfolding around us is so important, many ecocritics would agree, so acutely pressing, that it demands the attention of all thinkers and the action of all citizens. Global warming, mass extinctions, overpopulation, and the unsustainable exploitation of the Earth's resources are now far too important to be left to scientists or (even worse) politicians. The global environmental crisis provides an ineluctable context for everything we do, leaving nothing untouched. It is this feeling, the feeling that we all must do something to address ecological matters in our work—whatever is within our capabilities—that provides the overarching project for ecocriticism. As sea levels rise, even the uncalloused hands of the theorists and critics must man the pumps.

New modes of literary criticism are unlikely to save the world, however. Indeed, it is a feature of my argument in this book that the world (as we have always known it) is past saving and that our focus should be on new types of world-building, new realms of possibility in the wake of the collapse of humanity's ancien régime of separation from, antagonism toward, and exploitation of what we have been pleased to call Nature—a thing that never existed as such in the first place.

Bruno Latour calls Nature "a premature unification of all existents, probably political in origin," which strikes me as an excellent definition if modified by the caveat that, for some, Nature encompasses all existents minus the (Western) human subject, at least when that distinction is politically expedient for them.[4] Elsewhere, Latour has expanded on this definition:

> Nature is not a thing, a domain, a realm, an ontological territory. It is (or rather, it was during the short modern parenthesis) a way of organizing the division (what Alfred North Whitehead has called the Bifurcation) between appearances and reality, subjectivity and objectivity, history and immutability. A fully transcendent, yet a fully historical construct, a deeply religious way (but not in the truly religious sense of the word) of creating the difference of potential between what human souls were attached to and what was really out there.[5]

It is a commonplace among ecocritics currently to assert that our ecological crisis arises ultimately from certain human cultures' strictly dualistic world-views, worldviews that insist upon the separateness of mankind from a reified Nature which exists only so far as it exists for our benefit. This dualism, as Val Plumwood has laid out so convincingly, is particularly prevalent in Western patriarchal cultures and requires the deployment of enormous resources of power to maintain. For Plumwood, dualisms are "not just freefloating systems of ideas; they are closely associated with domination and accumulations, and are their major cultural expressions and justifications." Human domination of Nature is wrapped up with all other oppressive regimes of dualistic thought, including those which insist upon clear and inevitable distinctions of gender, race, and class, for example. These dualisms are far from transcendentally natural. Rather,

> their development has been a historical process, following a historical
> sequence of evolution. Thus dualisms such as reason/nature may be ancient,
> but others such as human/nature and subject/object are associated especially
> with modern, post-enlightenment consciousness. But even the ancient forms
> do not necessarily fade away because their original context has changed;
> they are often preserved in our conceptual framework as residues, layers of
> sediment deposited by past oppressions.[6]

If our current ecological predicament is the result of historical processes, as Plumwood claims, we may be able to work back through human history, stripping away these "layers of sediment" and revealing mentalities that precede and undermine the modern West's systematic and oppressive dualisms.

Accordingly, though all work in the ecological humanities should aim to lead us toward new paradigms for a more successful mode of being-in-the-world in the future, much literary ecocriticism has been explicitly backward looking, even nostalgic. This book is, in one way, no exception to this trend. It deals, after all, with texts that were written down seven or eight centuries ago, and delves into cultural traditions of even greater antiquity. The basic goal of historically oriented ecocriticism of this sort is to seek alternative ways of looking at our place in the world and our interactions with the world through our reading of texts that represent Nature, Society, and their inter-relationships in ways that are less ecologically disastrous than our own (post) modern conditions of thought. And since the catastrophe is taking place in the present—since it is frequently argued to be a direct product of modernity, in fact—one way of preparing ourselves for a different possible future is to look for examples from many possible pasts. How did we live before we divorced ourselves from the rest of the universe, before we regarded Nature as mankind's dominion? When did the separation of the world into two onto-logical zones that must never overlap—human/nonhuman, or Nature/Society, or Us/Other (there are many names for the same fundamental divide)—take place, and how might we achieve a reintegration of these two zones into a harmonious and sustainable prelapsarian unity? As Carl Phelpstead puts it, the hope of premodernist ecocriticism is that "knowledge that things have been different in the past and so need not be the way that they are now offers encouragement to those who seek to ensure that things will be different again in the future."[7]

Medievalists therefore increasingly believe that we might have a particular contribution to make to ecocritical studies because, as Vin Nardizzi writes, "medieval and Renaissance ecocriticisms can help to imagine for our world a range of futures unfolding from banned, censored and forgotten pasts."[8] If the origin of global warming lies in technologies of the Industrial Revolution, or if the equation of the human/nonhuman and subject/object dichotomies is the product of Enlightenment thought, those of us who study periods before these points of fracture believe that we may have special new insights to con-tribute to ecocritical study. Frankly, we also appreciate this opportunity to imagine that medieval studies (and medievalists) might be relevant to a bur-geoning discipline that has the advantage of being fashionable and therefore more than normally visible to our peers working on other periods and in other disciplines—and to do work that feels important, even imperative, in our cur-rent perilous situation.

What Ecocriticism Has to Offer
Old Norse–Icelandic Studies

Ecocritical medieval studies has thus become an increasingly vibrant field of research in the discipline over the past decade or so. To date, however, Old Norse–Icelandic literary culture, which is the subject of this book, has received hardly any attention from ecocritics. Carl Phelpstead has led the way with the first explicitly ecocritical study of an Icelandic saga, and other scholars have produced studies of medieval Scandinavian landscapes that are certainly ecocriticism adjacent, but scholarship on Old Norse has lagged behind work done by ecocritics working on different linguistic and literary tra-ditions.[9] Our field has traditionally been resistant to theoretical or politically inspired modes of criticism; indeed, Old Norse–Icelandic studies could fairly

be described as a methodologically conservative enterprise. Things are changing, as younger scholars (belatedly) embrace poststructuralist critique with
as much enthusiasm as a previous generation of Scandinavianists (belatedly)
embraced structuralism. But there remains a certain anxiety of influence
among critics working in a tradition that has foregrounded empirical philology
and resisted status quo–challenging hermeneutics. Part of the attraction that
an ecocritical approach to Old Norse–Icelandic literature has for me thus lies
precisely in its novelty. As Graham Harman notes in another context, "From
time to time something new is needed to awaken us from various dogmatic
slumbers. Properly pursued, the search for 'the next big thing' is not a form of
hip posturing or capitalist commodification, but of hope."[10] It is my hope that
this book will provide a stimulus to readers of Old Norse who are open to new
approaches—the theory curious or those who might be anxious about the contemporary reception of their work outside their home discipline, perhaps—to
embark with confidence on new interpretative adventures.

It is my contention in these pages that ecocriticism has much to offer Old
Norse–Icelandic studies. In many important ways, this literature, the vast bulk
of which originated in Iceland between about 1150 and 1400, is an intrinsically ecopoetical project, an act of literary world-making unparalleled in other
regions of medieval Europe. Nowhere else in the Old World was such a new
world to be found. Iceland, itself a remarkably young landmass in geological terms, was an effectively pristine ecosystem, untouched by human hand,
when it was discovered and settled, allegedly by a few Irish monks and then
by droves of Norwegian colonists in the ninth and tenth centuries. With its
constant volcanic activity, marginal climate, and unique flora and fauna, Iceland presented its Norse settlers with a new *oikos* that was both uncannily like
home—like Norway, it has fjords on its coastlines and uninhabitable mountains in its center—and almost entirely alien. As any visitor to present-day
Iceland will attest, there are places where the landscape feels more lunar
than earthly. For outsiders, Iceland can be profoundly unsettling, and the first
Icelanders were faced with the task of settling it.

These new Icelanders had to imagine new ways of being-in-the-world that
made sense in, and of, their new home; or rather, they had to make a home
in and out of a new and presumably to them dramatically strange ecological
situation. If we are to understand fully the political and cultural development
of Iceland in its foundational centuries, we omit consideration of nonhuman
factors—climate, natural disasters, changing patterns of resource availabil-
ity—at our peril: such is the claim of ecohistoricism, an increasingly important
mode of ecological humanistic discourse that bridges the political and cultural

concerns of the ecocritical project and the more data-driven methodologies of ecological history and anthropology. Without reverting to a crude determinism—suggesting, for example, that a certain Icelandic national character arises from the relative inhospitableness of the weather, or that the origins of the sagas lie in the fact that there wasn't very much else to do during Iceland's interminable winter darkness—ecohistorical approaches can attempt to explain, in Gillen D'Arcy Wood's terms, what the "hard data of historical climatology *meant* in cultural terms, in the minds and lived experience of the people who endured or benefited from a specific meteorological regime, and how human cultures have both adapted to and shaped environmental change."[11] As we have seen, there is ample evidence of how Iceland's constant seismic activity and intermittent episodes of near-apocalyptic catastrophe have always imposed a unique set of environmental pressures on its inhabitants. We can thus attempt to trace the impact of these physical phenomena on the Icelanders and the development of their worldviews, ways of life, and social and political institutions as they are reflected in the society's cultural responses to the land and its climate, geology, flora, and fauna.

Or we can look at the question from the opposite direction. We know that medieval Iceland was for three centuries or so a polity unique among European nations, a decentralized "commonwealth" that lacked a monarchy or other form of ultimate executive authority. We know, too, that the Icelanders produced one of the largest and most varied of medieval Europe's vernacular literary corpuses, which includes in the *Íslendinga sögur* (sagas of Icelanders) a sui generis form of prose narrative that arguably anticipates some of the concerns and aesthetic mores of the much later realist novel. These texts and the society that produced them have an ecohistorical context just as much as the social or political contexts that literary critics are so comfortable exploring. They arise in and out of particular moments of human interaction with the physical environment just as much as from historical moments of interaction between different people and groups of people. Because Iceland's climate, geology, and landscape are so unusual in a European context, we might assume that they have shaped Iceland, the Icelanders, and the Icelanders' cultural production in particularly influential ways. In considering these suggestions, an ecocritically oriented cultural history merges with a historically aware literary ecocriticism to produce a picture of a natureculture that attempts to account for both the human and nonhuman actants that work together to make up the totality of what we know as "Iceland."

This book mostly treats mythological writings, however, and it is difficult to contextualize myths in time or space in the way that we are accustomed to treat other forms of literature. In the case of Norse mythology, we have to deal with the fact—directly relevant to this investigation—that although the textual records of the myths were mostly made in Iceland, they derive from a religious culture that originated in mainland Scandinavia as a branch of a wider Germanic mythology, much of which has been lost. There is no doubt that the myths that are inscribed in Old Norse–Icelandic texts existed in some form in other locations, before the settlement of Iceland. Should we identify an ecological context for them in Iceland, or in Scandinavia, or in some remote fastness of time and space that we can only speculate about? It becomes necessary always to hold in mind the idea that myths are somehow always both local and universal, which often presents unusual interpretative challenges.

In the most important treatment of Norse mythology from an environmental perspective so far written, Mathias Valentin Nordvig outlines the principles of what he calls "ecomythology":

> [An ecomythological approach] consists of the understanding of mythopoesis in concert with the surrounding environment and ecosystem. It is not an attempt to *perceive* nature that sparks mythogenesis and subsequently propels mythopoesis. It is rather the case that landscape, nature, ecosystems, and environment offer Memory Spaces with which myth can be associated. This can be myth in terms of folktales preserved in Communicative Memory, telling about a landscape feature connected with ancient ritual practice, or it may be myth in terms of the narrativization of natural landscape features, providing them at times with etiologies that involve supernatural species and events. This is myth as a function of the Mythical Charter of Tradition that preserves technical knowledge which is crucial to survival.[12]

Declan Taggart, meanwhile, has taken a similar approach to geological phenomena in myths associated with the god Þórr, suggesting that Þórr's common association with thunder in the modern imagination obscures the fact that his reputation as a noisy, violent, earth-disturbing figure may in fact mythologize seismic activity—landslides in Norway, or earthquakes and volcanic eruptions in Iceland.[13] Taggart's and Nordvig's work shows the value of contextualizing myth in its physical environment, but their projects are only—I believe it is fair to say—ecocritical in the loosest sense of the term. They do not submit the myths they study to critique on ecological lines. Although I have been inspired by Nordvig's work, I do not follow his example, even when my analysis focuses on mythological material. Rather than seeking to identify the ecological background of the Norse myths, I am instead mostly interested in using these texts as a way to foreground and interrogate ecological issues that are relevant both to the medieval past and to a future-focused ecocritical praxis in the present.

What Old Norse Has to Offer Ecocriticism

In his pioneering ecocritical study of *Eyrbyggja saga,* Carl Phelpstead lays out a twofold aim for work in this direction. Following Phelpstead's example, I hope in this book to "demonstrate the difference that taking an environmentally aware approach may make" to a reading of Old Norse–Icelandic texts and "to suggest the difference that ecocritical readings of sagas [and other forms and genres of Old Norse literature] might make to ecocriticism."[14] The balance in my book tips slightly toward the latter concern, as I believe that Old Norse literature provides us with distinctively different and at times advantageous viewpoints on matters of fundamental concern to ecocriticism. In my view, there are five key characteristics of Old Norse–Icelandic literary culture that make it a potentially valuable contributor to the ongoing development of several strands of ecocritical thought.

1. Old Norse–Icelandic literature preserves elements of a pre-Christian mythology.

I have already mentioned the belief, commonplace among ecocritics, that dualistic worldviews, modes of being-in-the-world that insist on the absolute separation of the human from the nonhuman and of Society from Nature, can be blamed for humanity's estrangement from the rest of creation and its disastrous consequences for ecosystems and the ultimate fate of life on Earth. These dualisms have a long heritage but are particularly associated with the Enlightenment's Cartesian revolution that reconfigured the human subject as the sole arbiter of reality; the combined efforts of the scientific revolution and the Industrial Revolution in providing the tools by which our mastery over the nonhuman world could be implemented; and capitalism's legitimization of economic growth, resource exploitation, and individual wealth accumulation as the motors and measures of social progress that has resulted in the commodification of the planet's goods. Old Norse–Icelandic literature originates in a precapitalist, preindustrial, pre-Enlightenment world and thus could in principle be expected, along with other medieval cultures, to reflect a less dualistic worldview than that of Western modernity. Moreover, as medieval Iceland was never a truly feudal society, even after the kings of Norway gained sovereignty over the colony in the second half of the thirteenth century, it also offers an alternative sociopolitical trajectory to that followed by much of Western Europe in this period. Feudalism has been identified as having significant and distinctive environmentally damaging impacts on the land, and may be seen as a precursor of modern capitalism in some respects. As Jason Moore puts it, "Feudalism consequently limited the surplus available for investment in agricultural improvement, which tended to undermine soil fertility. . . . Simply put, the lord-peasant relation was fundamentally antagonistic to long-run ecological sustainability . . . the feudal system of production exhausted the soil, which led to malnutrition, which prepared the ground for epidemic disease and, in short order, a terminal systemic crisis."[15] Iceland faced many of these problems during the Middle Ages, but classical feudalism cannot be blamed for them.

But one other dualistic worldview has also been thought particularly blameworthy in providing the conditions in which ecologically harmful worldviews could flourish: the Judeo-Christian tradition, which made mankind the proper owner, controller, and beneficiary of the whole nonhuman world on the basis of the text of Genesis 1:28–29: "God blessed them and said to them, 'Be fruitful and increase in number; fill the earth and subdue it. Rule over the fish in the sea and the birds in the sky and over every living creature that moves on the ground.' Then God said, 'Behold, I have given you every plant yielding seed that is on the surface of all the earth, and every tree which has fruit yielding seed; it shall be food for you.'" In one of the most influential—though certainly controversial—early discussions of the implication of premodern cultures in the "progress" of Western society toward an anticipated or actually unfolding ecological crisis, Lynn White Jr. placed the heaviest possible emphasis on the deleterious influence of Genesis on humanity's swift and early fall into disharmony with Nature.[16] "Christianity, in absolute contrast to ancient paganism and Asia's religions (except, perhaps, Zoroastrianism)," wrote White, "not only established a dualism of man and nature but also insisted that it is God's will that man exploit nature for his proper ends."[17] Anne Primavesi expands on these ideas, though she claims that they are based on only one (potentially erroneous) reading of many that are possible of Genesis:

> In western religious and cultural history, matter has been distinguished from mind, nature from culture, woman from man, body from spirit, emotion from reason, earth from heaven in order to devalue one compared with the other, the devalued being described as unclean, polluting, inferior and/or profane. The de-valuation or de-grading has meant that emotion, matter,

nature, woman and earth could then be treated as of lesser value, lesser importance. This degradation, in the case of women, nature and the earth, was taken to justify their exploitation.[18]

For these reasons, White called (Western) Christianity "the most anthropocentric religion the world has ever seen," and suggested that Christianity's victory over paganism in Europe was "the greatest psychic revolution in the history of our culture."[19]

These are bold claims, but they immediately catch the attention of readers of Old Norse, a literature which is almost unique among its contemporaries in its preservation of a substantial body of mythological material that derives from indigenous European pagan religions beyond the classical Greco-Roman canon.[20] The first claim in favor of Norse culture's value to an ecocritical project is that the existence of a substantial body of non-Christian myth in this corpus will allow us to test White's confident assertions about the advantages from an ecological perspective of a pagan worldview over a Christian one. If, as Shepard Krech puts it, White's "implication is that in 'pagan animism,' both prior to the arrival of Christian thought and outside the orb of Christian influence, there existed kinder and gentler ways of thinking about and acting toward the natural world, which Christianity, if and when it arrived, would undermine and even obliterate," then Norse mythology may be a good place to look for these "kinder and gentler ways of thinking."[21]

The relative "greenness" of pagan culture in general has been claimed on multiple grounds, some of which stand up to scrutiny better than others. Joan and River Higginbotham, for example, subtitle their 2003 study of paganism "an introduction to earth-centered religions."[22] Graham Harvey goes further, writing that "paganism is primarily a Green Spirituality, a Natural religion, a Religion with roots in Nature," while Matthew Hall claims that paganism evinces a "sense of humanity situated in a heterarchical natural world [that] closely mirrors the depiction of consubstantiality and relatedness found in the old pagan texts."[23] If that is the case, then these "old pagan texts" are surely worthy of ecocritical attention.

Before we get carried away, however, there are some necessary words of caution that attend our attempts to use Norse myth as a way into White's lost universe of a harmoniously integrated naturecultural pagan worldview. We know more about the pre-Christian religious culture of Scandinavia than that of many other regions, for the simple reason that the conversion of the northern realms to Christianity took place much later here than elsewhere. (Parts of Sweden, for example, were identifiably pagan well into the twelfth century, whereas England became officially Christian from 597 CE onward.) Our record of Norse paganism—both textual and archaeological—is relatively full. Traditions, particularly poetic traditions, with origins in pagan culture retained a good deal of prestige in Iceland after that country accepted Christianity in 999 or 1000, leading to greater attempts being made to preserve in memory and subsequently on parchment these artifacts of paganism here than in other European regions.[24]

Nonetheless, the textual sources on which our knowledge of Norse mythology depends are the products not of paganism but of postconversion interest in paganism, mediated by and for Christians. *Snorra Edda* and the *Poetic Edda*, the most important repositories of mythological narratives from medieval Iceland, were both written in the thirteenth century, and though both these anthologies probably stand at the end of traditions that are genuinely old, there is no avoiding the fact that the myths they contain have all passed through an unknowable number of hands in the postpagan era. They exist because they served a purpose in a cultural milieu that was literate, educated, and unambiguously Christian.

To make Norse mythology as it exists today represent the same worldview as White claims for an undifferentiated mass of non-Christian religions is to ignore a great deal about where it comes from and what jobs it was supposed to do in its contemporary contexts. At the same time, however, the Norse myths presumably take us several stages closer to an actual, historical, non-Christian ecological worldview than we are able to get by reading the medieval (or modern) literature of most other Western cultures. If this mythology is the product of a less anthropocentric worldview than that promoted by Genesis, there is a high likelihood that traces of this worldview will survive into its textual manifestations, however "inauthentic" we may believe them to be.

Myth may also have a deanthropocentrizing tendency in comparison to other forms of literature in general. Operating beyond conventional notions of history and geography, myth may be an important form of eco-discourse precisely because it does not center on relations between humans and their real-world "environment." The inhabitants of the world of myth are very often not properly human at all, and the nonhuman world is often represented in a livelier and weirder way than we find in anthropocentric literature. Perhaps for this reason this type of narrative will allow us to bypass or short-circuit some of the hermeneutic feedback loops that ecocriticism works hard to destabilize but can often end up reinforcing. As Patsy Callaghan argues, "Myths as a genre often invite us to read the spaces around the protagonist by giving the natural world itself agency and identity and complexity; in this way, our most ancient stories, read ecocritically, can provide an antidote to the anthropocentrism that might be said to motivate, perpetuate, and aggravate the ecological crises of our time."[25] Callaghan concludes by asking, "What better way to identify with those 'natural things' than to engage ecocritically with stories that give voice and agency to complex, challenging presentations of nature and of humans as a part of nature?"; and she answers her own question: "Read ecocritically, stories like these [myths] make it harder to believe in and validate the anthropocentric universe, harder to believe in rewards earned by loving ourselves the best of all."[26]

2. Norse pagan culture had no concept of Nature.

It may seem perverse that the lack of a concept analogous to Nature in Old Norse–Icelandic sources could be one of this culture's main ecological credentials. But the work of Timothy Morton, among others, has now problematized the mainstream Western idea of Nature as a thing apart from humanity so thoroughly as to make its deployment in the service of a progressive ecological agenda problematic, if not untenable. Morton, whose work has been highly influential in developing the ideas for this book, argues that there is no such thing as Nature. He claims, moreover, that making an imaginary thing called Nature the main object of our concerns and desires as ecologically minded citizens is to perpetuate the very dualism between Us and the rest of the world that earlier ecocritics had identified as lying at the heart of our current predicament. This is only one of several contradictions that Morton sees as unavoidable in deploying this concept in ecocritical discourse:

> Since the Romantic period, nature has been used to support the capitalist theory of value and to undermine it; to point out what is intrinsically human, and to exclude the human; to inspire kindness and compassion, and to justify competition and cruelty. . . . In short, nature has been on both sides of the equation ever since it was invented. . . . We discover how nature always slips out of reach in the very act of grasping it. At the very moment at which writing seems to be dissolving in the face of the compelling reality it is describing, writing overwhelms what it is depicting and makes it impossible to find anything behind its opaque texture. Even as it establishes a middle ground "in between" terms such as subject and object, or inside and outside, nature without fail excludes certain terms, thus reproducing the difference between inside and outside in other ways. Just when it brings us into proximity with the nonhuman "other," nature reestablishes a comfortable distance between "us" and "them."[27]

Other thinkers echo Morton's renunciation of Nature. Bruno Latour celebrates the death of a Nature that he believes to have been a stultifying political invention: "Thank God, nature is going to die. Yes, the great Pan is dead. After the death of God and the death of man, nature, too, had to give up the ghost. It was time: we were about to be unable to engage in politics any more at all."[28] Slavoj Žižek adopts a Mortonian rallying cry: "What we need is an ecology without nature: the ultimate obstacle to protecting nature is the very notion of nature we rely on."[29] Sam Mickey, whose concept of "coexistentialism" owes much to Morton's ideas, sees Nature's demise as an unambiguously positive development: "While the death of living beings, extinction of species, degradation of ecosystems, and destabilization of the climate are real problems, unbearably real, the loss of nature is good. The death of God and the death of nature are emancipatory events. With them gone, it is possible to engage in the perplexing complexity of events that weave together knots of nature and culture, ecology and religion, and science and politics."[30]

But while these writers have in different ways and for different reasons identified Nature as a state of the world (whether real or conceptual) whose time has passed, their opinions are not as radical as Morton's insistence that Nature is not even a thing, or Graham Harman's ringing claim that "nature is not natural and can never be naturalized."[31] Rather than thinking of Nature as existing no longer, we can imagine it as a dream that the West is just now waking up from: not only has Nature never been natural, it simply has never been. Bracketing Nature as a sort of cultural chimera allows us to sidestep some infuriating contradictions in the term's use: Did the so-called scientific revolution result in the "death of Nature," as Carolyn Merchant suggests? Or did the scientific revolution call the idea of Nature into being? In the first of these options, the Nature that Merchant sees the likes of Francis Bacon bringing under patriarchal control is an ancient, active, disorderly, organic cosmology that serves as a "nurturing mother" to humanity.[32] But this very concept of Nature as separate from a Society that presses Nature into its service, of the distinction of an organic versus mechanistic mode of being-in-the-world, arguably only comes into focus when the human-subject/natural-object dichotomy begins to be strictly enforced in Enlightenment thinking. Nature is killed in the act of creating it, leaving us, in Morton's words, with "the ghost of 'Nature,' a brand-new entity dressed up like a relic from a past age, haunt[ing] the modernity in which it was born."[33]

Premodern ecologies may provide salutary examples of how to live not in harmony with Nature, ironically, but in the absence of Nature as a category of being. If we need to move toward a notion of "ecology without Nature," as

Morton and Žižek aver, then the absence of Nature (as a reified concept) from premodern worldviews may show us some possible ways forward. If we have managed without Nature before, we can find ways to do so again.

Once again, a note of caution must temper my confidence in the medieval world's alleged pre-Natural status, for plenty of scholars have written about medieval Nature as if it certainly did exist. Indeed, for Marie-Dominique Chenu and his followers, the discovery of Nature was one of the most import-ant developments in the Western Christian thought of the twelfth-century "renaissance" of European learning.[34] (It is worth noting that this same renaissance has also often been identified as the site of "the discovery of the individual," implying that the full human-subject/natural-object binary may already have been at least immanent at this stage in medieval thought, though the notion of "the discovery of the individual" is to say the least con-troversial.)[35] Hugh White, for example, is sure that the concept of Nature was a key feature of medieval mentalities: "How people conceive Nature is intimately and ineluctably bound up with their opinions on all sorts of important matters—on the existential predicament of human beings, on the possibilities for moral behavior, on God. If we are wrong about what people think about Nature, we will be hopelessly wrong about what they think—and feel—full stop."[36]

This may be true, but what do we mean by "Nature," and indeed what do we mean by "people"? As Sara Ritchey shows in a brilliant critique of the "discovery of Nature" narrative, medievalists have focused their attention on the personified figure of Natura, who does indeed have an important place in Latin poetry of the twelfth century. But Natura is not a personification of what we normally mean by Nature: in Bernard Silvestris's *Cosmographia* (1147), Natura is a creative force, a shaper of the matter that comes to make up the physical cosmos, a bridge between God and the world. She is not coextensive with Nature—indeed, in order to shape creation, she must exist beyond it. So when we speak of Natura, we should be careful not to slip into talking about Nature, as Ritchey cautions: "Scholars often conflate twentieth- and twenty-first-century concepts of nature as the physical world with *natura* and descriptions of the phenomenal world found in the theol-ogy, poetry, architecture, and technology of the twelfth century. *Nature*, however, as an abstraction in the twelfth century, did not connote the con-glomeration of physical objects in the material world; *creation* did. Nature was an immaterial force that oversaw the orderly processes of generation."[37] We should also be wary of attributing greater influence and currency to a worldview founded in an idea of Natura than it deserves. The personified Natura is important to the work of philosopher-poets like Bernard, Alain of Lille, and William of Conches, but the evidence in favor of this figure—or a putative notion of Nature that she might represent—having widespread importance in the worldview or religious practices of twelfth-century Christians seems to have been stretched quite thin by twentieth- and twenty-first-century scholars.

None of the indigenous Norse deities has anything resembling the function of representing the totality of creation. As is often the case with polytheistic religious systems, the Scandinavian gods and goddesses are associated with specific aspects of the world and its operations, rather than with an abstracted idea of the whole physical realm. Although there is a female-gendered personification of Earth in Norse myth, Jǫrð, whom I will discuss in some depth in chapter 3, I argue that she always personifies only the Earth-as-physical-thing, the land, and must never be assumed to represent some sort of Gaia figure, a totalizing symbol of a global life system, and still less to be equivalent with either the Latin figure of Natura or modern Nature.

When Christian Old Norse–Icelandic authors use the loanword *náttúra*, as they do fairly frequently in learned works and translations from the second half of the thirteenth century onward, they seem to have no inkling of Nature as a "unification of all existents," and certainly none of it representing half of a dualism with a concept of Society or Culture or Humanity. *Náttúra,* for these writers, seems to connote most frequently an ordering principle—the order of creation, perhaps, or the characteristics proper to individual constituents of the world. *Náttúra* can also be a numinous power, or a Christian virtue, or perhaps once again a female personification: *Alexanders saga* (a translation of the Latin *Alexandreis*) names her as the "first mother" (*natturan sialf en fyrst moðer*), though this appears to be an isolated occurrence of this trope.[38] The Norse usages of the term are congruent with the Latin exemplars whence both the word and the concept have been borrowed. But if we go back to the older poetry, those texts that might provide glimpses into the worldviews of Norse pagan religion, we find that Nature disappears from the scene entirely. This pagan cosmology is the product of an ecology without Nature.

3. Scandinavian paganisms were animistic.

When Christian missionaries had to try to convince northern European pagans of the benefits of converting to the new religion, one of their main strategies was to undermine the reality of the pagans' traditional beliefs and practices.

They would insist, for example, that the idols the pagans worshipped were nothing more than the wood from which they were made; they would deny absolutely the idea that sacred groves, springs, or stones possessed any sort of living spirit inside them, any power or independent agency.[39] They were, in short, staunchly anti-animistic.

Animism is currently enjoying something of a revival among ecologically oriented scholars of religion and culture, although it is not the same sort of the animism that Christian missionaries throughout history have dismissed and denigrated in the worldviews of their target populations. While the Christian party line was that God held the monopoly on numinous existence beyond direct human experience, pagan cultures were represented as naive enough to imagine a vast plurality of spiritual potentialities behind the scenes of everyday life. For Victorian anthropologists like Edward Tylor, "animism" was a convenient label for this fundamental credulity—all spiritual beings are imaginary (with the politically expedient exception of the Christian God), but some are more imaginary than others. Animism was seen as a characteristic of a "primitive" stage in a culture's evolution toward scientific rationality. For these reasons, Graham Harvey notes that "the term *animism* is now largely ghettoized as an example of an early phase of academic thought and of the entanglement of our academic ancestors with colonialism."[40] But for Harvey and a growing number of colleagues, a revision of "animism" is providing a fruitful framework for discussions of human-world interactions in the twenty-first century. This new animism has at its heart the idea that the "world is found to be, and treated as, a community of persons not all of whom are human."[41] Morton echoes this conception in his call for an "upgraded" animism: "The ethics of the ecological thought is to regard beings as people even when they aren't people."[42] And whereas much second-wave animistic theory is founded in relations between living creatures in contemporary indigenous cultures, Morton's deployment of the term—anticipating his later turn toward an object-oriented ontology—requires us to consider as beings, and thus as people, inanimate as well as animate objects, the dead as well as the living.[43]

Old Norse–Icelandic pagan religious culture was animistic in the old sense of the word: the tenacious belief in Iceland and Norway's *landvættir* (land-spirits), normally invisible, protective entities that dwelled in groves or mounds according to the thirteenth-century (Christian) Gulaþing law from central Norway, could certainly be classed as indicating a belief in a wider range of nonempirical beings than the pagan gods alone.[44] As Nicolas Meylan discusses, too, and as the Gulaþing law's reference to them indicates, the *landvættir* remained real to Scandinavians long into the Christian era.[45] They are certainly related to the elves (or *huldufólk,* "hidden people") who—as is so often gleefully reported by a world media keen to maintain the country's reputation for kookiness—must be considered before a new civil engineering project in Iceland can go ahead.[46]

While there is clearly some ecocritical resonance in the existence of spirits that animate the landscape and protect areas of wilderness from development, my interest in this book lies firmly in the potentially illuminating symbiosis of Old Norse–Icelandic worldviews with neo-animism—the possibility that Old Norse–Icelandic literature endows nonhuman entities of all types with a sort of personhood that helps to dissolve artificial ontological boundaries between humans and nonhumans.

4. Old Norse–Icelandic mimesis has a place for the
supernatural; it troubles the boundaries of literary realism.

The sagas of Icelanders have a unique reputation as a mimetic form of medieval prose "fiction" and a pioneer of literary realism in Europe. Though these claims are open to debate, the sagas' mode of mimesis places them in the orbit of the types of representations of the "real world" that have often attracted ecocritics working in other periods. And, because the sagas are set in a premodern, decentralized, arguably "organic" society, their representations of the physical environment could well prove of value to ecocritical inquiries. As Lawrence Buell puts it, this type of criticism must place special emphasis on "literature's capacity for articulating the nonhuman environment."[47]

But I tend to agree with Serpil Oppermann when she problematizes ecocriticism's preoccupation with realist modes of literature. "Ecocriticism today," writes Oppermann, "finds itself struggling with hermeneutic closure as well as facing an ambivalent openness in its interpretative approach. This paradox is due to the fact that many prominent ecocritics who aligned themselves with the perspectives of realist epistemology, think it enables ecocriticism to be an open field of inquiry. They ignore the conceptual problems the realist perspectives conjure."[48] These problems include, but are not limited to, a naive or disingenuous acceptance of the referential quality of realist literature, a strong antipathy to poststructuralist theories about the discursive constructedness of textual representations of the world, and an uncritical approbation of "nature writing." Since, as we have observed, native Old Norse–Icelandic literary traditions possess no concept analogous to Nature, it follows that we must not identify any of its constituent texts as "nature writing." The sagas and poetry of medieval Scandinavia may help an ecocritical revaluation of the nature of literary representation in other ways, too. As we saw in the first part of this introduction, Norse myth is a distinctly nonmimetic form of literature that has no referential relationship to the physical environments in which it was produced—but it is unquestionably a nexus of ecological concerns. And even the sagas of Icelanders—those paragons of medieval realism—trouble our complacent notions of literary mimesis by their treatment of the supernatural.

For Phelpstead, the sagas' treatment of the supernatural is one of the most distinctive contributions that Old Norse–Icelandic literature can make to ecocritical inquiry. The sagas' brand of mimesis includes a host of supernatural beings and occurrences that are represented exactly as realistically as the quotidian details of human life on the farmstead. For Phelpstead, this easy acceptance of the supernatural "may have something to teach ecocritics":

> When it takes for granted that the non-human is limited to the natural, ecocriticism is an unreflective child of its time. Medieval literature, including a text such as *Eyrbyggja saga,* reminds us that such an assumption is characteristic of a tiny minority of the human beings who have so far existed on earth. The environmentally aware reader might be moved to reflect that it is only in the last couple of hundred years, precisely the period during which the natural environment has come under gravest threat from human beings, that belief in the supernatural has disappeared among sizable parts of the human population.[49]

He goes on to conclude that the realistic presentation of the supernatural in the sagas challenges twenty-first-century critics to rethink relationships between Nature and Culture, and between the human and the nonhuman, and to reintegrate a sense of the world's numinousness. It also disturbs, I think, our too-casual acceptance of the idea that the Western canon of realistic literature has a particular claim to a referential relationship with Nature.[50] If nineteenth-century realist fiction has no place in its mimesis for the weird and uncanny supernature that was taken for granted by the authors of the Icelandic sagas, and is still taken for granted among many indigenous cultures in the world, can it truly be called realistic? Or must we claim that the sagas are not realistic literature because they evince an acceptance of the existence of nonempirical entities, despite the manifest realism of their mode of description? These questions illustrate the simple fact that realism has no intrinsic claim to referentiality over and above myth, say, or poetry or speculative fiction. Just as Morton provocatively proposes that we need "ecology without Nature," I am tempted to suggest that one slogan for future critical work in the field might be "ecocriticism without nature writing."[51]

5. Catastrophe is immanent in Norse mythology (and medieval Icelandic culture more generally).

My sixth and seventh chapters deal with the end of the world, using the Norse mythology surrounding Ragnarǫk as way into a theorization of the apocalyptic qualities of the Anthropocene. I contend that the pervasive apocalypticism of Scandinavian mythology helps us to understand more clearly the benefits, and risks, of thinking of our current era of ecological crisis as a world-ending scenario. The narrative of Ragnarǫk is normally explained in human terms— the world ends because the pagan gods fail to maintain social cohesion in the face of the giants' hostility. But an ecocritical reading of Ragnarǫk reveals that the cause of all the Æsir's problems is an ecological failure, the result of their determination to maintain at all costs the same dualistic systems of thought that are so often implicated in our own descent into ecocide on a massive scale; the effects of Ragnarǫk, too, touch the whole of creation, including physical systems like climate and geology.

Apocalypticism is a quintessential ecocritical trope, whether one believes in its potential as a spur to political action or questions its efficacy as potentially paralyzing. J. L. Schatz, for instance, suggests that apocalyptic rhetoric is invaluable in raising consciousness about the urgency of ecological crisis and creating pressure for change: "Oftentimes it takes images of planetary annihilation to motivate people into action after years of sitting idly by watching things slowly decay. In reality it takes awareness of impending disaster to compel policymakers to enact even piecemeal reform. On the screen it takes the actual appearance of ecological apocalypse to set the plot in motion."[52] Ragnarǫk is an alternate myth of "planetary annihilation" that supports in some ways, and in other ways challenges, Schatz's claims of the importance of apocalyptic thinking in effecting change. The issue as I see it is that Icelandic culture seems to use apocalyptic mythmaking as a way of displacing immanent catastrophe, moving it from the here and now into Mircea Eliade's *illud tempus,* the never-and-always that is characteristic of mythic time.[53] We have already seen how volcanic eruptions, the most threatening feature of the Icelandic landscape and a genuinely world-ending phenomenon, cast hardly a cloud over the realistic descriptions of Iceland that appear in the sagas. Rather, this real-world catastrophe is dealt with, it seems, by constant deferral, by sublimation, and by mythologizing. All these things can also happen, I argue, with apocalyptic imaginings in the twenty-first century. Because I am alive to type these words and you are, I hope, alive to read them, because the sun came up this morning and life went on as normal, we find it difficult to relate the end of the world to our own experiences: for us, it is a myth that the world is going to end because of global warming, even though it is true that the world is going to end because of global warming—even if it is true, as Morton claims, that the world has ended already.[54] It is my hope that analyzing apocalyptic myths as myths will illuminate the responses to ecological catastrophe that are possible to us in the conditions created by the Anthropocene. I conclude that the end of the world mandates the creation of new worlds, and that we must strive to do better than the Norse gods, whose doom Ragnarǫk truly turns out to be.

These five features of Old Norse–Icelandic literary culture—its roots in a non-Christian belief system and its expression through myth, the absence of Nature from its worldview, its animism, the weird (super)realism of its representational literature, and its origins in a natureculture that has always lived under the shadow of ecological catastrophe—make ecocriticism particularly important to Old Norse studies, and Old Norse particularly relevant to the ecocritical project as a whole.

Epilogue: A Non-apology for Anachronism

Over the course of this book, I will frequently commit (or, better, "perform") anachronisms. In the court of medievalists' opinion, the charge of anachronism is a damning one, frequently raised. A 2016 blog post by Michael Johnston and Alex Mueller describes the current situation thus: "The charge of anachronism is so common and so promiscuously leveled in book reviews that just about any work of historical scholarship is vulnerable to it. By anachronism, we don't mean the creative kind, such as Dante being quoted within the Arthurian age of the *Wife of Bath's Tale*. We mean the sort where reviewers accuse reviewees of the 'mistaken' use of a modern term for a medieval phenomenon or of making an 'armchair' judgment about an ancient form of xenophobia."[55] In anticipation of these charges, I observe that this book embraces anachronism as an inevitable and even welcome condition of any ecologically oriented medievalism. As a critical response to contemporary ecological issues, all ecocriticism is founded in a concern with the present and future state of the world. When ecocritics study an earlier period, they do so through frames of reference developed in response to twentieth- and twenty-first-century problems, with the intention that learning from the (ecological) past might help us understand the (ecological) present and prepare us for our (ecological) future. As I outlined above, this work is not primarily an ecohistorical project—understanding the environmental contexts that have helped shape Old Norse literary culture is a worthwhile and fascinating endeavor in its own right, but it is not my main concern here. Rather, this book is concerned with reading contemporary eco-logical issues *into* the medieval past so that we can read *out of* medieval texts ideas that inform our responses to the world that we live in now. For, as John Parham puts it, "it is the case that the practice of what might be called histor-ical ecocriticism is not so much about excavating past environmental anxiet-ies—interesting and informative as these are—as about examining antecedent attitudes toward nature for clues in the attempt to understand our own."[56]

So, when I claim in chapters 6 and 7 that the myth of Ragnarǫk holds up a mirror to the Anthropocene narrative of economic growth, technological advancement, and ecological collapse, it will be easy to criticize my work for anachronism. Poets and mythmakers in medieval Scandinavia did not have any conception of anthropogenic global warming; nor am I claiming that memories of historical climactic crises have necessarily informed the produc-tion of these stories—though I do not discount that idea. Instead, I simply propose that what we know about global warming tells us something about the nature and import of the Ragnarǫk myth's apocalypticism, while what we can learn about the end of the world from the Ragnarǫk myth complex speaks to us, in compelling and potentially transformational terms, of our own situation as citizens of the Anthropocene.

As I have struggled, as a medievalist trained in a historicist tradition, to come to terms with my new attraction to anachronism, I have been much encouraged and comforted by J. Hillis Miller's example in an article simply entitled "Anachronistic Reading." "Literary works," writes Miller,

> program or encode their future readings, though in an unpredictable
> way. . . . A free reading would try to identify the way a poem or other literary
> work mirrors the future. Such a reading, it follows, is anachronistic. It takes
> possession of the old work for present uses and in a new context. . . . A poem
> encrypts, though not predictably, the effects it may have when at some
> future moment, in another context, it happens to be read and inscribed
> in a new situation, in "an interpretation that transforms the very thing it
> interprets," as Jacques Derrida puts it in *Specters of Marx*. The effects of a
> transformative reading exceed any intentions or intended meanings that may
> have been in the poet's mind when he put the words down on paper.[57]

In his article, Miller goes on to provide a reading of a poem by Wallace Ste-vens that sees "the old text as somehow a proleptic foretelling of a present situation . . . a reading that sees a text as prefiguring a future event that comes to seem what the text predicted, foresaw, or forecast."[58] As it happens, the future that Miller identifies Stevens's "The Man on the Dump" as presaging is the environmental catastrophe of overpopulation and mass extinction in the face of anthropogenic pollution, which the poet cannot have known about and had no particular reason to predict in the act of composition. But just as Miller comes to the conclusion that to him "The Man on the Dump" inevitably leads to a reading that flashes forward to the twenty-first century's ecological predicament, my ecocritical reading of an ancient poem like Vǫluspá leads me, quite naturally, to the conclusion that immanent in its descriptions of Ragnarǫk is an unintended foreshadowing of global warming and other ecocatastrophes that we identify as quintessentially modern. The ways in which Norse poets transfigure people into trees and endow trees with agency, emotion, and sociability foreshadows recent work in plant communication studies, while the sagas' representation of pre-settlement Iceland as a pristine wilderness, full of resources ripe for the plundering, calls to mind debates over the economic exploitation of the Icelandic interior (and elsewhere) in the twenty-first century. All these readings, which come from my own experience as an ecologically concerned inhabitant of late modernity, now seem thoroughly natural to me, even inevitable. My conception of Old Norse literature is richer for these readings, and my conception of the world is much the richer for my reading of Old Norse.

Above all, I hope that the free readings of Old Norse–Icelandic texts that I put forward here will be transformative in the way that Miller suggests that all readings can be. Reading ourselves, our anxieties, and our worldviews into the medieval text transforms the text into something it was not before; reading the text transforms us into something we have never been before. The meeting of the reader and the text is a site of pure, unbounded potential, and if the price of tapping some of that potential is to be accused of anachronism, it is a price I am well prepared to pay.

2   Remembering and Dismembering
a Transcorporeal Cosmos

IF LYNN WHITE'S FAMOUS HYPOTHESIS about the per-
nicious impact of the Judeo-Christian creation myth on the ecological trajectory of Western culture is true, the twenty-eighth and twenty-ninth verses of
the first chapter of Genesis become a singularly harmful text in the history of
life on Earth. By making the sustenance of human beings the whole world's
raison d'être and by commanding Adam and Eve to go forth and multiply
while subduing and ruling the nonhuman, God sows the seeds of the ecological disaster that threatens, millennia later, to cause the end of the world.
An old creation myth has led to a new sort of apocalypse that happens to be
unfolding before our eyes.

If the West's foundational ecological myths were (or had been, or could
be) different, how would (or would have been, or could be) our past, present, and future as Earth dwellers be different? If Genesis did not exist or
if Christianity did not become the overwhelmingly dominant cultural force
in Western Europe and, eventually, in Europe's colonial sphere of influence,
how would our ecological situation be different today? We can play a variant
of the alternate-universe time-travel game: if a time traveler could go back
and destroy the first chapter of Genesis, how would our lives change? Would
the Anthropocene happen, the Industrial Revolution, the Atomic Age? Would
the Earth's population have been kept in check? What about global warming?
If White's theory holds, we might expect that these phenomena, all of which
implicate the great divorce of people from the nonhuman world that Genesis
sanctions, would at least have happened differently in a world without Genesis.

It may seem that to place so much emphasis on the text, rather than the
attitudes that it encodes, is to stretch White's thesis too far. But one of the
strengths of White's theory is precisely the weight it places on mythmaking's
significance in the formation of worldviews. The importance of worldview to
the formation of habits of thought and modes of life—all those things that

determine the course of human/nonhuman interactions through history—is obvious. We make and use myths to explain our beliefs, justify our actions, and impose our vision of the world onto (what we view as) our surroundings. As Bruce Lincoln so memorably defined it, "Myth is ideology in narrative form,"[1] and the ideologies that are especially implicated in the twenty-first century's ecological crises—capitalism, technocracy, patriarchy, and other forms of hierarchic oppression, including those perpetuated by organized religion— continue to mythologize the hard distinction between Nature and Society that Genesis anticipates. And those of us who believe we are on the side of the world-beyond-us also create and deploy myths over and over again. Consider the famous example of James Lovelock's Gaia theory. Lovelock's Gaia is doubly mythic, in that it takes other people's myths—the Greek stories of Gaia, in this case—and makes them emblematic of Lovelock's own "ideology in narrative form," his belief in a prehistoric global matriarchy that cherished the Earth as a living being:

> In times that are ancient by human measure, as far back as the earliest artefacts can be found, it seems that the Earth was worshipped as a goddess and believed to be alive. The myth of the great Mother is part of most early religions. The Mother is a compassionate, feminine figure; spring of all life, of fecundity, of gentleness. She is also the stern and unforgiving bringer of death. . . . At some time not more than a few thousand years ago the concept of a remote master God, an overseer of Gaia, took root.[2]

This mythic Gaia has become a potent and popular symbol around which the ecologically inclined have rallied. For such people, Gaia can provide a positive counterexample to the Genesis myth's damaging insistence on man's divinely ordained separation from, and superiority to, the rest of the world. But to recognize something as mythic is also always to cast some doubt about its claims to veracity. We can say that Lovelock's Gaia is a myth and mean it as a simple statement of fact that alludes to the origins of this figure in a body of narratives that we identify as mythology; but if we say that his concept of Gaia is "just a myth," we are using the term to cast doubt on the very reality of the story he tells. It is telling that as I write this chapter, the Google internet search engine's first suggestion for how the phrase "Global warming is . . . ." might be completed is ". . . a myth." And indeed, even as someone who accepts absolutely the scientific evidence that tells us that global warming is already a fait accompli, I can see that this phenomenon has important mythic aspects. Narratives cluster around the concept of global warming, and they are narratives that are always ideologically invested in either asserting or denying its existence. These narratives seek to explain, convince, justify, or (when turned against those on the other side of the debate) cast doubt on deeply entrenched worldviews that have important ramifications for how people really live their lives.

Myths remain and have always been narrative vehicles for the formation, expression, and testing of worldviews. As such, looking to myths beyond the Judeo-Christian mainstream for alternative ways of being-in-the-world has proven an important tool for creating new metaphors that can contribute to the construction of different forms of ecological consciousness. Gaia has been the most influential example of an alternative ecomyth that can be set up in direct opposition to Genesis's hierarchies of being, perhaps, but there have been others, and there is room for more. In this chapter, therefore, I explore the ecological potential of Old Norse worldviews, especially as they are preserved in those myths that deal with the creation of the universe.

As I discussed in the previous chapter, Norse mythology has its roots in a pre-Christian cultural system, a set of interconnected pagan religions (or, perhaps better, religiosities) that stretches back at least into the northern European Iron Age. At the same time, however, the textual sources on which our knowledge of these myths rest were all preserved in a Christian milieu, and untangling for once and for all which aspects of Norse myth are genuinely pagan, or even what "pagan" means in this context, often seems impossible. In interrogating these world-building myths, therefore, my plan is to suspend judgment about the *origins* of these texts and their worldviews and instead to concentrate on their (potential) effects. Myths can do various sorts of work in the world regardless of where they ultimately come from, and we do not need to insist upon some sort of pagan purity for the Norse myths for them to represent worldviews that are nonetheless different from the more familiar structures of Judeo-Christian or classical traditions. Reading the Norse creation myths against Genesis's cosmogony may show us an alternative mode of world-building that could prove to be less disastrous and more sustainable than our prevailing models.

Norse Myths of Creation: Sources and Challenges to Interpretation

No single master narrative of the creation of the Norse mythological cosmos survives. Rather, there are four main sources whose myths are clearly interrelated but the nature of whose interrelationships is not altogether clear. These four texts are all, in their current forms, products of a remarkable renewal of interest in traditional poetry and pre-Christian culture in thirteenth-century Iceland. Perhaps the most important are three mythological poems that have been preserved in the Codex Regius (*Konungsbók* in Icelandic) manuscript of the so-called *Poetic Edda*, which was probably written around 1270. On the basis of the surviving evidence, poetry of the Eddic type must have been the prime vehicle for the preservation of mythological and legendary narratives in pre-Christian Scandinavia. The poems of the *Poetic Edda* show many hallmarks of their origins in an oral tradition: they are composed in rhythmical, alliterative meters, and they make frequent use of formulas—repeated units of semantically and metrically identical lines or phrases that occur multiple times within single poems and across the corpus as a whole, sometimes with variation. These texts are, in many cases, much older than the manuscript that preserves them. We know, for example, that Icelandic and Norwegian court poets, some of whose occasional verse survives and is datable back to the tenth century, sprinkled their poems with formulaic allusions to mythological poems of the Eddic type.[3]

The first poem in the *Poetic Edda* is *Vǫluspá* ("The Seeress's Prophecy"), which is of unique value to our understanding of Old Norse cosmogony (and eschatology) because it provides a complete, though strange and elusive, narrative of the universe's entire history—from its coming into being to its eventual destruction in the apocalypse of Ragnarǫk and its subsequent rebirth. But while *Vǫluspá*'s apparent cohesiveness is beguiling, it cannot safely be taken as giving an authorized or even authoritative version of a pre-Christian worldview. Although this poem is usually thought to have been composed in the period during which Norway and Iceland were undergoing their turbulent conversion to Christianity (within half a century or so either side of the year 1000), it now displays quite clear evidence of having been composed by a poet who was either a Christian, well on his or her way to becoming a Christian, or somehow surprisingly knowledgeable amount about Christianity for a person otherwise deeply immersed in pagan traditions.[4] We do not know whether the Christian elements in *Vǫluspá* were always integral to the poem or, if they were not, at what point or under what circumstances they were incorporated into its tradition. We are also faced with the challenge that *Vǫluspá* is preserved entire in two separate versions. Along with the Codex Regius, a manuscript miscellany known as *Hauksbók*—written by an Icelander in Norway around 1300—has a text of *Vǫluspá*, and the two versions agree with each other in neither overall form nor individual details. *Vǫluspá* is a mysterious text, entirely in keeping with its sinister tone and often esoteric subject matter, but it is often the only source that allows us to make sense of the disparate snippets of mythological information that we find in other poems. However, it deals with the origins of the universe in much less detail than the end of the world receives. It would be difficult to use *Vǫluspá* on its own to tell the full story of the Norse creation.

Two further Eddic poems, *Vafþrúðnismál* and *Grímnismál,* neighbors in the Codex Regius and members of the same genre of wisdom exchange–contest poem, also narrate the origins of the pagan cosmos. Each poem is named after a character who takes part in a battle of wits that is designed to try the participants' knowledge of the mythological universe and its inhabitants. In the former poem, the god Óðinn interrogates the wise giant Vafþrúðnir to see if he can obtain any further information about the fate of the gods. *Grímnismál* sees Óðinn disguise himself as a man named Grímnir in order to test the hospitality of a human king called Geirrøðr. After Geirrøðr suspends the disguised Óðinn between two fires for eight long nights, close enough to singe his cloak, Óðinn utters a stream of mythological knowledge as a soliloquy, apparently a propos of nothing. Both these poems contain information relating to the creation of the cosmos, though it appears piecemeal: their generic form as question-and-answer knowledge exchanges precludes them from telling a cohesive narrative.[5]

The only source to narrate the origins of the mythological cosmos in full and in detail, therefore, is *Snorra Edda. Snorra Edda* (alternately called the *Prose Edda,* or the *Younger Edda*) is a four-part work, composed in the first half of the thirteenth century by the Icelandic chieftain, lawyer, and poet Snorri Sturluson.[6] It provides a comprehensive overview of traditional Old Norse poetics and a conspectus of the mythological knowledge that contemporary Christian audiences would need to know to understand the poetry of their pagan ancestors. Modeling his prose narrative closely on the timeline of events given by *Vǫluspá* but quoting widely from other Eddic poems, Snorri weaves together a synoptic history of the pagan gods and their universe more cohesive and comprehensive even than *Vǫluspá*'s. *Snorra Edda* is truly the one indispensable written source for the Norse myths. Without it, we would lose almost all knowledge of certain myths; we would, moreover, often find it impossible to interpret those myths that do survive in older Old Norse–Icelandic poetry. Snorri explains away ambiguities in the source texts and smooths over narrative gaps and inconsistencies. He has done so much of the interpretative work for us that it is hard to imagine where we would begin if *Snorra Edda* did not exist.

The great strength of *Snorra Edda* is also its weakness, however, if we consider it as a potential source of information about pagan beliefs and worldviews.

Snorri's reworking of the myths is so coherent and his explanations of them so convincing—and so essential to our understanding of other mythological texts—that we are inclined to overlook the fact that our best source for pagan mythology in Scandinavia is the one that in some ways is furthest removed from the culture whose beliefs it purports to represent. Snorri was an accomplished poet, who clearly had at his disposal a rich array of verse by others, either written in manuscripts now lost or held in his memory. Some of his poetic inheritance, like the texts that find their way into the *Poetic Edda,* is likely to have been genuinely antique—the product of a pre-Christian era. But Snorri was a Christian, and one of his purposes in writing his *Edda* was not merely to harmonize different stories from Norse mythology with each other but to harmonize the whole within a (relatively) orthodox Christian schema of history and cosmology. In its present form, *Snorra Edda* begins with an apologetic prologue that seeks to explain away Scandinavian paganism within the parameters of Christian universal history as an unfortunate—but not altogether blameworthy—blip in human progress. In the Prologue, the Norse gods are shown to be nothing more than historical personages—characters from the Trojan War, as it happens—whose prowess and valor led to their being deified by pagans. The pagans, Snorri says, were those people who had neglected their obedience to God in the aftermath of Noah's flood, becoming capable of understanding the world only through rational thought, blind to the deeper spiritual meaning of things.[7]

The conceit that paganism is a form of delusion is maintained in the second section of *Snorra Edda, Gylfaginning* (Gylfi's tricking). *Gylfaginning* is the most purely mythological part of the *Edda;* it is here that Snorri's overarching narrative of the pagan cosmos and its downfall is related. But the reader is distanced from *Gylfaginning*'s myths by a framing device that places all information about the pagan gods in speeches uttered by a triune manifestation of Óðinn, figured here as three human kings in accordance with Snorri's explanation of the origins of paganism in the Prologue. At the end of *Gylfaginning,* the pagan world vanishes, almost in a puff of smoke, leaving us with the impression that the whole edifice of paganism is no more solid than a stage set in front of which the old gods' surrogates are made to act out a masquerade—an imitation of something that never really existed.

Thus *Snorra Edda* is a conundrum. It is, by the standards of its age, sympathetic to pagans, accepting of paganism, and admiring of pagan culture. But it is a highly self-conscious exercise in framing pagan myths as witnesses to a worldview that was seen as being built on sand, a misstep on the path toward Christian enlightenment that humanity otherwise had been following. And while Snorri's attitude toward paganism is often made quite explicit, once we penetrate the narrative frame and enter the pagan world that he conjures up so vividly, elements of Snorri's Christian viewpoint can bleed into what seem like perfectly straightforward representations of pre-Christian myths. *Snorra Edda*'s cosmogonic narratives are a case in point.

The Prologue to *Snorra Edda* begins, as we might expect in a work firmly aligned with Christian universal history, with a potted account of the Judeo-Christian creation modeled on Genesis: "Almighty God created heaven and earth and all things in them, and lastly two humans from whom generations are descended, Adam and Eve, and their stock multiplied and spread over the world. But as time passed mankind became diverse: some were good and orthodox in faith, but many more turned aside to follow the lusts of the world and neglected God's commandments, and so God drowned the world except those who were in the ark with Noah."[8] From an ecological perspective, we might say that Snorri's brief synopsis of the Judeo-Christian creation myth at least has the advantage of not specifying that Adam and Eve were given dominion over the nonhuman world, but there is little here to suggest that Snorri is thinking beyond Genesis's paradigms. Nor should we expect him to: in the Prologue, we are still within the parameters of a Christian worldview, and Snorri's deployment of a conventional cosmogony allows him briefly to establish the orthodox credentials of his discussion of paganism. But when the curtain lifts on the dialog between King Gylfi and the three mouthpieces of paganism, Hár, Jafnhár, and Þriði ("High," "Just-as-High," and "Third"), Snorri's first attempt at an account of a Norse creation myth produces an uncomfortable hybrid of pagan and Christian ideas.[9]

Like the Eddic poem *Vafþrúðnismál, Gylfaginning* is an exchange of knowledge that is presented in a question-and-answer format. Gylfi, a bewildered neighbor of the (human) Æsir—falsely etymologized as "people of Asia" in the Prologue—disguises himself as a man called Gangleri and asks questions; Hár, Jafnhár, and Þriði take turns to answer. Hár, Jafnhár, and Þriði are human hypostases of the god Óðinn; part of the joke of *Gylfaginning* is that the pagans are hopelessly confused about who is a god and who is not a god.[10] These human surrogates for Óðinn worship another, fully divine figure whom we might identify with Óðinn, but whom they do not call by that name, as their first response makes clear:

Gangleri began his questioning thus:
    "Who is the highest and most ancient of all gods?"
    Hár said: "He is called All-Father in our language, but in Old Ásgarðr he had twelve names" [. . .]

Then Gangleri asked: "Where is this god, what power has he, and what great works has he performed?"

Hár said: "He lives throughout all ages and rules all his kingdom and governs all things great and small."

Then spoke Just-as-high: "He made heaven and earth and the skies and everything in them."

Then spoke Þriði: "But his greatest work is that he made man and gave him a soul that shall live and never perish though the body decay to dust or burn to ashes. And all men who are righteous shall live and dwell with him in the place called Gimlé or Vingólf, but wicked men go to Hel and on to Niflhel; that is down in the ninth world."[11]

These human Æsir worship a creator deity who is functionally identical to the Christian God. Although Alfǫðr (All-father) is an attested byname for Óðinn, its use here is obviously meant to evoke God the Father's paternal relationship to his creation.[12] Alfǫðr controls the universe—time, space, and "all things great and small"—in an ontological hierarchy that closely resembles the Judeo-Christian creation. The people that this Alfǫðr creates do not explicitly receive dominion over the nonhuman, but it is revealing that Þriði still regards the creation of soul-bearing humans as the creator's greatest achievement: the apparent goal of creation in this universe, like that of Genesis, is to provide a home for people, an environment in which they can attempt to live righteously in the hope of achieving a postmortem existence with the godhead. The explicit link between morality and soteriology is another reconfiguration of a pagan myth along Christian lines: while the names Gimlé, Vingólf, Hel, and Niflhel are all found in other contexts, it is only in *Snorra Edda* that a clear distinction is made between them on the basis of the "righteousness" of who gets to go where in the afterlife.

If Snorri's aim in his second creation myth was to harmonize pagan conceptions of the origins of the universe with the authorized Christian version, he has done so by thoroughly reshaping the pagan cosmogony in the image of Genesis's account, though there are many details from scripture that do not find their way into the Æsir's statements. The Æsir—as the Prologue suggests they should be—are deluded in some ways because, as pagans, they have had no access to the spiritual truth revealed through Christ's incarnation. At the same time, though, these figures are shown to have arrived autonomously at something pretty close to a true belief in God the Father. All of this means that neither the opening of the Prologue nor the opening exchange of *Gylfaginning* can yield much hope of a cosmology that takes us beyond Genesis's hierarchies. The whole point of these introductory sections is to establish that pagan myths are in fact a distortion, almost a parody, of Christian truth. Happily, Snorri soon feels comfortable in dropping this façade, beginning to work with his mythological sources directly. And so, as *Gylfaginning* continues, we forget—though never entirely—that Gylfi's encounter with the Æsir is supposed to be taking place in a particular hermeneutic context that maintains a sort of cordon sanitaire around paganism, keeping a Christian audience from getting its hands dirty, as it were. We gradually enter the world of Norse myth, the world that we also see in the Eddic poems that Snorri uses as his sources. Finally, we begin to get an inkling that the structures of the pagan cosmos might indeed offer alternative mythical paradigms for our being-in-the world.

Everything, Incorporated: Embodying and Dismembering the World beyond the Human

In the beginning, there was nothing:

> Gangleri spoke: "What was the beginning? And how did things start? And what was there before?"
> High replied: "As it says in *Vǫluspá*:
>
>> It was at the beginning of time,
>> when nothing was; sand was not, nor sea, nor cool waves.
>> Earth did not exist, nor heaven on high.
>> The mighty gap was, but no growth."[13]

While creation ex nihilo is also characteristic of the Judeo-Christian myth, the initial vision of the pagan cosmos that Snorri gives us is more radically devoid of substance because there is, in this myth, no preexisting creator deity. As Richard Cole puts it, this void is an example of a "perfect Absence, [since] it is from here that all things present or absent must come. It is a place devoid of observers, and so it exists before the absence-tainting act of signification."[14] We might see correspondences with Genesis 1:1's "Now the earth was formless and empty" in the second half of the stanza that Hár quotes from *Vǫluspá*, but nothing can precede God and therefore nothing *cannot* precede the universe. But in *Vǫluspá*, the void, the "mighty gap," exists (*gap var ginnunga*), and there is no divine power beyond or outside this gap, nothing at all except absence. Notably, what is defined as being absent from this preemptive shadow of a cosmos is not people, but those things that might be tagged as Nature—earth, water, land, sky, vegetation. (The God of Genesis creates humankind as the last and greatest of his deeds, it is true, but the Norse myths' relative lack of interest in the creation of humanity is striking, as we will see.)

In the two versions of *Vǫluspá* that circulate independently of *Snorra Edda,* the second line of this stanza, the third in the poem, is different, reading *þar er Ymir byggði* ("there when [or where] Ymir dwelled" or "made a dwelling"). Thus, rather than the absolute emptiness of Snorri's account, *Vǫluspá* places emphasis on the fact that the early universe was indeed inhabited. But Ymir is not a god: he is a primeval giant, as all versions of the cosmogony attest. Ymir's absence from *Gylfaginning*'s first citation of *Vǫluspá* is puzzling. Has Snorri omitted him deliberately, to make the precosmic void even voider? Or did Snorri have access to an alternate version of *Vǫluspá* that differed in this way, for similarly obscure reasons? In a way, it makes little difference to an ecocritical reading of the passage, since we can construe Ymir's act of "dwelling" as being synchronous (and synonymous) with the universe's coming into being. The most likely explanation for Snorri's alteration of the verse, in my view, is simply that introducing Ymir at this point would create an extra layer of uncertainty, as it might imply that Ymir preexisted the moment of creation, and thus mean that Ymir must have come into being separately. Snorri has his own explanation for Ymir's birth, which would be inconsistent with the possibility of Ymir preexisting the rest of the cosmos.

Snorri's account of how the universe transitioned from absolute absence to a teeming abundance of life is convoluted and often strikes readers as somewhat ridiculous. His main source for the chronology of the pagan cosmos, *Vǫluspá,* only makes a single reference to Ymir, and Snorri either did not know that reading or rejected it. The Eddic poems *Vafþrúðnismál* and *Grímnismál* both mention Ymir's cosmological significance, but they do not speak of where Ymir comes from or how he comes to be:

> From Ymir's flesh was the world shaped,
> and the mountains from his bones;
> the sky from the skull of the frost-cold giant,
> and the sea from his blood. (*Vafþrúðnismál* 21)[15]

> From Ymir's flesh the world was made,
> and from his blood, the sea,
> mountains from his bones, trees from his hair,
> and from his skull the sky.

And from his eyelashes the cheerful gods
made Miðgarðr for men's sons;
and from his brain the hard-tempered clouds
were all created. (*Grímnismál* 40–41)[16]

In making sense of these sources, Snorri turns the creation of the universe into
a spontaneous process completely at odds with the Judeo-Christian schema,
though he cannot entirely avoid inconsistencies. (Indeed, I suspect that the
difficulty that the Æsir have in telling a coherent creation narrative is part of
Snorri's strategy of having pagan characters reveal from their own mouths the
logical flaws and spiritual inadequacies of their worldview, considered in the
light of Christian truth.)

According to the three Æsir, the first stage in the origins of the universe
is a sort of elemental fusion, although they do not explain whence these elements came. First, there was a realm called Niflheimr (world of mist), a cold
and damp underworld that is presumably related to the Niflhel that Þriði
mentioned in the second, hybridized creation myth told in *Gylfaginning*. We
do not learn how Niflheimr came into being. In opposition to Niflheimr was a
region named Muspell, so torrid as to be constantly aflame. Again, we receive
no information about whether Muspell had always existed or, if not, how it
originated. Between Niflheimr and Muspell flowed rivers of poison, which
changed state depending on how close they passed by the two realms of heat
and cold. First they turned to ice, then the heat blowing from Muspell melted
that ice, which dripped into Ginnungagap, which is *Vǫluspá*'s total abyss now
turned into a localized geographical feature. Ginnungagap is "as mild as a
windless sky" and so provides the appropriate climatic conditions in which life
can flourish: "Then spoke Þriði: 'Just as from Niflheimr there arose coldness
and all things grim, so what was facing close to Muspell was hot and bright,
but Ginnungagap was as mild as a winter sky. And when the rime and the
blowing of the warmth met so that it thawed and dripped, there was a quick-
ening from these flowing drops due to the power of the source of the heat,
and it became the form of a man, and he was given the name Ymir.'"[17] There
is something almost modern in this account of the origins of a primordial life-
form, with its insistence that life can only develop in certain circumstances:
for the cosmos to be hospitable to life, it must have a habitable zone neither
too close to a source of energy—here Muspell plays the role of the sun—nor
too far away from it. Life, in this version of pagan cosmogony, is not the prov-
ince of a god in whose gift all existence resides, but a contingent, haphazard
development arising out of a fortuitous set of circumstances.

So Ymir becomes the first living being in the universe. He is not a god, as Hár is at pains to emphasize, but nor he is created by a god. He is not human, either, though he has the appearance of a human (*manns líkandi*). Rather, he is the source of all life in the cosmos, as well as the origin of the actual substance that will constitute the living Earth. We might almost see him as a symbolic personification somewhat similar to Gaia, were it not for the fact that Ymir's violent death is the essential prerequisite for the world to come into being.

Ymir is briefly alone in the largely empty cosmos. But while he sleeps, he sweats, and in the warmth and moisture of his left armpit grow a male and a female giant. One of his legs, meanwhile, "begot a son with the other." We assume that Ymir's offspring are all giants, because he is identified as a giant, and because the race of frost-giants is said to descend from his peculiarly begotten children, but the terms that Snorri uses here, *maðr ok kona,* are the conventional Old Norse words for "man" and "woman" (though *maðr* can also be used as a gender-neutral term denoting "person" or "human being.")[18]

Since Ymir has apparently come to life and started a family in the middle of an enormous void, the next question that Gangleri asks addresses an important lacuna in the creation myth so far: where did Ymir live, and what did he eat? Conveniently, the second being to grow out of the ice melting in Ginnungagap is a cow named Auðhumla, whose teats provide four rivers of milk for Ymir to subsist on.[19] Auðhumla, in turn, lives by licking the salty stones that have hardened out of the frozen rivers of poison; eventually, she licks away so much salt and rime that the figure of a man begins to appear. This man is called Búri, and Hár tells Gylfi that Búri marries a female giant named Bestla. Bestla is the daughter of one Bǫlþorn, of whose origins we hear nothing: perhaps he is one of the giants that Ymir sired on himself. Bestla and Bǫlþorn have three sons, Óðinn, Vili, and Vé: "And it is my belief that this Óðinn and his brothers must be the rulers of heaven and earth; it is our opinion that this must be what he is called. This is the name of the one who is the greatest and most glorious that we know, and you would do well to agree to call him that too."[20] It does not seem to perturb Hár that he has already called Alfǫðr the ruler of heaven and earth: either he is identifying Óðinn with the Christian creator's surrogate or else his speech demonstrates once again the hopeless confusion into which these pagans have fallen. While we know Óðinn very well to be a god, it is notable that Hár uses the word *maðr* for Óðinn, which Faulkes for some reason omits from his translation. The divinity or humanity of the pagan gods is, from the start, open to question. They are, in any case, not fully transcendent beings, and though they come to rule the cosmos, they are not responsible for calling it into being.

To this point in the creation myth that Snorri weaves out of his three main sources we find suggestive differences between the ontological schema of Genesis and its Norse equivalent. Lacking a transcendent creator god, the Norse universe comes into being in a more haphazard, messy fashion. Because it does not establish a single, ultimate point of origin for the cosmos, it leaves unanswered the question of what was there before; Snorri's vision of the beginning does away with the total void that precedes creation in *Vǫluspá,* implying instead that something has always been in place, in which and out of which other things can grow and in which, eventually, life can begin. In this, the third creation myth told in *Gylfaginning,* matter exists all the way down. This pagan cosmos is an intensely material universe, one that operates not through divine will or word but by the constant interaction of various bodies. The Norse cosmos is a transcorporeal system, to borrow Stacy Alaimo's term. It is an embodied universe.

The idea of transcorporeality, as Alaimo defines it, disturbs the boundaries of the human and nonhuman, Nature and Society, by insisting on the inseparability, on a material level, of people from the rest of the world. It is

the time-space where human corporeality, in all its material fleshiness, is inseparable from "nature" or "environment." . . . Imagining human corporeality as trans-corporeality, in which the human is always intermeshed with the more-than-human world, underlines the extent to which the corporeal substance of the human is ultimately inseparable from "the environment." It makes it difficult to pose nature as a mere background for the exploits of the human, since "nature" is always as close as one's own skin. Indeed, thinking across bodies may catalyze the recognition that the "environment," which is too often imagined as inert, empty space or as a "resource" for human use, is, in fact, a world of fleshy beings, with their own needs, claims, and actions. By emphasizing the movement across bodies, trans-corporeality reveals the interchanges and interconnections between human corporeality and the more-than-human. But by underscoring that "trans" indicates movement across different sites, transcorporeality opens up an epistemological "space" that acknowledges the often unpredictable and unwanted actions of human bodies, nonhuman creatures, ecological systems, chemical agents, and other actors.[21]

The actors who have played a role in the creation of life in *Gylfaginning's* cosmogony include the elemental forces heat and cold; chemical processes that transmute the poisonous rivers that flow between Muspell and Niflheimr into a mineral substance; the animal, in the form of a titanic space cow who works at this stone with her tongue until a fully fleshly humanoid emerges from it. At the same time, Auðhumla nourishes the giant who had coalesced out of the early universe's combination of heat and cold, wet and dry. The giant Ymir, meanwhile, exhibits a queer form of reproduction that does not require the existence of biological sex. He is not asexual—the frottage that his legs engage in reads like a sexual act, and a somewhat kinky one, to boot—but he confounds all notions of the necessity of heterosexuality for reproduction. Although recognizably humanoid, and the ancestor of fully social beings, Ymir embodies a concept of a universe free from gendered reproduction. He represents the possibility of male motherhood, of parenthood without paternity. And in this he is perhaps more natural than we realize. As Myra Hird points out, "The *vast* majority of cells in the human body are intersex," and "most of the organisms in four out of the five kingdoms do not require sex for reproduction."[22] Hird's overarching thesis is that Nature is queer and that queerness is natural. By my reading, Ymir could be held up as a mythical exemplar of these principles.

In its earliest phases, this version of the pagan cosmos is nonhierarchical and nonteleological. The universe does not exist for a purpose: it just exists. There is no ontological distinction to be drawn between human, giant, god, animal, vegetable, and mineral; nobody occupies a subject position, because everything is "just" a body. All the actors in this cosmic drama are enmeshed in a convoluted web of mutual obligations: Ymir cannot live without Auðhumla, Auðhumla cannot live without the salty stones, which could not exist without the climatic conditions created by Muspell's heat and Niflheimr's cold. Everything is essential to the existence of everything else.

But if this is what Nature looks like in a transcorporeal system, it is not long before Nature crumbles, to be replaced by or to turn into something else. As we have seen, the spontaneous generation of the figures Búri and Bestla leads to the earliest occurrence of heterosexual reproduction in the universe. As if by magic, this act of un-queering leads, in effect, to the establishment of patriarchy and the patriarchy's imposition of a dualistic hierarchy that assigns Nature to the realm of the feminine, and vice versa. We have already seen that the Æsir regard Óðinn, Vili, and Vé as "rulers of heaven and earth," but we do not know how they have gained that status. The answer, unsurprisingly, is that they have taken it for themselves through the exercise of murderous power: as soon as they are able, they kill Ymir.

Then Hár replied: "Borr's sons killed the giant Ymir. And when he fell, so much blood flowed from his wounds that with it they drowned all the race of frost-giants, except that one escaped with his household. [. . .] They took

Ymir and transported him to the middle of Ginnungagap, and out of him made the earth, out of his blood the sea and the lakes. The earth was made of the flesh and the rocks of the bones, stone and scree they made out of the teeth and molars and of the bones that had been broken."[23]

Ymir's murder is a creative act, in a sense: his death is necessary for the Earth to take form. As Jeffrey Jerome Cohen puts it, "The monster's body becomes the raw material of cosmogenesis," although in this instance I disagree with Cohen when he says that the universe was fashioned "from the corpse of the ur-giant Ymir."[24] It is not the whole universe that results from Ymir's dismemberment, but specifically the world-as-home-for-us: there was already a cosmos in which Ymir could dwell. Rather than an act of cosmogenesis proper, I see Óðinn and his brothers' butchery of Ymir's corpse as a restructuring of preexisting matter into a new type of world, a world which separated from the rest of creation and which exists to serve as an *oikos* specific to the figures who come to be regarded—at first, it seems, by themselves—as gods. It is also an act of political violence that almost succeeds in wiping out all the frost-giants, who are suddenly figured as the antagonists of Óðinn's party, absent any explanation of this newfound enmity.

The earliest cosmos, the time-space in which, as *Vǫluspá* puts it, Ymir made his dwelling, was a site of transcorporeal interactions, with everything created with and from everything else, and everything implicated in the survival and thriving of all things. The new gods' plans insist on a different spatial and symbolic order. If Ymir represents the fully enmeshed cosmos that would deserve the name Nature (in the sense of a genuine "unification of all actants," as Latour phrases it, but one neither "premature" nor driven by politics), the gods' killing of Ymir is the death of Nature-as-All and its replacement with Nature-as-Other. Once Ymir has been dismembered, he cannot be re-membered; there is no going back, no hope of reunification. And Ymir is hardly even mourned: the Æsir regard him and all his descendants as "evil," and if his flood of blood had successfully drowned the last of the line of frost-giants we might have forgotten that he ever existed. (It is important to note that two of the speakers of the cosmogonic poems in the *Poetic Edda*—the narrator of *Vǫluspá* and the protagonist of *Vafþrúðnismál*—are either giants or closely connected to giants. These two poems are notably less antagonistic toward the giants than Snorri's retelling of the same events. The version of the story told in *Gylfaginning* reflects the Æsir's perspective throughout.)

The creation of any cosmos tends to be a messy, confusing, sometimes deadly affair. But the Norse cosmogonic myths are especially brutal. As far as we know, Ymir committed no crime beyond the crime of giving birth to the race of giants. And, in any case, the creator gods/Ymir murderers Óðinn, Vili, and Vé were of giantish descent on their mother's side. Somehow the fact that their paternal ancestor had been licked out of a stone by a massive cow—another product of the transcorporeal phase of cosmic history—allowed them to conceive of themselves as belonging to a different order of creation. But the Norse gods *are* created beings, and they can create nothing from nothing: their primal act of creation—the making of a world from the devastated ruins of Ymir's body—is an act of horrific destruction that results in the almost complete ethnic cleansing of a neighboring people, a people, moreover, to whom the gods were (or should have been) bound with close ties of kinship. Then again, we should probably expect no less from them. The gods quickly come to represent, and to represent themselves as, a force of Culture, of Civilization. And as we know from bitter historical experience, the cost of human Civilization is high, whether it is paid by the nonhuman inhabitants of the universe or by those people branded as non-Civilized. Ymir has to die so that the world as we know it can be born, dragged from the bloody and broken trans-body of the queer paternal-maternal ancestor who gave life to everything.

Constructing Miðgarðr

The world that the gods construct from Ymir's violated form is not just a new physical space, though "space" is certainly one of the orders that they impose on the universe: it reveals a different conception of what a world is. The fundamental development that takes place across this point of fracture is a transition from a transcorporeal, enmeshed heterarchy of mutually dependent beings to a structured anthropocentrism that attempts to impose fixed ontological and spatial boundaries upon the cosmos. After Ymir's initial dismemberment, the gods are quick to establish a new spatial order in which one's location in the cosmos correlates to one's status in the new schematization of the world as *oikos:* The purpose of the world becomes now to provide a place to live and thrive *for the gods*—and, eventually, for mankind. Since the giants have somehow managed to cling on to life, they must also be accommodated in this new schema. From this point forward, all the way up to the cataclysm of Ragnarǫk, Norse cosmology—especially as it is explained in *Snorra Edda*—comes to resemble uncomfortably closely other Western worldviews that assert and maintain the Nature/Society dualism. The gods occupy the place normally reserved for (Western) humanity on the civilized/cultural side of the structure; the giants are assigned the status of the gods' perpetual Out-group, the binary counterpart against which the gods construct and defend their identity and place in the world. They are aligned with Nature/savagery/the wild.

We have already seen that *Grímnismál* includes two stanzas that detail the fate of Ymir's body. The second of these verses mentions for the first time the construction of Miðgarðr, which is an extremely important step in the imposition of a spatial order onto the nonspace of the early cosmos: "And from his eyelashes the cheerful gods / made Miðgarðr for men's sons." That the gods are called "cheerful" (*blíð*) here may reflect the fact that one of their own number, Óðinn, utters this statement. *Vafþrúðnismál*, which is spoken by a giant, does not mention the creation of Miðgarðr. But stanza 4 of *Vǫluspá*, a poem that is by no means sympathetic to the Æsir, also calls Miðgarðr "glorious" (*mærr*)—and *Vǫluspá*, oddly, does not mention Ymir's killing directly. The creation of the world in this version of the myth is much more serene than we read about in other sources.

> . . . before the sons of Burr brought up the land-surface,[25]
> those who shaped glorious Miðgarðr;
> the sun shone from the south on the stone-hall,
> then the ground was grown over with vegetation. (*Vǫluspá* [K] 4)[26]

Miðgarðr ("middle-yard" or "middle-enclosure")—which is directly cognate with the Old English term *middangeard,* whence Tolkien appropriated his idea of a "Middle-earth"—is a spatial structuring device, but its precise nature is not at once clear from these descriptions. *Grímnismál* states that Miðgarðr exists "for men's sons," presumably meaning humanity in general. So we might assume that the gods intend Miðgarðr as an *oikos* for humanity, with *Vǫluspá* conjuring up a vision of a pacific and bountiful green homeland, warmed by the sun. However, in Snorri's elaboration of this passage, Miðgarðr sounds rather more sinister:

> Then spoke Gangleri: "This is important information that I have just heard. That [i.e., Jǫrð, the earth] is an amazingly large construction and skillfully made. How was the earth arranged?"
>   Then Hár replied: "It is circular round the edge, and around it lies the deep sea, and along the shore of this sea they gave lands to live to the races of giants. But on the earth on the inner side they made a fortification

round the world against the hostility of giants, and for this fortification they used the giant Ymir's eyelashes, and they called the fortification Miðgarðr. They also took his brains and threw them into the sky and made out of them the clouds."[27]

In Snorri's version, Miðgarðr is a "fortification" (*borg*) and its construction is motivated not by the desire to build a habitat for humanity but by the gods' anxiety over the giants' alleged hostility. The giants have ample cause to be hostile toward the gods—their entire ethnos had nearly been destroyed in the act of killing their ancestor, and they have since been banished to the very margins of the new world—but we have not so far heard anything about this hostility; paranoia will quickly become a hallmark of the gods' society, as we shall see. Miðgarðr is a concrete manifestation of the division between Nature and Society that has been so fundamental to structuralist anthropology's analysis of worldviews, but it is not an intrinsic part of the world. The opposition of the "social" with the "wild" (and so on) that Miðgarðr reifies is not natural, as Lévi-Strauss himself recognized, but a creation of culture, "a protective rampart thrown up around [culture] because it only felt able to assert its existence and uniqueness by destroying all the links that lead back to its original association with other manifestations of life."[28]

It soon becomes impossible to keep the two conceptions of Miðgarðr separate from one another. The term seems always able to imply both the fortification that protects its interior and the interior that is so protected. The gods always dwell within the fortified bounds of Miðgarðr, but they establish their own realm, known as Ásgarðr, within Miðgarðr's zone of protection and thereby maintain their separation from human beings as well as the giants. This dichotomy is reinforced by the naming of the giants' realm as Útgarðr ("outer-enclosure" or "beyond-the-enclosure"), although this term is used only rarely in mythological sources.[29] For the structuralist critics following in Snorri's wake, however, the distinction between Miðgarðr and Útgarðr has become fundamental to the ordering of the Norse cosmos.

According to the structuralist anthropologist Kirsten Hastrup, the binary opposition of Miðgarðr and Útgarðr maps directly onto the psychospatial realities of life in medieval Iceland.[30] The Icelandic farmhouse was surrounded by a physical and conceptual boundary known as a *garðr*, which term comes to encompass both the physical structure by which the farmstead was enclosed—in practice, normally a wall of stacked turfs—and the area that was enclosed by the wall, which is sometimes called the *tún* ("meadow" or "homefield"). In the sagas of Icelanders, the term *útgarðar* is used (in the plural), though uncommonly, to refer to spaces beyond the homestead wall, and this out-space is conceptualized as the realm of the wild, the untamable, the unproductive, and the non- or antisocial.[31] As Hastrup summarizes the situation: "In Iceland, the cultural category of 'the wild' included untamed nature. . . . 'The social' was everywhere the law obtained. It was the conceptual inside of the boundaries of society, with its centre at the Althing.[32] Outside was 'the wild.' It was all over the physical space, yet it formed a distinct 'space,' inhabited by distinct categories of non-social beings."[33] In-space is the realm of law and order in medieval Icelandic worldviews: to be made an outlaw entailed a banishment into out-space, as that was defined in Icelandic terms.[34] Outlawry was called *útlegð*—"lying outside"; or an outlaw could be called a *skógamaðr*, a "man of the forests," with the "forest" representing another symbolic wilderness space. (He could also be known as a *vargr* [wolf], aligning him with another aspect of "untamed Nature.")[35] This equation of outlawry with dwelling in a forest that did not really exist in Iceland—the term *skógamaðr* is an inheritance from Norway—confirms that we are dealing with conceptual categories that are imposed upon physical space, rather than conceptual categories that arise directly out of an experience of a particular place. However, Hastrup also notes that the lava field that occupies much of the center of Iceland, the *ódáðahraun,* an uninhabited, almost desert region, should be seen as a physical instantiation of the wild/social binary. Forming a formidable physical boundary between the inhabited areas around the coastal periphery of Iceland, the *ódáðahraun,* Hastrup claims, "was at once metonymically related to 'the wild' as one of the places where the *útilegumenn* were thought to live, and metaphorically related to it as a condensed notion of the anti-social, the 'outside.'"[36] It is perhaps ironic, in that case, that this spatialization of "outside" is physically located at the heart of the Icelandic *interior,* but for Icelanders and Norwegians alike the coastal lowlands and fjord valleys have always provided the best hope of making a living, while the mountainous centers of these landmasses have indeed remained largely untouched by civilization.

The structure of the mythological cosmos, especially as we reconstruct it from Snorri's account, is therefore a spatial inversion of the Icelandic conceptual binary. The giants—who are associated with rocky, icy, and inaccessible landscapes in Nordic folklore (including forests)—occupy the periphery of the cosmos on the other side of Miðgarðr, whereas the space that conceptually maps Útgarðr-as-inhospitable-space in Iceland occupies the middle of the country.[37] The two systems are, in one sense, inside out, suggesting perhaps that the universe of the gods and giants is not a reflection of the geographic realities of the society that produced these myths—that the myths have not grown out of the real-world environment of the people who created them and perhaps held them to be true. But in a structuralist analysis, the conceptual superbinaries encoded by In and Out are of much greater significance than their actual location.[38]

The gods' construction of Miðgarðr as a structuring device by which they may impose order onto the cosmos is just that: a construction. Miðgarðr is categorically not natural, but the concrete manifestation of a culture's desire to dominate "the wild." Helga Kress goes so far as to suggest that "the whole of Norse mythology is geared to illustrate how the gods conquered nature, the untamed and wild, and established a society."[39] In order to dominate "the wild," however, "the wild" first needs to be constructed, since wildness is itself a construction. The undifferentiated, messy, enmeshed cosmos of the earliest phases of the creation is an affront to the Æsir, something they are unable to control. But once Miðgarðr has been built, it becomes possible, even inevitable, for everything to be either In or Out, with Us or against Us. Everything that gets assigned to the (conceptual) *útgarðr* is automatically Othered, and we are no longer able to conceive of these Others as occupying the gods' subject position, their position at the conceptual center of the universe. These Others are nonhuman or subhuman. In Iceland, the outlaw, the *skógamaðr*, lost his right to life along with his recourse to the law. He could be killed with impunity for as long as his banishment lasted. In the mythological cosmos, the giants are fair game for all forms of exploitation and violence at the hands of the gods; but they are forbidden to come across Miðgarðr, which was supposedly built because of *their* hostility.[40] Quite typically, the gods are able to move freely through the "wilderness" to which the giants have been assigned, but they are utterly paranoid about the threat that these Others would pose, should Miðgarðr fall or fail, letting the outside in—which naturally is exactly what happens.

In chapters 6 and 7 of this book, I will claim that the building of Miðgarðr and the gods' inevitable failures to maintain its integrity are thoroughly implicated in the end of the world at Ragnarǫk. They may, indeed, be the main root cause of the apocalypse. The type of conceptual structure that Miðgarðr stands for, though well-nigh universal in human culture, is not "natural"—in the sense of innate or transcendent—nor is it sustainable. It requires massive expenditures of energy (and time, and money, and resources of all sorts) to maintain, but it cannot defeat entropy. Things fall apart, and the center cannot hold.

The creation myths of Nordic paganism, as they are preserved and rewritten in the two Eddas, did not originate in a prestructural(ist) worldview. They impose a schematization on the cosmos that reflects the spatial-conceptual schema that underlay early Icelanders' structural categorizations of their own world, but this schema is itself a sociocultural construct that was overlaid onto a physical environment whose strongly dichotomized landscape lent itself to such a project. There are possibly hints of a prestructuralist (or less structuralist) cosmology in the Eddic poems *Vǫluspá*, *Grímnismál*, and *Vafþrúðnismál*, when they imagine the transcorporeal entanglement of elements and beings in the period before and during Ymir's murder, in the absence of a preexistent creator. But overall, the full creation story as Snorri tells it is mostly concerned with the imposition of structures, categories, and dualisms onto the physical universe. It is a narrative about the exercise of divine beings' power and discretion just as much as Genesis's creation myth is, and the world that comes about is hardly less anthropocentric than the Judeo-Christian world, as long as we read the Æsir as occupying the human subject position, as I think we must.

The spontaneity and fluidity of the initial moment of creation, the sense of the infinite possibilities for life in this universe, last for but an instant in cosmic terms. And it is the moment when Óðinn and his brothers, the gods who will impose structure onto the chaos out of which they will make for themselves an *oikos,* arrive on the scene that the familiar conceptual regime of the In/Out, Nature/Society, Wild/Civilized binaries is imposed upon the world. For many ecocritics, it is this regime that underlies mankind's spectacularly poor record of living equitably and sustainably in fellowship with the world-beyond-the-human. And for the Norse gods, it is a regime that will lead ultimately to annihilation, just as it seems to be accelerating humanity toward an unknown cataclysm in the twenty-first century.

All this makes it sound as if there is relatively little to separate the structures of a notionally pre-Christian Norse cosmology from those which White identified as being particularly problematic in Christian theology. I do, in fact, believe that to be the case, at least as far as the surviving mythological evidence indicates. We must remain alive to the possibility, however, that the cosmological conceptions of *Snorra Edda* in particular, but also of the Eddic poems, owe something to Christian influence. Snorri was trying to impose order on a disparate range of narrative material, to create a coherent worldview that was simultaneously true to the beliefs of his pagan ancestors (as he understood them), safe for consumption by Christian audiences in the thirteenth century, and consistent with the Christian master narrative of universal history, which also had a spatial dimension.[41] Snorri's organizing principles owe something to his Christian upbringing: his insistence on imposing a vertical axis onto mythological space, in which the chthonic realm of the dead,

Hel, is balanced by placing a distinctly heaven-sounding Ásgarðr in the sky, is at least a conscious manipulation of the evidence from older poetic sources in imitation of Christian cosmology, if not Snorri's actual invention.[42] But the horizontal spatial structures of the cosmos, and the dualism of in-space and out-space that they map, are already present in the Eddic poems. Snorri has perhaps worked them into a tidier, more coherent system, but these structures already permeate the older forms of the myths. We might assume some degree of Christian influence in the Eddic poems, especially *Vǫluspá,* but to reject their evidence as being tainted by the cosmology of the incoming religion would be unfounded, and it defeats our purpose. Instead, we must conclude on the basis of the available evidence that the structures of Old Norse pagan cosmology, as mediated through the extant creation myths preserved in medieval manuscripts, are intrinsically dualistic. They encode precisely the human/world and Nature/Society binaries that we have been looking to these myths to disrupt or circumvent.

3   The Nature of World in
       a World without Nature

Heimr, Verǫld, Jǫrð

IN HIS IMPORTANT RECENT BOOK *Ecocriticism on the Edge,* Timothy Clark expresses some frustration with our inability to differentiate between the concepts of "earth" and "world":

> The Earth is obviously implicit and assumed in our existence in any conceivable respect, including how we talk and think. It is all-pervasive, assumed but unthematized. The question of the meaning of the Earth is latent even in the simple pervasive confusion about the words "earth" and "world." Does the term name the physical planet or the universe? When we speak of "the world," the referent is almost always to the specific planet (as in "the deepest seas in the world"), yet to speak of a person's "world view" is to imply a view of the cosmos in the broad sense. The idiom, "what on earth?" seems to hover between one sense and the other, as if they made no difference. Yet, why is the conflation of the terms "earth" and "world" so prevalent and so hard to avoid?[1]

In Norse mythology, there is no "planet Earth" to worry about. But the difficulties that Clark identifies in untangling various conceptions of "world" persist. There are three principle terms used to denote "world" in Old Norse. Two of them, *verǫld* and *jǫrð*, are directly cognate with the English words "world" and "earth," respectively (though the latter does not refer to the planet conceived as a separate entity in space but to the physical substance under our feet). The third and most common term for "world" in Old Norse is *heimr* (home). All three of these words have significance in the mythological universe as well as currency in mimetic writing, but it seems that *heimr* bears a special significance as an aspect of the spatial-conceptual structure of the cosmos.

Heimr

To this point, we have been looking at cosmogonic myths that represent the spontaneous creation of matter ex nihilo, followed by a series of structuring events that impose order on an initially chaotic nonsystem. Once Miðgarðr has been created, we can begin to speak of the existence of a world, or rather of worlds, since there are nine of them in the universe, according to Vǫluspá:

> I remember giants born early in time
> those nurtured me long ago;
> I remember nine worlds, I remember nine giant-women,
> the mighty Measuring-Tree below the earth. (Vǫluspá [K] 2)[2]

This ninefold structure is found elsewhere in the myths, although nowhere are the nine worlds listed together in one place.[3] Two of them are certainly Miðgarðr and Ásgarðr. As we have seen, these are the "enclosures" in which humankind and the gods dwell, the gated communities whose borders are so heavily guarded and jealously maintained by the Æsir. The realms of the giants are called Jǫtunheimar (always plural). The remaining six worlds of the cosmos are, to varying degrees, obscure. Hel is the realm of the dead, a shadowy and dismal underworld; the dwarfs, or "dark elves," live in Svartálfa-heimr, while their nondark counterparts have a world called Álfaheimr. Snorri claims that the Vanir—the deities associated with fertility whom the Æsir defeat in the first war in mythic history—also had their own dwelling place, Vanaheimar (also given as a plural). Finally, we have seen that Snorri names the two primordial regions of elemental power Niflheimr and Muspellsheimr: these are the sources of the cold and heat out of which all matter coalesces in Snorri's cosmogony.[4]

With the exception of Hel, all these worlds are given names that include the elements -garðr or -heimr. At first glance, heimr (home) strikes one as an ecological idiom analogous to the Greek word oikos, whence all our eco-vocabulary derives. But there are some unresolved tensions in our use of the concepts of "home equals world" and "world equals home." In one of the foun-dational statements of the principles of ecocriticism, William Howarth wrote that "oikos is nature, a place Edward Hoagland calls 'our widest home.'"[5] The immediate problem with this definition, so crucial to first-wave ecocriticism, is the word "our." The Greek term oikos refers to a house, a dwelling place, a construction by and of and for human Society; by deploying oikos to speak about humanity's place in the order of things vis-à-vis the nonhuman we once again begin to reify the Nature/Society dualism. To think of Nature as our dwelling place is, in one sense, appropriate, for Nature is an edifice that we have constructed for ourselves to live in. But this is an inescapably anthropocentric way of thinking, which perpetuates the problems that arise when talking about the "environment." Both terms define the world by reference to humanity: "the environment" is the world around *us;* the *oikos* is the world as a home for *us.* Indeed, we need the world to be a home *for us,* a place of safety and nourishment, and there might be eco-political advantages to thinking of the world in these terms. By making human society the central reference point for thinking about issues like overpopulation and global warming, we hope that self-interest may lead to a political situation that enables the conditions of life for the beyond-human as well as the human to be improved. Just think what *we* lose if the Amazonian rainforest is chopped down—there might be a cure for (human) cancer in there! How sad if the Great Barrier Reef dies—what will snorkelers look at?

But to treat Nature as humanity's *oikos,* "our widest home," does nothing to reconfigure anthropocentric notions of world-building that have been catastrophically damaging to the biosphere. When we build a house, we clear a patch of ground, chop down trees, pour concrete, chase away critters. We erect a fence around it to stop those critters, and all other Others, for that matter, from returning. As we have seen, the construction of Miðgarðr is an excellent mythological example of this type of home-making world-building. Yet Miðgarðr is named for its boundary, with this circumscription essential to its function as a dwelling place for the gods and, eventually, human beings. It is the realms of the gods' various Out-groups that are called *heimar.* This might challenge the idea that the giants, dwarfs, and other subaltern groups in the cosmos are to be identified with the Natural, as opposed to cultural, sphere. If *heimr* equals *oikos,* and *oikos* means the world as a home for people, then people living in a *heimr* must all occupy the same sort of subject position. This is probably true up to a point: the giants are a civilization, they build, they exploit their environment just as the gods exploit their environment. At the same time, there is something almost ironic, perhaps even sinister, in the way that gods and humans live inside a *garðr* while their antagonists are all assigned to *heimar* beyond the walls, physical and conceptual, that the Æsir have built. There is almost something of the Nature preserve or even North American "Indian" reservations in the relationship between the gods and the giants and their respective homes: a "home" can be a place where one puts someone, like an inconveniently aged relative. It was the gods who drew up the boundaries between the different worlds, who got to decide who lives where. The giants are in fact the true first nation of the cosmos, since they are of the direct bloodline of Ymir, the source of all life. But after their near extinction in the Æsir's genocidal murder of Ymir, they have been made marginal, both spatially and politically, to a world over which the Æsir had no intrinsic rights whatever. The gods are able to visit Jǫtunheimar, to marry (or rape) giant women or gain giantish wisdom, but the giants are supposed to be restricted to their homelands. The borders are closed, and when one or more giant does manage to penetrate Miðgarðr, it is always a cause of panic for the Æsir, as we will see in chapter 6.

At best, then, the term *heimr* is neutral in its mythological contexts, used unthinkingly as a spatial term perhaps akin to our speaking of "the globe." Or it could be used conceptually to refer to the entirety of the cosmos as we know it, as in one's "worldview," which is never defined entirely by spatial aware- ness. In Norse mythology, it does not seem to offer a conceptual break from the anthropocentric worldings familiar from mainstream Western traditions. The *heimar* into which the universe is subdivided are structuring devices, an imposition of an artificial, hierarchical order onto an originally much more fluid and heterarchical cosmos. Their boundaries are not quite as rigid as those denoted by the term *garðr*, perhaps, but they are nonetheless another facet of the In-group's spatial reification of its categories of domination. The concept of "world as home" loses some of its cozy domesticity when we realize that most of the inhabitants of the universe are assigned a home on the basis of the desires of a ruling class rather than by reference to their own rights, needs, or wishes. The giants and other Out-groups in the universe have no choice but to make a home out of their assigned *heimr*, but it hardly seems as though the term encodes any sort of ecological oneness between these Others and the Othered environments in which they have been placed.

Verǫld

The second main Old Norse world word has temporal as well as spatial con- notations. *Verǫld* shares a common ancestor with English word "world," a term that in Proto-Germanic looked something like the form °*wer-ald:* this word breaks down into two elements meaning, respectively, "man" and "age." Etymologically, this conception of "world" is one determined by mankind's relationship with time, measured on a human scale. *Verǫld* is the world of history—the world of which it is possible to write a "history of the world," a narrative of humanity's existence in time. In Iceland, *Veraldar saga* (History of the *verǫld*) was the title given to a twelfth-century work of universal history that divides the time-bound world into six *aetates mundi* in the conventional medieval manner, taking us from God's creation of the planet via Troy and Rome to the reign of the German emperor Konrad III.[6] *Veraldar saga* is of course not a work of pagan myth but of Christian scholarship, and its choice of *verǫld* for its title is etymologically apposite to its subject matter.

In *Snorra Edda*, *verǫld* occurs first in a familiarly (pseudo)historical frame of reference in the Prologue: "After Noah's flood there lived eight people who inhabited the world [*heimr*] and from them generations have descended, and it happened just as before that as the *verǫld* came to be peopled and settled it turned out to be the vast majority of mankind that cultivated desire for wealth and glory and neglected obedience to God, and this reached such a pass that they refused to mention the name of God."[7] Here, *verǫld* refers to the totality of human-inhabitable space—the space that is available for people to fill—and if Snorri intends a distinction between this term and the *heimr* he mentions earlier in the same sentence, it is not clear what he means by it. The temporality that *verǫld*'s etymology suggests has become less definitional, analogous with an early stage in the concept's development in English: even during the Anglo-Saxon period, *woruld* was used without discrimination to refer to the universe considered spatially, as well as to universal history.[8] But if the Prologue to *Snorra Edda* uses *verǫld* as a spatial term, it does so within a specific frame of historical reference. This vision of *verǫld* is specific to the demands of a Christian universal history—it exists for (a chosen) people to occupy and to make use of in their pursuit of "wealth and glory."

The same holds true for other occurrences of the word in *Snorra Edda*. In the Prologue's cosmography, "the *verǫld* was divided into three parts," which are named as "Africa," "Europe or Enea," and "Asia."[9] Although this statement sounds like a neutral geographical description, it remains very much in the realm of human geography: the names of the continents are cultural artifacts that encode cultural differences between peoples as much as spatial realities. Snorri's threefold conception of the *verǫld* reflects mainstream medieval (Christian) conceptions of geography, as frequently and vividly expressed in so-called T-O maps. In the Prologue, which seeks to explain paganism as a largely accidental—and largely blameless—outcome of historical processes in the light of revealed Christian truth, Snorri's concept of "world" offers little for the ecocritic to work with.

Vǫluspá, Snorri's most important source for the chronology of mythological history, is the only poem in the mythological section of the *Poetic Edda* that uses the word *verǫld* at all. *Verǫld* occurs twice in the poem. In stanza 29, the word's usage seems happenstance and is possibly the result of the poet needing a world word beginning with *v* to alliterate with preceding words in a couplet:

> Father of Hosts chose for her rings and necklaces,
> received wise speech, and spirits of divination;
> she saw widely, widely about every *verǫld*. (*Vǫluspá* [K], 29)[10]

Here, *verǫld* is clearly being used as a spatial term, and as a plural: the seeress who narrates the poem can see into all worlds, just as she remembers multiple worlds at the start of her account of the creation, which she calls *heimar*. There does not seem to be much to be made of her use of *verǫld* in this context. And indeed, the scarcity of this term in the extant mythological sources suggests that it was much less prevalent a world concept than *heimr* in traditional cosmological thought. Nonetheless, the distinction between a temporally figured world and one that is conceived in spatial terms may be useful to an ecocritical reading of *Vǫluspá*. When the *vǫlva* uses the term *verǫld* for the second time, she does so at precisely the moment when the end of the world is beginning to enact itself:

> Brother will fight brother and be his slayer,
> sister's sons will violate the kinship-bond;
> hard it is in the *heimr,* whoredom abounds,
> axe-age, sword-age, shields are cleft asunder,
> wind-age, wolf-age, before the *verǫld* plunges headlong;
> no man will spare another. (*Vǫluspá* [K], 44)[11]

Disregarding the pusillanimous impulse to attribute the poem's use of *verǫld* here to the need for a word that alliterates with *vindǫld* and *vargǫld*, this stanza marks an important shift in how the world is represented in *Vǫluspá*. It is no longer a *heimr,* because it no longer provides the familiar environmental conditions that allow people to treat it as a home. At the very start of Ragnarǫk—which has been named for the first time in the preceding stanza— the "age of men" crumbles and a "wind-age" and "wolf-age" takes its place. The nonhuman Other, in other words, is now in the ascendancy as humankind's malfeasances cause not just the ethical structures of human society to collapse but also the physical structures of the cosmos. The old order, the order so carefully created and jealously guarded by the Æsir, is poignantly represented by the term *verǫld*. It is the temporally delimited "age of men"— which is also the age of the mythological Æsir—that has passed.

Although there is no hard-and-fast distinction in the corpus between instances where *verǫld* is more semantically appropriate than *heimr,* the tension between the etymologies of the two words will be useful in discussing the ways in which worlds end. *Verǫld* can stand for History, *heimr* for Nature, with the full and problematic connotations of both these terms. If *heimr* suggests a world outside the human in which the human can dwell, a (perhaps misleadingly) cozy-sounding place that will shelter and nurture us, *verǫld* is in more of a hurry: the world is an age of men—the use of the gendered term is appropriate both etymologically and politically—a bounded period, a phase we're going through. Perhaps it will come to an end. In my reading of the Ragnarǫk myths in chapters 6 and 7, I equate *verǫld* with the etymologically similar term "Anthropocene," the epoch of human intervention in Earth's systems that has caused catastrophic, and arguably apocalyptic, damage to the planet's ability to sustain a fully diverse lifeworld. But while the *verǫld* world seems to encode its end in its very etymology, let's not be fooled into thinking that *heimr* is eternal. We leave home; we can be forced from our homes; our homes can be repossessed; homes can blow away in hurricanes or wash away in floods. Many of us are homeless; many are homesick. Ecocriticism would suggest, perhaps, that the demands and pressures of history, of "progress," have displaced us from Nature, from our true ecological home, and denied us the possibility of dwelling ecologically. We yearn for the *heimr* as the *verǫld* sweeps us along at breakneck speed. If we want to refind or rebuild a *heimr* for ourselves, the *verǫld* is not enough. But as we have seen, even the concept of world-as-*heimr* carries with it anti-ecological baggage, for how do we build a home world for ourselves without impinging on or diminishing the worlds of Others, both human and nonhuman? Whether conceived as a primarily spatial phenomenon or a temporal one, an anthropocentric conception of "world" is a construction of human society for the benefit of human society, just as the idea of the *heimr* in Norse mythology is a construction designed, at bottom, to keep the gods' undesirable cosmic cohabitants in "their" place—and out of "our" place.

Timothy Morton has interrogated these worldings from the standpoint of what he regards as the "ecological thought"—the idea that all life forms are bound up with all other life forms, all inanimate objects, chemical processes, the climate, and so on, in a radically nonhierarchical "mesh."[12] Morton argues that

"world" is an aesthetic construct—it's more compelling than it is real. For there is a more fundamental problem with worlds: they do not exist. It is ecological thinking itself that implies that there is no world. The system of life forms is open-ended and infinite. Since there is no such thing as "species" (just read Darwin), the life/non-life distinction is untenable; thus there had to be a pre-living "life" as biologist Sol Spiegelman showed. Since all life forms coexist (symbiosis, explored by Lynn Margulis), we cannot draw a line around them, a horizon, and construct a "within" (where life lives) and a "without" (where it doesn't). Where do you stop? The biosphere? The Earth's gravitational field? The Sun? The Solar System? Life forms are connected in a mesh without a center or an edge. There is no way to achieve the appropriate distance from which to observe anything like a world.[13]

The worlding that takes place in the Old Norse cosmological myths that I have analyzed so far seems to perpetuate the dualistic delusion that Morton identifies as being at the heart of Western culture's anti-ecological modes of thought. The creation myths show us how the gods do "draw a line around [certain life forms], a horizon, and construct a 'within' (where life lives) and a 'without' (where it doesn't)," with the addition of a strongly hierarchical conception of the differences between different classes of life forms which are the gods' own invention. Like all such worldings, the Æsir's constructed world is a mirage—a mirage created for ideological reasons and one that will not persist. It is riven from the start with the contradictions that will bring about its downfall. Ragnarǫk is always already on its way.

Jǫrð

If neither *verǫld* nor *heimr* helps us to conceive of the nature of "world" in a new and perhaps more enlightened way, or to move beyond "world," if we follow Morton and think that the very idea of "worlding" is hopelessly anthropocentric and anti-ecological, perhaps we would be on firmer ground with the Old Norse term *jǫrð*. *Jǫrð* is directly cognate with English "earth," and it has as its primary signification the physical substance of the planet, conceived of holistically or in part: in different contexts it can be interpreted as "ground," "soil," or "land." As we saw, one of the things that specifically did not exist before the universe was filled with matter was *jǫrð*, which is associated with green vegetation in stanza 3 of *Vǫluspá*: "earth there was nowhere nor the sky above, a void of yawning chaos, grass was there nowhere," as Larrington translates it. We might assume that *jǫrð* is thus more substantial, to a lesser extent predicated on the needs and experiences of humans (or their divine surrogates) than either *heimr* or *verǫld*. *Jǫrð* cannot refer to earth in the sense of "little blue planet that we live on," but in answer to Timothy Clark's difficulty with telling "earth" and "world" apart we can say that the difference seems to have been clearer in Old Norse than it is in modern English usage. *Jǫrð* is what we would touch if we were to bend to the ground in an Old Norse–speaking community, while *heimr* and *verǫld*, like modern English "world," are ineffable abstractions that can encompass the physical substance of the planet but are never coterminous with it.

The Eddic poem *Alvíssmál* functions, in part, as a repository of possible synonyms for different features of the mythological universe. In its tenth stanza, the dwarf Alvíss (All-wise) gives Óðinn an idea of the range of alternative words that can be given for "earth":

> Earth (*jǫrð*) it's called among men, and ground (*fold*) by the Æsir,
> the Vanir call it ways (*vega*);
> the giants splendid-green (*ígrœnn*), the elves the growing one (*gróandi*),
> the Powers above call it loam (*aurr*). (*Alvíssmál* 10)[14]

These terms seem to encode the same conception of earth as substance, with additional connotations of nurturing fecundity. *Fold* is related to the identical, now obsolete English noun (translated as "ground" by Larrington), which the *OED* glosses as (a) the surface of the earth; the ground, and (b) dry land; the earth, as the dwelling place of man. In *Vǫluspá* 55, this term is used to describe the land sinking into the sea at the climax of Ragnarǫk. *Ígrœnn* reminds us of the description of Yggdrasill as the tree which *stendr æ yfir grœnn* (green it always stands over) in stanza 19 of *Vǫluspá*: the tree as symbol of steadfast protection beyond the chronology of mortals.[15] It also recalls once again the beginning of *Vǫluspá* and its pacific vision of the uninhabited cosmos. Although critics of *Alvíssmál* generally regard the ascription of different synonyms to different classes of beings as an effectively happenstance structural device in the poem, often driven by the demands of alliteration, it is worth noting that Alvíss says that the ground is thought of as "green" among the giants.[16] If the earth is defined by its greenness, fecundity, and nurturing properties, it is so defined for all its inhabitants, and not just for the Æsir's In-group. The same is true for the elves, for whom earth is "the growing one," while among the "heavenly powers" (*uppregin*) the word used is *aurr*, "loam," "dirt," or "mud"—something earthily organic sounding.[17]

Jǫrð is thus surrounded by a set of associations to do with the physical matter of the land, the ground beneath our feet—and not just *our* feet. In contrast to the worldings of *heimr* and *verǫld*, *jǫrð* and its synonyms are not exclusive to one or other class of life forms. They transcend the artificial boundaries between gods and giants, between Nature and Society. All subsequent structures and categories apprehend and depend on *jǫrð*, which is the true sine qua non of life in habitable space. Until *jǫrð* exists, nothing can exist, and when *jǫrð* sinks into the sea at Ragnarǫk, all life as we know it will come to an end. (Though, as we shall see, a new earth soon replaces the old one.)

All this makes *jǫrð* sound like a conceptually, as well as literally, "greener" notion of "world" (or perhaps "non-world") than the ethically problematic *heimr* or the anthropocentric *verǫld*. It sounds, in fact, as if *jǫrð* is what we should be working on saving and preserving: we can rally around the idea of saving the Earth even if we think that the worlds we inhabit—the worlds of the Anthropocene, late capitalism, patriarchy, and so on—need to be done away with. It seems to have something in common with our idea of the biosphere, the space in which physical conditions are such that life can exist, but it reaches beneath the biosphere into deeper strata of being: it is that which enables the biosphere to exist, which gives life to the zone that provides the conditions of life for the living. It has a numinous quality quite independent of any god or gods: *jǫrð* is not created by the Æsir. It is, rather, what needs to be in order for the gods to perform their acts of (sub)creation. It is also possible and probably desirable to align *jǫrð* against the patriarchal, top-down modes of structuralization that the Æsir enact. As well as being a cosmic entity that was not created through the desire of male deities, *jǫrð*, the nurturing materfamilias of everything, is a feminine noun.

Jǫrð, in other words, sounds more like Lovelock's Gaia than the other alternatives that Old Norse mythology has so far presented us with. In a recent explanation of Gaia theory and its development over some forty years, Lovelock gives a neat and now widely accepted definition: "The Earth System behaves as a single, self-regulating system comprised of physical, chemical, biological and human components."[18] Gaia is quite simply a name given to this Earth system. We do not have enough information to say that, in Norse mythology, there is a *jǫrð* system that regulates itself to provide the conditions in which life may flourish in the ways that Lovelock and other Earth systems scientists propose Gaia does. Nonetheless, there are similarities between the two entities. Neither can be said to be coterminous with any other conception of "world," but both are necessary for any "world" to exist; both are nonhierarchical and nonlocalized, encompassing instead all the networks that are necessary for any and all life forms to flourish. Like Gaia, *jǫrð* is an actant that responds to stimulus and works actively to maintain the equilibrium (called homeostasis) necessary to maintain the conditions that support life in the biosphere. Gaia theory emphasizes that it is not merely that organisms adapt to their environment but that the whole system is capable of adapting in response to the effects that the evolution of different organisms has upon it, as well as to changing external conditions.[19] One of Lovelock's more sobering suggestions is that Anthropocene humanity's effect upon Gaia is that of a pathogen in an organism: "We have grown in number to the point where our presence is perceptibly disabling the planet like a disease. As in human diseases there are four possible outcomes: destruction of the invading disease organisms; chronic infection; destruction of the host; or symbiosis—a lasting relationship of mutual benefit to the host and the invader."[20]

The ecological crises of the twenty-first century point toward a lasting period of the stage Lovelock identifies with "chronic infection." The planet will not implode any time soon; nor will human beings be wiped out as a species in the immediate future. Humanity will limp along, causing more ever harm to its nonhuman coexistents, which will in turn make the conditions under which human life must proceed ever more dreadful. In the long term, unless some sort of symbiosis can be attained, either humanity will disappear or else the systems of Gaia will cease to function, in which case humanity will also disappear. In an effective piece of polemic, Lovelock's 2006 book is called *The Revenge of Gaia* and states in its subtitle that "the Earth is fighting back" against humanity. The planet is poised to fight off its human "infection." Global warming is akin to Gaia having a fever: perhaps her rising temperature will get rid of some of the (human) bugs in her system; perhaps the patient herself will succumb before a cure is effected and her fever subsides.

There are problems with this rhetoric. Viewing humanity in its current form as a pathogen, as a bug in the system, runs the risk of treating people as something foreign to Gaia, something unnatural. This move can actually perpetuate the separation of Nature from Society that so much ecological thinking works to challenge. It can also lead to a sort of self-abnegating fatalism: if Gaia is an organism, and we are her cancer, for example, wouldn't the planet be better off if she underwent a radical humanectomy? Nuclear war could then even be figured as a form of radiotherapy. Once again, to think like this is to sidestep humanity's fundamental entanglement with the rest of the cosmos, ironically attempting to prolong our regimes of power over Nature by making martyrs of ourselves at Gaia's altar. Morton suggests that thinking like this is a form of cynicism that actually impedes ecological progress: "One common Gaian assertion is that there is something wrong with humans. Nonhumans are more Natural. Humans have deviated from the path and will be wiped out (poor fools!). No one says the same about dolphins, but it's just as true. If dolphins do go extinct, why worry? The parts are greater than the whole. . . . The parts are replaceable. Gaia will replace humans with a less defective component."[21] By this analysis, the human/world and Nature/ Culture dichotomies are strengthened, rather than dissolved, in the Gaian model. Certainly, a sort of fatalism can arise from viewing humanity as wrong or unnatural. If Gaia is going to reject us anyway and replace us, eventually, with something better, why should we do anything to mitigate the damage that we are doing to her?

The idea of a ridding the world of all or part of humanity as a sort of beneficial planetary detox is an ancient and popular one. It happens in Noah's flood, and it has already happened in the Norse cosmos before the worlds have even come into being, in the form of the Æsir's drowning of the frost-giants in Ymir's blood. In the myths of Ragnarǫk that I will discuss in chapter 7, I discern a similar dynamic at play: the gods' actions cause damage to the system that provides the conditions in which all life can exist, which is represented at its climax by *jǫrð* sinking into the sea, symbolically cleansing itself of the infection that had prevented it from performing its proper life-sustaining functions.

The final point of similarity between *jǫrð* and Gaia, and one with important ecocritical resonances, is that both are connected to female mythological figures. Lovelock's Earth system is named after the Greek earth goddess who gives birth to the sky (personified as Uranus), with whom she mates to produce the Titans, themselves ancestral figures for gods and giants alike. In Norse myth, Jǫrð has an identity similar to Gaia's, but a different function, since she has no place in the creation narratives. The earth, *jǫrð*, comes into being, then this substance is personified by means that are never made clear. There is no extant myth that tells us how earth became flesh—though we know through the example of Ymir how intimately flesh and the stuff of the cosmos were connected.

The personified Jǫrð is a relatively obscure figure, one of several deities or pseudodeities about whom no independent narratives survive but who are alluded to quite frequently by poets, though traces of her are few and far between in the *Poetic Edda* itself. Snorri tells us that Jǫrð is "counted among the Ásynjur [i.e., the female Æsir]" and that she is the mother of Þórr.[22] (Þórr is called *Jarðar burr* [Jǫrð's son] in the opening stanza of *Þrymskviða* and presumably also in *Lokasenna* 58, though the manuscript has omitted the word *burr* here.) Snorri also states that Óðinn is both father and husband to *jǫrðin*. There is, however, no myth that narrates their relationship in any such way, and Anthony Faulkes prefers to read this instance of *jǫrð* as meaning "the earth" rather than the personification because the word is accompanied by a definite article here.[23] At this point in *Gylfaginning*, Snorri has just told us how Óðinn came to be "father of all gods and men," which explains why he can be identified with the creator figure Alfǫðr. If Jǫrð is one of the Ásynjur, she must therefore be a descendant of Óðinn. And since Jǫrð is well known as Þórr's mother and Óðinn as his father, it is follows, according to Snorri's logic, that Óðinn and Jǫrð are man and wife. Snorri goes on to tell us that Jǫrð is of the kindred of the giants, the daughter of Nótt (Night) and her second husband, Annarr—which, rather suspiciously, means "second."[24] Making Jǫrð a giantess aligns her even more closely with the Æsir's Out-groups, rendering her even riper for the gods' exploitation. Nonetheless, I doubt whether her status as a giantess is very well founded. She is a personified earth goddess in both origin and function.

However, as soon as *jǫrð* becomes personified and gendered female we have to take into account the implications of this gendering. In Snorri's reading of the figure, her most important roles are wife and mother, aligning her with Gaia and other analogous "Mother Earth" figures that are so widespread across world mythologies and plunging her straight into the controversies surrounding the feminization of Nature that have dominated much ecofeminist debate over several decades. For some critics, identifying Nature as female has done useful work in pointing to the fundamentally patriarchal origins of ecological degradation, for, as Ynestra King puts it, "the ecological crisis is related to the systems of hatred of all that is natural and female by the white, male western formulators of philosophy, technology, and death inventions. . . . Nature did not declare war on humanity; patriarchal humanity declared war on women and on living nature."[25] Other feminist scholars have been more cautious about equating women with Nature—or have rejected this move outright—on the grounds that it is a short and hazardous step from feminizing Nature to naturalizing femininity. These two moves, in discourses of patriarchal domination, are complementary and mutually reinforcing.[26]

In her ecofeminist reading of Plato's *Timaeus*, Val Plumwood has demonstrated that the figure of Gaia is implicated in a problematic gendering of the Nature/Culture binary in Greek mythology, and several of her points are also germane to Jǫrð's position relative to the male powers who shape the universe. Plumwood argues that "Platonic philosophy is organised around the hierarchical dualism of the sphere of reason over the sphere of nature." In this dualism, "reason" is overwhelmingly gendered male while the "lower" functions of Nature, the body and the "realm of becoming," are aligned with the feminine and personified in Gaia.[27] Norse cosmology, as we have seen—and especially as it is represented in Snorri's rationalizing synthesis—is also a system whereby male creator figures impose order upon a chaos that includes a feminized realm of Nature whose functions are all gender norms that fit into a broadly Platonic schema. Jǫrð is little more than a body and an embodiment, who exists to fulfill a maternal function that is always inferior to the rational creating and organizing of the universe which the male gods have undertaken. As *Vǫluspá* tells the story, the first phases of the gods' creation of the new cosmos—all of which take place in the absolute absence of women—are driven by a desire to impose order onto chaos. Although the universe has its origins in some form of spontaneous generation, it is the Æsir who decide how creation must be ordered: the courses the sun and moon must follow and the imposition of temporal structures by which to track their progress, for example.

For Plumwood, it is precisely this separation of the organized, rational (and masculine) cosmos from its disorganized, irrational (and feminine) chaos that also characterizes the cosmogony of the *Timaeus:*

> God as maker and fabricator of the universe imposes on the natural disorder of nature of nature (chaos) a properly regular, rational and perfect shape, motion and form. . . . Primal nature (chaos) is conceived as initially fallen and disordered; *logos* undertakes to do for this disorderly other that he finds in nature the same task that he undertakes for slaves, free-living animals, female forces and other "disorderly" elements; *logos* orders and rules the world of nature conceived as chaotic and disorderly, in a relation of domination conceived as the imposition of a rational order. . . . Thus Plato separates world-body and world-soul and insists on the world-soul's priority.[28]

Jǫrð can be read as the pagan Norse reflex of this world-body, while her husband Óðinn will do well as a personification of the world-soul in this Platonic sense. In his guise as the All-father he performs the role of a pseudo-Christian creator god; as part of the world-building triumvirate of Æsir he rationalizes a whole cosmos out of the chaotic, unplanned, but absolutely real substantiality of the giant Ymir. He is always associated with "higher" cultural functions in the wider mythology—with warfare, magic, kingship, and poetry, the skillful deployment of words to achieve his ends. The Norse creation myths are not themselves explicitly logocentric—word does not have precedence over substance—but nonetheless Óðinn could, with only minor modifications, fit into Plato's hierarchies as a creator god and a representative of the superiority of *logos* over a feminized realm of Nature. Nowhere in Old Norse literature do we hear Jǫrð speak for herself.

Óðinn's marriage to Jǫrð represents a culmination of the domination of the body-chaos-Nature-woman complex by the soul-reason-order-Culture-man set of associations. As a member of the stigmatized lower half of the binary, Jǫrð is subject to the regimes of control that the upper half of the binary may choose to impose upon its subordinates in pursuit of "progress," "security," and "civilization." And although we do not see much evidence of how Jǫrð is treated at the hands of her husband in the myths, Norwegian and Icelandic poets working in other genres were greatly attracted by the things that it is possible to do to a personified, feminine earth—and none of these things offer salutary examples of respect or affection for either women or the physical world.

Although Jǫrð is an obscure figure in myth, and even more obscure is her possible role in pagan religious culture, she enjoyed sporadic but significant prominence among poets who wished to celebrate political and martial victories using images of rape, abduction, and marriage. As Roberta Frank notes, "The seduction or rape of a woman is a popular image for the conquest of one political entity by another."[29] In poetry associated with the court of Earl Hákon Sigurðarson of Hlaðir, who was the de facto ruler of Norway from about 975 to 995, such visualizations appear to have enjoyed some cachet. We find them in the work of poets who delight in exploiting the feminization of jǫrð to produce erotically charged and obviously misogynistic images of the ruler's dominance over both land and women. Hákon was a notorious seducer of other men's wives, a fact his poets play on with every indication of approval.[30] As an example, we can look at a sequence of stanzas attributed to Hallfreðr Óttarsson, which were probably composed toward the end of Hákon's reign, ca. 990, and which are preserved only in manuscripts of *Snorra Edda*.[31] In these verses, Jǫrð's identity is disguised by making her the referent of a kenning, a poetic device in which an object is referred to through the juxtaposition of two other objects that are in a relationship with one another that is not identical to their relationship with the referent. In the following text, the referent or solution of the kenning is placed within square brackets, as has become conventional in the presentation of this type of poetry.

> The swift receiver of the horse of the breeze [SHIP > SEAFARER] draws
>   under himself the foliage-haired waiting wife of Þriði <= Óðinn >
>   [= Jǫrð] by means of true words of swords.
> Because of that I think the renowned flinger [of riches] [GENEROUS
>   MAN] is very reluctant to let Auðr's <giant's> sister [= Jǫrð] alone; Jǫrð
>   submits to the glorious ring-diminisher [GENEROUS MAN].
> The marriage was concluded, so that shrewdly-advising king's intimate
>   [RULER] afterward possessed the only daughter of Ónarr <giant>
>   [= Jǫrð], grown with forest.

The steerer of the Hrafnar <legendary horses> of the harbor [SHIPS
> SEAFARER] managed to allure to himself the broad-faced bride
of Báleygr <= Óðinn> [= Jǫrð] with sovereign speeches of swords
[BATTLE].[32]

In each of these vignettes, we see Hákon taking possession of land and the
land morphing into the personified Jǫrð, who in three of the four stanzas is
already identified by her relationship to male authority figures—her father
and her husband.[33] She is a prize to be fought over and a chattel to be possessed: Hákon wins her in battle, and there are distinct overtones of rape and
forced marriage in the first and last verses in the sequence.

Much traditional criticism has seen in these stanzas vestiges of a form of
ritualized sacred marriage, often dignified with the label *hieros gamos*. Folke
Ström exemplifies this tendency when he writes that "using erotic metaphors,
the poet develops the idea, known from other parts of the world, of a holy
wedding between the ruler and the land, the latter identical with the earth,
seen also as a female being, the earth-goddess."[34] The existence of some form
of *hieros gamos* in pagan Scandinavia is still widely assumed, and the stanzas by
Hallfreðr cited above are almost always offered as evidence of it.[35] But Frank
has demonstrated that the ruler's sexual domination of the land is a poetic
motif that cannot be tied to particular religious traditions, since Norse poets
maintain the conceit when talking about later kings who certainly did not enter
into a ritualized marriage with the territory they commanded. Poetry survives
from the courts of the Christian kings Óláfr skǫtkonung of Sweden, Knútr
(Cnut the Great) of Denmark and England, and Haraldr harðráði of Norway
that treats Jǫrð in similarly eroticized terms.[36] Perhaps the apogee of this tradition, however, is found in a verse by Snorri Sturluson himself, who attempts,
as a sort of poetic exercise, to push this image as far as he can manage, using
four different mythological land kennings in the eight lines available to him:

The hater of the precious pyre of the sea [GOLD > GENEROUS MAN]
defends the wife of the wolf's enemy [= Óðinn > = Jǫrð]; prows are
placed before the steep edge of the confidante of Mímir's friend [= Óðinn
> = Jǫrð]. The glorious mighty ruler can hold the mother of the serpent's
harmer [= Þórr > = Jǫrð]; necklace-destroyer [GENEROUS MAN],
enjoy the mother of the giantess's enemy [= Þórr > = Jǫrð] until old age.[37]

In Snorri's verse, Jǫrð and the land for which she must act as surrogate
are both subject to regimes of masculine domination. Jǫrð is defined, once

more, by her relationships with male figures; she is primarily a wife and mother, but also now a *mála,* a "female friend"/"confidante" and a *rúna,* a "confidante"/"sharer of secrets." Perhaps these cognomens, which seem to suggest the king will entrust the land with his secret counsels, indicate that the partnership between the man and his earth-wife will have a less asymmetrical power dynamic than is normal in this situation. But the verbs of which Jǫrð is the object—and she is always the object—all subordinate her to the king, who will "protect" (*verja*) her. We might think that "protecting" the earth is something we should look for in an enlightened leader, but the verse strongly implies that this protection is a function of the king's ownership. And, just as with Hallfreðr's earlier stanzas along the same lines, the other verbs which Snorri deploys have sexual overtones: the king will *njóta* (enjoy/make use of) her, because he, the *allvaldr* (ruler of all), knows how to *halda* (hold) her.[38] Both *njóta* and *halda* have attested sexual connotations, and Snorri is not being particularly subtle in the image he conveys.

Lacking in all these poetic and mythological references to Jǫrð are any signs of agency and any indication of consent. By feminizing the earth, we are immediately invited to begin treating her like a woman. This means that, in the vast majority of cultural situations in which we can assess this type of mythos, and certainly in the case of the Old Norse texts I've discussed here, the earth is subordinated, marginalized, disregarded, oppressed, taken possession of, exploited, and violated in the same ways that women are in patriarchies. Her function is reduced to that of wife and mother, and though she is celebrated for her maternal qualities (and demure, wifely compliance), this celebration does nothing to reconfigure the fundamental disparity in power between the embodied feminized world and the disembodied rational authority of men. To put it bluntly: personifying the physical world as female only ensures that the earth gets fucked.[39]

"Mother Earth" is part of the environmental movement's historical imaginary, and the earth-goddess figure has much greater importance in many indigenous religions than she does in Judeo-Christian-Islamic traditions. But as we have seen with Gaia's Scandinavian sister Jǫrð, the feminization of the physical world (or whole Earth system) is just as problematic as any gendering of an abstracted idea of Nature. If we think of the world as our mother, we expect the world to nurture, protect, and love us, provide for our needs and forgive us our sins. We are also accustomed to think of mothers as figures who will "do anything" for their children, up to and including laying down their lives for them. We certainly expect the woman-as-mother to subordinate her own needs and desires to those of her offspring. "The strength of the [Nature or Earth as] mother archetype is that it is a universal and powerful image which communicates clearly the need for an unconditional commitment to protect and sustain the environment," writes Lynn Stearney. But she goes on to problematize ecofeminists' use of the mother metaphor, because it "returns women to a primary identification as mothers, and reinforces the notion of women's roles and natures as inextricably connected to their reproductive capacity."[40] Whether we think of Gaia as doting mother or spurned femme fatale, we are defining her by her gendered Otherness from ourselves—and we are still thinking of "ourselves" as a masculinized Culture within a Nature/Culture hierarchy. The bind that we saw in Plumwood's reading of Plato is still in operation in Lovelock's Gaia, and it is certainly fundamental to the portrayal of Jǫrð in Norse mythology.

Jǫrð's treatment at the hands of Norse gods and poets alike shows that Scandinavian paganism was hardly some sort of ecofeminist utopia. Jǫrð is a passive object, a victim, defined by her inferiority to those men who possess her. Unlike Gaia, I am not sure she is capable of fighting back. If the giantess named by Snorri as the mother of Day and/or Night can be considered separately from the personification, we learn nothing of the ultimate fate of this figure. But the destiny of the physical world is clear. In the fifty-fifth stanza of *Vǫluspá*, the *fold*, the "land," sinks into the sea at the climax of the apocalyptic sequence of events known as Ragnarǫk:[41]

> The sun turns black, *fold* sinks into the sea,
> the bright stars vanish from the sky;
> steam rises up in the conflagration,
> hot flame plays high against heaven itself.
> (*Vǫluspá* [K] 55; 54 in Larrington)[42]

I regard *fold* as being metonymic with *jǫrð* in this verse, since stanza 57 shows new land emerging from the waters and uses the latter term to refer to it:

> She sees, coming up a second time,
> *jǫrð* from the ocean, eternally green;
> the waterfalls plunge, and eagle soars above them,
> over the mountain hunting fish.
> (*Vǫluspá* [K] 57; 56 in Larrington)[43]

When the *fold* sinks into the sea—with its poignant resonances with anthropogenic sea-level increases that we expect to have devastating effects upon ecosystems and human habitations in the near future—it does not do so as a last-ditch attempt to save itself from the actions of those who have caused Ragnarǫk. The worlds of gods, giants, and people have already ended, and everyone is dead. The cosmos could not regulate itself, could not prevent disaster.

However, the vision of a new and pristine *jǫrð* rising back up out of the sea gives us hope for a second chance, a new vision of a world full of the possibility of a harmonious *oikos* for fish and eagles, with humans and gods nowhere to be found. As we will see, however, this blessed interlude lasts but a moment, as some of the Æsir return to repopulate the virgin *jǫrð* and re-create their patriarchy in a postapocalyptic parody of their old ways of life. We do not learn about the ultimate fate of this second *jǫrð*—but we know what tends to happen to "virgin territory," and to virgins, in patriarchal societies.

The presence of a female personification of the physical world in Norse cosmology cannot be taken as indicative of an especially ecologically enlightened worldview. In the myths and mythologically inspired poems I have analyzed here, in fact, this feminization of the Earth seems particularly problematic from an ecofeminist standpoint. As Tzeporah Berman puts it,

> The Gaia and Mother Earth image limits our imagination, giving us an image of the Earth as human and female, limiting the image we could create. It is essential for humans to forge a new understanding of the Earth as a powerful sacred entity of which humans are but one constituent. Engendering the earth as female limits this possibility and reinforces the subordination and oppression of women and Nature and perpetuates the patriarchal ideology of domination.[44]

Jǫrð's status as wife, lover, mother, and possession of various male figures is always inferior, and often degrading. Her status as female is figured as an invitation, rather than an impediment, to her oppression. She has no agency; she has no voice. A passive cipher, Jǫrð cannot take a Gaian revenge upon her abusers, and so she will perish along with them at Ragnarǫk, only to be reborn into more or less the same structures of domination that pertained under the Æsir's rule.

Three Worlds, One Worldview

The three conceptions of "world" that I have identified as underlying the terms *heimr, verǫld,* and *jǫrð* in Norse mythological sources are all anthropocentric. *Heimr* considers the world as the "home" of mankind, conceived of primarily in geographic terms. We might think of it as analogous to "space" as Morton describes it—a "constant-presencing machine for making things appear consistent and solid, to make them easier to colonize, enslave, and plunder. Constant presence was part of an anthropocentric colonization protocol."[45] Many of the worlds that are bracketed by the cosmological concept of *heimr* are the dwelling places of the universe's subaltern groups, those the Æsir have cast out of their *garðr* into outer-spaces that then become sites of conquest and exploitation. The giants and dwarves are given *heimar* to dwell in, and their spaces are constantly invaded by the Æsir in search of wealth, sexual partners, and adventure in exotic realms.

Verǫld is a less fully determined concept of "world" in Norse mythological sources, but its etymology suggests that it has a temporal dimension. A world, in this reading, is a "time of men"—and the gendered noun is probably appropriate to this conception. This sort of worlding privileges men as agents of causality and can be equated with "history." We can speak confidently of "the world of the Vikings" or the "modern world" and know that we will be understood as referring to space and time and culture simultaneously. *Verǫld* is a term that encodes the idea of a world-from-a-human-perspective, rather than a concept analogous to everything-apart-from-a-human-perspective, as we sometimes perceive in ideas of Nature or "the natural world."

If the idea of a "natural world" did exist in Norse pagan worldview—if it was possible to think of a separate world beyond humans or their mythological surrogates—then *jǫrð* is probably the word that comes closest to representing it. *Jǫrð*'s most salient feature is its physicality, its embodiment. *Jǫrð* is a thing that we can touch—and it is therefore something that exists beyond ourselves. It cannot do quite the same job as our modern conception of Earth, since medieval Scandinavians lacked the planetary perspective that is a very recent addition to humanity's perception of itself. Nonetheless, *jǫrð* has plenty of earthy, organic connotations that make it feel like the "greenest" of the three Norse worldings. However, as we have seen, the personification of the physical world as a female figure, and her treatment at the hands of men, subvert any naive expectations of the benefits of thinking about the world as the soil that nurtures us, the cocoon that protects us, or the womb from which we emerge. The idea of *jǫrð* is perhaps less anthropocentric in its origins than either *heimr* or *verǫld*—but when Jǫrð becomes the constant object of exploitation by men (and, again, it really is men, and not people in general, that are the problem here), her status as universal mother, wife, and chattel puts her at the service of a phallocentric worldview. The physical world (*jǫrð*) is something for men to possess and exploit, just like as a woman Jǫrð is something for men to exploit—this hardly seems like an improvement on the anthropocentric worlding we find in Genesis and traditions that derive from it.

After seeing some promising signs of non- or even anti-anthropocentric thinking in the earliest, transcorporeal phases of the Eddic creation myths, the structuration of the universe that the gods embark on quite quickly produces a worldview that seems mostly identical with mainstream Western dualisms. The Norse cosmos becomes a structured system of hierarchies, of In-groups and Out-groups, of Us and Them, men and women, even if this system is not inherent in the universe but an imposition on it. Part of the problem is undoubtedly that Snorri Sturluson was a structuralist *avant la lettre,* as well as a Christian interpreter of pagan mythology. Snorri's account of the Norse creation(s) has been influenced—quite explicitly in places—by Genesis's cosmogony, which leads to the suspicion that his anthropocentrism has distorted myths that could have been more "ecological" in earlier forms. But as we have seen, *Vǫluspá* also sees the gods impose structural binaries onto the universe that are familiar to us from the Christian schema. While many critics have pointed out *Vǫluspá*'s indebtedness to contemporary Christian narratives and motifs, this poem—along with *Grímnismál* and *Vafþrúðnismál*—remains our best source for genuinely pre-Christian cosmological traditions in Scandinavia. To reject any elements of these poems' worldview as inauthentic because they do not agree with our preconceptions about the supposed "greenness" of Norse paganisms is fruitless. The structural correspondences between Christian and pagan cosmogonies that come to light in this analysis could represent a deep-rooted similarity between the two systems of thought that transcends questions of intercultural influence. In other words: the apparent anthropocentrism of the Norse myths may reflect a fundamental anthropocentrism in pagan Norse worldviews that is not significantly different from the Judeo-Christian dualisms that Lynn White claimed underlie the ecological crises of modernity.

4 Tree-People and People-Trees

Yggdrasill, the great ash, is central to Norse cosmology, both conceptually and literally. According to the character Hár in *Gylfaginning*, the "chief centre or holy place of the gods . . . is at the ash Yggdrasill," where the gods must hold their courts each day.[1] On hearing of this most holy and important tree, Gylfi immediately asks for more detail, and detail he receives:

> Then said Just-as-high: "The ash is of all trees the biggest and the best. Its branches spread out over all the world and extend across the sky. Three of the roots support it and extend very, very far. One is among the Æsir, the second among the frost-giants, where Ginnungagap once was. The third extends over Niflheimr, and under that root is Hvergelmir, and Níðhǫggr gnaws the bottom of the root. But under the root that reaches towards the frost-giants, there is where Mímir's well is, which has wisdom and intelligence contained in it . . . The third root of the ash extends to heaven, and beneath that root is a well which is very holy, called Urðr's well. There the gods have their court.[2]

Snorri Sturluson, the Icelandic author of this passage, lived in a largely treeless landscape. He might have seen a mature specimen of an ash tree on a visit to Norway, but by the thirteenth century trees large enough to imagine as containing whole worlds would have been rare indeed in Iceland. Timber was scarce and had to be imported or recycled. In an Icelandic context, it seems strange that one could conceive of an arborocentric cosmos. The Icelanders' chief parliament and law court, their equivalent of the gods' *hǫfuðstaðr*, was at Þingvellir, a gully formed along a fissure between the Eurasian and North American tectonic plates. The central place of this central place was a rock, the *lǫgberg*. Trees could not serve as central places or points of orientation for a people that had no trees.

The world-ash Yggdrasill, however, is an inheritance from a world and worldview that long predates the settlement of Iceland. Snorri's ancestors were pagans, and their paganism had its roots in the densely forested land-scapes of Norway and, ultimately, the European homelands of the Germanic peoples. Northern European pagans did not simply live in forests; they wor-shipped in them, and they revered the trees they contained.[3] Trees were at the very heart of their religious life. In the Norse myths, the universe is rep-resented as having Yggdrasill at its center, supporting the nine worlds of the cosmos, sheltering and nurturing all their inhabitants. In pagan Sweden and Norway, an objective correlative to the mythological ash was often found on farms that had a special protective tree—known respectively as a *vårdträd* or *tuntre*—in the middle of the *tún*, the enclosure that immediately surrounded the farmhouse.[4] This tree marked the conceptual center of householders' worldview, which itself was, in its arrangement of concentric circles around a tree that serves as the *axis mundi*, a microcosm of the whole pagan cosmos.[5]

In this chapter, I return to the idea that pre-Christian Nordic world-views offer the possibility of a nonhierarchical, possibly even transcorporeal approach to the interrelationships between people and the nonhuman—the latter represented now by trees, and trees represented, at first, by Yggdrasill. It strikes me as apt that this part of my book feels like its "greenest" and most optimistic section, in that it discusses ways of being-in-the-world that do seem to challenge and disrupt human myths of our ontological separation from, and concomitant superiority over, members of other species—even plants. Trees are always potent ecological symbols. But we should bear in mind, as we read these Icelandic myths about "evergreen ashes," that the early settlers of Ice-land cut down almost all the island's trees within a few decades of its discov-ery. However holy Yggdrasill might have been to these pagan pioneers, their reverence for this tree and for all trees did not prevent the rapid deforestation of their new homeland. We will return to this ecocide and its ramifications for Icelandic life and literature in chapter 5.

Tree Time

We met Yggdrasill in the prologue of this book, where I sought inspiration for an ecocritical approach to Old Norse myth from this uncanny ash, which stands greenly forever, outside of time and immune to the cataclysmic effects of Ragnarǫk. Because it is at least quasi-eternal, Yggdrasill can symbolize per-manence, stability, hope for a future beyond ecological catastrophe. Trees are often made to carry such symbolic freight, principally because of their capacity to achieve great age, transcending by far the lifespans of humans. An encounter with an ancient tree can have a humbling effect as we consider the generations of people who it has outlived. The tree is so old and we are so young; it is so large and we are so small; it was here before us and it will be here long after we are gone. In comparison with the great mature trees, the life of human beings seems like a mayfly's day in the sun, like the work of a moment. People have chainsaws, though, so we can soon get over these intimations of our smallness and transitoriness.

But Yggdrasill is forever. The gods cannot alter Yggdrasill; they cannot bend it to their purposes in the way that we saw them construct the inhabited realms of the cosmos for their own benefit. Yggdrasill stands in temporal relationship to the gods as the most ancient trees in our world stand in relationship to us: it was here before they came into being and it will be here after we are gone, barring some sort of disaster. The natural lifespan of a European ash is up to four hundred years: many other species have much longer lives than this. They might as well be immortal, as far as we are concerned. In *Vǫluspá*, Yggdrasill is called the "famous measuring-tree" (*mjǫtviðr mærr*), and it pre-exists every element of the created cosmos. It is present before Ymir makes his settlement; it does not need to be made out of anything else, nor is it the result of any formative processes. It simply is. As a *mjǫtviðr*, Yggdrasill limns the limits of the universe, but it also provides a temporal framework against which all other livings can be measured. The tree can provide definition for the cosmos because it is always already predefined.

When Yggdrasill is first mentioned under its familiar name in *Vǫluspá*, its associations with the fate of mortal beings is made clear:

An ash I know that stands, Yggdrasill it's called,
a tall tree, drenched with shining loam;
from there come the dews which fall in the valley,
green, it stands always over the well of fate.

From there come girls, knowing a great deal,
three from the lake standing under the tree;
Urð one is called, Verðandi another—
they carved on a wooden slip—Skuld the third;
they laid down laws, they chose lives
for the sons of men, the fates of men.
    (*Vǫluspá* [K] 19–20; 19–21 in Larrington)[6]

Yggdrasill now has a name, an identity; it acquires something like subjectivity, perhaps, through its naming. It has a certain amount of power, since it is the source of the waters that nourish creation and it seems to guard over the "well of fate," where the female personifications of "became," "becoming," and "must become," collectively known as the Norns, determine the destiny of all mortals.[7] But we do not get the impression that Yggdrasill itself is subject to time, decay, or death: it stands "always," and there is nothing to suggest, at this point in the poem, that this situation is likely to change. As we saw from Yggdrasill's introduction in *Gylfaginning*, the tree has a consistent connection with fate and judgment: it is where things happen, where decisions get made, where the course of events is determined. The Norns' prescriptions for the course of human lives are inscribed in wood.

If Yggdrasill's prominence in Norse mythology reflects the reality of pagan cultures in which trees, or groups of trees, were indeed chief and holy places in the community's life, the places where judgments might be made and the gods invoked, then the mythical world-tree is a reflection of cultural practices, or vice versa. We might argue, however, that this aspect of Yggdrasill's identity has little to do with the quotidian quiddity of actual trees—but our fate and the fate of trees are inextricably linked. Without trees to absorb carbon dioxide and respire oxygen in its place, Earth's climate would (and perhaps will) become ever more inhospitable to life as we know it. Although we seem hell-bent on trying it, humanity may not be able to survive without trees. Yggdrasill's involvement in measuring out the fate of the cosmos is a symbolic reminder of our dependence on them. But it also calls attention to a difference in the timescales according to which our species live and die. In Norse mythology, gods, giants, humans, dwarfs, and elves are all subject to fate; Yggdrasill exists beyond fate. Perhaps it is the only thing in the universe that exists beyond fate, beyond time. Just as an oak or redwood or yew confounds our own sense of temporal scale with its longevity, so Yggdrasill outspans and overshadows the whole of history and all of the deeds of the gods. I won't propose that we should take Yggdrasill as a surrogate for Nature, since Nature doesn't exist—but the great tree seems like a good, if perhaps clichéd, mascot for Life.

Arbor-Reality in the *Poetic Edda*

Yggdrasill's atemporality is but one aspect of its life that can be read as evoking a sense of the difference between human and arboreal existences. In other respects, Yggdrasill's authentic treeishness depends upon its interrelationships with other entities. Despite being radically outside the worlds that the gods create for mortal beings to inhabit, Yggdrasill's representation in Eddic poetry places the tree in a nonhierarchical mesh—to use Morton's favorite term once more—in which everything in the cosmos is also implicated. Yggdrasill is a central place for the gods, a point around which to orient themselves, but it is also everywhere for everyone and everything. It defies conventional mapping just as much as it challenges human-scale notions of temporality.

The main source for *Gylfaginning*'s account of Yggdrasill, with which the present chapter began, is the Eddic knowledge-exchange poem *Grímnismál*. *Grímnismál* starts by introducing the world-tree as the gods' judgment place, just as Snorri does. Then the poem discusses the trees' roots:

> Three roots there grow in different directions
> under Yggdrasill's ash;
> Hel lives under one, under the second, the frost-giants,
> under the third, humankind. (*Grímnismál* 31)[8]

This stanza presents problems for certain structuralist interpretations of the Norse cosmos which require Miðgarðr—the fortified "middle-yard" in which humankind is meant to live along with the gods—to be on the middle level of a vertical schematization of the universe. In the vertical model, Hel is the only entity from *Grímnismál* who should really live below the horizontal plane.[9] The frost-giants, as we have seen, are on the same ontological level as the gods, but cast out from the Æsir's center. In order to travel to the lands of the giants, there is no indication elsewhere in the myths that one has to move up or down in space. The Æsir's home at Ásgarðr is the only realm in the cosmos that is ever represented as existing above Miðgarðr, and its location is controversial and varies according to which source we read.[10]

Grímnismál 31 places humans on the same level as the world of the dead and the realm of the Æsir's implacable enemies. Read naturalistically, it places the dead and the living alike down below the ground, beneath the roots of the tree: perhaps, from Yggdrasill's atemporal perspective, all mortals are dead already, or might as well be. Rather than trying to imagine Yggdrasill's roots as curling unnaturally through the ether in order to reach realms in the cosmos that elsewhere seem to be regarded as existing at ground level or above it, I think it is worth thinking about where a real ash's roots go and what they do for the tree. The tree's roots spread out and down; they anchor it, preventing it toppling over. Water and nutrients travel from the soil to the tree via the root system. We are accustomed, I think, to imagine Yggdrasill as hanging suspended in the cosmic void—but as a tree, it must be rooted somewhere. Its roots are down among the living and dying, those beings who are part of the natural life cycle of Yggdrasill's *oikos:* those whose bodies will, as Snorri puts it, "decay into earth" (*fúni at moldu*).[11] In this reading, we are all in the process of becoming the dirt in which Yggdrasill can flourish. The gods, meanwhile, possess a sort of conditional immortality that keeps them separate from this organic process. As we will see in chapter 7, the Æsir will die at Ragnarǫk, but Ragnarǫk is something like a nuclear holocaust, wiping out very nearly all traces of the gods and their worlds and leaving a blank slate for the creation of a new naturecultural order. The gods do not die of natural causes.

Yggdrasill relies on us, therefore—on the dirt that we're made of and that we return to—for its ability to remain upright as a "standing ash" (*askr standandi*). Its roots are deep and wide and strong enough that it will not fall over even at Ragnarǫk. In return, Yggdrasill is the source of life for many types of creature. We have already seen that the tree is closely associated with liquid: the well of Urðr is where the Norns decide the fate of mortal people; Mímir also has a well at the base of the tree, which is a source of numinous wisdom. More prosaically, *Grímnismál* tells us that all the waterways of the worlds originate with a tree named "Læraðr," which is probably identical with Yggdrasill:

> Eikþyrnir is the hart's name, who stands on Father of Hosts' hall
> and browses on Læraðr's branches;
> and from his antlers there's dripping into Hvergelmir,
> from thence all waters make their way. (*Grímnismál* 26)[12]

Læraðr is an utterly obscure epithet, either for Yggdrasill or for any other tree. Its only other occurrence is Snorri's paraphrase of this part of *Grímnismál* in *Gylfaginning*, where no additional information is given save an alternative spelling of the name—*léraðr*.[13] The functional similarity between this Læraðr, from which drips the origin of the world's rivers, and *Vǫluspá*'s Yggdrasill, whose dews fill the valleys, suggests to me that the two moisture-bearing trees are the same tree. In any case, this tree has an important role in the mythological biosphere's water cycle. Earthly trees play a similar role: as much as 10 percent of the water in our atmosphere is produced by plant transpiration, and a large oak can transpire 151,000 liters of water per year.[14] The role of the hart Eikþyrnir—whose name means "oak-antlers"—in the process does not suggest that the author of *Grímnismál* understood the mechanics of transpiration, but this poem, like *Vǫluspá*, intuits the importance of trees to the biome in their participation in the production of life-giving fresh water.

Yggdrasill supports a wide variety of life forms directly, as well as indirectly as both an *oikos* and a source of water for the inhabited worlds. The tree is home to squirrels, serpents, birds, and a dragon, and a source of food for another group of deer. These creatures exist in full symbiosis with Yggdrasill, who provides them with all their needs, even though it suffers on account of its hospitality. Once again, *Grímnismál* is our main source for this information:

> Ratatoskr is the squirrel's name, who must scurry
> about on Yggdrasill's ash;
> the eagle's utterance he must bring from above
> and tell to Níðhǫggr below.

> There are four harts too, who browse on its shoots,
> with their necks tilted back;
> Dáinn and Dvalinn,
> Dúneyrr and Duraþrór. (*Grímnismál* 32–33)[15]

The next stanza lists six snakes who live under Yggdrasill, about which the narrator comments, "I think [they] will erode the tree forever" (*hygg ek at æ skyli / meiðs kvistu má*). *Gylfaginning* adds further species that Yggdrasill supports in some way: two swans swim around in Urðr's well, while honeybees feed on the dew (called "honey-fall") that drips from the tree.[16]

Yggdrasill is a food source, a nesting site, and a network of movement and communication for multiple species. In this light, its identification as an ash is perhaps particularly appropriate, as *Fraxinus excelsior* is associated with an extremely diverse range of other organisms: in British contexts, the ash is used by twenty-six types of mammal, who treat it as a larder or dormitory or simply prefer habitats that include this sort of tree, as do twelve species of bird. There is no association between British ash trees and serpents (or dragons), but an enormous diversity of smaller creatures thrive in symbiosis with the ash: 917 separate species of invertebrates, fungi, lichens, and bryophytes are recorded as living with ashes.[17] (If Yggdrasill were a yew we might see it as a problem that the foliage and seeds of that tree are highly toxic to most mammals, making it perhaps an unlikely choice for a prototypical tree of life. However, deer are almost unique in tolerating, and indeed relishing, yew as a food source. But if Læraðr is indeed identical with Yggdrasill, we would have to worry about the goat Heiðrún, who munches on Læraðr's branches in *Grímnismál* 25. Yew is poisonous to goats.)

Grímnismál treats Yggdrasill holistically and ecologically. The tree is represented as fully enmeshed with its surroundings and its symbiotes, creating an ecology out of its interrelationships that sustains a diversity of life. It cannot be reduced to those relationships, however: Yggdrasill transcends its roles as a food supply for deer or as an eagle's perch. Some of Yggdrasill's interrelationships are naturecultural—its function as the gods' central place or as the arbiter of human fate are not biological symbioses, but they are all part of the tree's true identity. Matthew Battles's comments about the nature of trees' engagements with their (and our) *oikos* are certainly applicable to Yggdrasill: "Even within itself, a tree will not to its own edges keep. And the forms trees take in connection with human lifeworld, meanwhile, engage the full panoply of our entanglement with questions of materiality, community, and design. As objects, trees inhabit or create an uncanny space in which they seem sessile, passive, pliably responsive to human acts and needs; and yet they carry on abundant and active lives of their own, with qualities and even varieties of affect remote to our experience."[18]

We get the clearest indication of what sort of life experience Yggdrasill endures from the last of *Grímnismál*'s sequence of tree stanzas, in which the suffering produced by the tree's involvement in symbiosis is vividly evoked:

> Yggdrasill's ash suffers agony
> more than men know,
> a stag nibbles it above, but at its side it's decaying,
> and Níðhǫggr rends it beneath. (*Grímnismál* 35)[19]

We think of Yggdrasill as a tree of life, and so it is, but this stanza reminds us that life continues always at the cost of something: for the deer to live, the tree must lose some of its leaves or bark. Presumably Níðhǫggr, the great dark subterranean dragon whose name means "corpse-striker," gets nourishment from Yggdrasill's roots. (It is not clear in the Norse myths what Yggdrasill gets in return for its generosity to its rapacious guests.) Here we get the first indication that Yggdrasill—though existing beyond human conceptions of time—is subject to change, to decay: perhaps it will not turn out to be immortal after all, although we cannot imagine a future without it. Above all, however, *Grímnismál* 35 makes it clear that Yggdrasill is a feeling tree: it suffers, it experiences agony (*erfiði*). Yggdrasill is no passive or inanimate object; it is a subject with which we might try to empathize, although the poem emphasizes that there are limits to how close we will ever get to understanding the full extent of the tree's pain. And, as Michael Bintley points out, Yggdrasill is by no means the only member of the plant kingdom to "experience suffering and loss in the same way as humans—in both physiological and psychological terms" in the Norse myths.[20]

The botanist Matthew Hall uses stanza 35 of *Grímnismál* to exemplify the ways in which Germanic pagans related to trees and other plants.[21] He argues that paganism—in contrast with Christianity, with its strictly hierarchical attitude toward Nature—incorporated a reverence for trees that did not depend on the imputation of some "higher" spirit that inhabited the tree or on any connection with a deity. Rather, the relationship between pagan people and trees was particularly close, he suggests, because of a perception of consubstantiality between all elements of creation: a feeling of kinship between man and the physical world around him that could lead to a close, respectful social bond and a degree of identification with the trees. Plants and people were not distinguished from one another on ontological grounds in the pagan worldview because pagan people did not set themselves apart from the nonhuman world, but rather recognized their own place within it. Hall claims that "fragments of old pagan texts recognize these real, corporeal kin [i.e., plants, from the human perspective] as subjective, aware, volitional, intelligent, relational beings."[22] Bintley adds that "the world tree Yggdrasill endures great and terrible hardships which, although distanced from human experience, remain nevertheless accessible to us through mythic and poetic discourse."[23] I certainly agree that this stanza imbues Yggdrasill with remarkable subjectivity: the description of the tree's "agony" (*erfiði*) is somehow the more powerful for its unexpectedness, since we are not accustomed to thinking of plants as susceptible to pain. But *Grímnismál* also emphasizes that people are incapable of true empathy with the suffering world-tree—its agony is "more than men can know." We can only represent the experience of a tree by relating it to our experience of the world, normally through verbal utterance or some other mediated performance, whereas the tree's life experience is encoded in its physical form, as Peter Del Tredici argues:

A direct consequence of the meristematic structure of trees is that everything that has ever happened to them over the course of their long lives is embedded in the very fiber of their being, which is to say, the structure of their wood. . . . At the risk of sounding anthropomorphic, one might say that the shape of an individual tree is analogous to the personality of a human, being the product of the complex interaction between genetic endowment (nature) and environmental pressures (nurture). Quite literally, everything that ever happens to a tree in the course of its long life is embedded in its form, even the little things that might have happened to the tree when it was just a sapling. The body language of trees speaks not only to the influence of the past in the present, but also to the promise of the future.[24]

In this attempt at a "gestalt" of treeishness, Del Tredici helps us to understand Yggdrasill's suffering from a more treelike perspective. We may have to think of bodily damage as causing pain, even "agony," because our bodies and brains are set up to process stimuli in that way. But a tree's response to tissue damage is to compartmentalize that tissue, to wall it off from the healthy wood and grow around it. Even the "decay" that the ash suffers can be dealt with in this way, and if the rot does not spread too far into the tree it will survive with no major damage. As long as it is capable of forming new growth, a tree will live. "A tree that is not expanding is a tree that is dying," writes Del Tredici.[25]

Grímnismál makes a bold attempt at empathy with Yggdrasill's life experiences, and its focus on the tree's subjectivity may indeed indicate some form of perceived interconnectedness between people and trees among Norse pagans, as Hall suggests. At the same time, this poem is self-aware enough to realize that anthropomorphic attempts to imagine what life is like for nonhumans—perhaps especially when we are dealing with an entity that so far exceeds our own experience of the world—can only be of limited success. They can succeed in making a tree more like us, but they do so at the price of making it less like itself.

Lotte Motz provides an excellent summary of Yggdrasill's portrayal in the extant Norse myths: "The tree, uniting the various geographic regions of the earth, assembles also its inhabitants. Itself being vegetable, it feeds and shelters beasts of land, air, and water, as well as creatures in human shape. It transmits a vision of unceasing activity, of continuous interactions and transformations, of birth and decay, of the generative power of moisture, and of life, tragically, feeding on life."[26] Motz goes on to discuss other iterations of the cosmic tree found in mythologies around the world, and finds that Yggdrasill has a number of significant correspondences with other "north-Eurasian" examples. She concludes by suggesting that Scandinavian peoples made their home in similar latitudes to the northern homelands of some Eurasian communities and therefore shared with them elements of ecology, geography, and culture.[27] Of these factors, however, I believe the ecological aspect of world-tree myths to be the most important. As Yggdrasill shows, the tree is a compelling metaphor for an intersubjective cosmos because absolutely real, nonmetaphorical trees are whole worlds in themselves, as well as full citizens of the ecosystems to which they belong. Trees exist in symbiotic relationships with myriad organisms and with the soil, rocks, and water of the earth they inhabit. They are fully actant: they respond to stimulus and—as botanists are increasingly coming to realize—they have an uncanny but important social life. Trees help each other.[28] In chapter 7, we will see that Yggdrasill does not suffer in silence or stillness through the upheaval of Ragnarǫk, but takes an active part in responding to the social and ecological collapse that is happening in the worlds around it. But mostly Yggdrasill's movements and experiences are inaccessible to us because, as with the lives of all trees, they simply occur on a temporal scale that is beyond our comprehension. They live too slowly. We die too soon.

Conifers and Confreres

To this point, I have argued that the Norse myths endow Yggdrasill with a degree of personhood that enables and encourages human subjects to feel empathy, and perhaps a sense of kinship, with the life experiences of trees. I have also suggested that this approach is perhaps too anthropomorphic to allow us to grasp the full, rich treeishness of Yggdrasill's "abor-reality." In another genre of Old Norse–Icelandic literature, however, poets approach the same task from the opposite direction, engaging in a sort of deanthropomorphizing game whereby people turn into trees. This second approach to human-tree interrelationships also suggests that Norse worldviews did indeed perceive the plant kingdom as existing on an ontological plane much closer to that of humanity than we are accustomed to allow.

When *Vǫluspá* tells of the creation of humankind (in stanza 17), it mentions that the first two people in the world are called Askr and Embla. *Askr* is "ash," of course, and his female counterpart may be "elm," although this identity has been disputed.[29] We do not learn much beyond the names of these two characters in *Vǫluspá,* but Snorri Sturluson fleshes out their story and emphasizes their arboreal origins: "As Borr's sons [i.e., the gods, named as Óðinn, Hœnir, and Loðurr in *Vǫluspá*] walked along the sea shore, they came across two logs, and created people out of them. The first gave breath and life, the second consciousness and movement, the third a face, speech and hearing and sight; they gave them clothes and names. The man was called Askr and the woman Embla, and from them were produced the mankind to whom the dwelling place under Miðgarðr was given."[30] *Vǫluspá* does not claim that the two primordial humans are actually made out of logs, but nor does it contradict the idea directly. The implication of Snorri's account is that Askr and Embla are created out of pieces of driftwood, since living trees seem unlikely to be found right on the shoreline. Driftwood became an increasingly important source of building material and firewood in Iceland as the native forests disappeared, and so the happy accident of the creation of human beings seems to have an Icelandic flavor to it: medieval Icelanders were accustomed to producing something useful out of flotsam and jetsam. As Michael Bintley points out, a similar impulse probably underlies stanza 49 of *Hávamál,* in which Óðinn gives clothes to two "tree-men" (*trémenn*), apparently bringing them to life, or at least endowing them with subjectivity.[31]

In these myths, the gods endow the two prototype humans with life, spirit, intelligence, and so on; but their substance, their nature at its most fundamental, is wooden. While we do not know how widespread this myth—or belief in Askr and Embla as progenitors of the human race—was among pagan Scandinavians, the idea that mankind is in origin and constitution of that same stuff that trees are made of could explain the apparent empathy between people and trees that we saw elsewhere in the mythological poems. Mankind's consubstantiality with treekind seems to be at the heart of this kinship. For the pagan Norse, trees were neither simply reserves of potential resources nor abstract symbols of something else—though they could be both of these things. They were connected by a shared subjectivity because they existed on the same ontological plane. Whereas we are used to thinking of humanity as a branch of the animal kingdom, Norse poetic culture regarded people as a species of feeling tree.

If humans are all essentially wooden actors, it's not surprising that aspects of their treeishness sometimes come to the surface. In Old Norse–Icelandic literature, the boundaries between the human and the arboreal become particularly blurry in skaldic poetry. We call poetry "skaldic" when it meets certain formal and generic criteria that differentiate it from the Eddic verse that we have read as the vehicle of much of the mythology.[32] (The term is, however, a tautology: "skaldic" derives from the Old Norse world *skáld,* which means "poet"; skaldic poetry is simply "poets' poetry.") In contrast to the always anonymous and usually undatable texts of the *Poetic Edda,* skaldic poetry is normally attributed to a named composer whom we can identify in the historical record. Norse skálds often served kings and other potentates, whose deeds they record in mostly glowing terms—the preservation of this verse owes partly to its high-status origins and function as a form of political propaganda. After a period of memorization and oral transmission, the authors of Icelandic sagas and histories used preexisting skaldic stanzas as evidence for their stories' authenticity, or just because they liked the sound of them. We owe the survival of much skaldic verse to these authors' decision to incorporate old poems into their narratives, though we should also be aware that they were not above making up a new stanza to fit their story if it suited them. The other main vector for the transmission of skaldic poetry is *Snorra Edda.* In the second part of this work, known as *Skáldskaparmál* (Language of poetry), Snorri provides a cornucopia of examples of the skáld's craft for the benefit of both readers and composers of this type of literature. The *Edda* concludes with a hundred-stanza tour de force called *Háttatal*, which Snorri composed to show off the full range of skaldic meters.

And what meters they are! Skaldic poetry is notoriously complex and dense, and its difficulty derives in large part from how strict its metrical requirements are. In the classical *dróttkvætt* (court meter) form, every stanza must adhere to unbending and highly artificial rules: each stanza must have eight lines; each four-line half stanza must be a complete sense unit; every pair of lines must have stressed syllables that participate in alliteration; and two different forms of internal rhyme are employed depending on whether the line is in an odd- or even-numbered position in the stanza. Every line must end with a disyllabic falling cadence. In order to accord with these strictures, skálds were forced to be extremely inventive and flexible with their word choice: they employ an enormous range of synonyms for mundane things, ready at a moment's notice to meet the need for a word for king that starts with a *d* and contains the vowel sound *ó,* for example. Trees have an important role in this complex, multibranched system of diction, for whenever a tree word appears in a skaldic stanza, its audience knows at once to expect not a leafy source of nuts or firewood but a person. The idea that "tree" equals "person" is one of the most commonplace images of this artistic idiom. By extension, any tree, any name of a tree, or any word for tree potentially can stand in for any human figure.

To clarify (!) their meaning, skaldic poets would often make the tree part of a kenning—one of the fiendish circumlocutions that are the most notable, enjoyable, and daunting feature of this poetry. A kenning is something like a metaphor, something like a riddle, and in some ways like nothing else whatever.[33] It is always easier to give examples than to define a kenning in the abstract. Let us say that we wish to mention a "warrior" in our verse; but "warrior" is boringly transparent, or perhaps it does not fit into the metrical structure of the stanza. We need to substitute something for "warrior" that will transform it into something else yet allow the hearer or reader of the poem to work out that we are really referring to a warrior. Often, this transformation will produce (or require) an interesting cognitive shift on the part of our audience.

At the most basic level, we could say that a warrior is a man, first of all; but "man" does not precisely denote "warrior." Therefore, we might modify the concept of man by reference to another aspect of the warrior's identity: that he carries weapons, for example. "Man of weapons" denotes a warrior neatly, if simplistically. Knowing that it is possible to substitute a tree word for a man word, however, we can produce a different effect if we alter the kenning to "tree of weapons." This phrase still means "warrior," but now the image is made more striking through (what strikes us) as the dissonance between the semantic field of the base word ("tree") and the determinant ("of weapons"). Kennings of this type are abundant in skaldic poetry of all periods.[34] A favorite of mine is one of the simpler examples: in a verse ascribed to Jórunn skáldmær, one of very few female skálds to whom extant verse is attributed, people are called *þollar gulls,* or "firs of gold."[35] If we try to read this kenning naturalistically, our mind's eye might picture conifers turning anachronistically yellow in the autumn, or glinting in evening sunlight; perhaps even a decorated Christmas tree. In fact, we must also think of people and trees as always being interchangeable—and people are also defined in the skaldic tradition by their fondness for gold and silver. While a tree might be golden, it can have no use for gold. Mankind is the only species of tree that has use for money. The kenning first inspires an image of the natural world that is then overlaid and finally replaced by the cultural connotations of its two elements.

Skaldic kennings often operate on this imagistic level: if a sword is described as a "fish of battle," we see it flashing and darting through a sea of enemies. But a tree and a man do not obviously resemble each other on a visual level. They are both upright, I suppose, and they both have limbs, but it is a stretch to imagine a tree as humanoid or a person as tree-shaped.[36] And while kennings have sometimes been viewed as being metaphorical, "tree" can be a direct substitution for "man" without the addition of a modifier: in poetry of this sort, a tree is simply a man and a man a tree, and we do not need to think of it in metaphorical or even imagistic terms.[37] In contrast to Askr and Embla, whose bark and sap turn into skin and blood by divine intervention, the people-trees of skaldic poetry might be seen simply as trees with hats on.[38] A reader of skaldic verse quickly becomes accustomed to regarding every tree word as shorthand for "man" or "woman." Familiarity with the trope—indeed, awareness that we are dealing with a trope at all—weakens the kennings' force. At the same time, the ubiquity of the device has a humbling, deanthropocentrizing effect: humanity and tree life are on the same ontological level. As we speculate about the possible weird realities of tree-feeling, we see that Norse poets were uncannily aware of the possibility that people are "merely" feeling (and fighting and loving and drinking) trees. Consider these examples of the kenning type that Snorri quotes in *Skáldskaparmál.* As skaldic verse offers possibly clinching evidence for the dictum (attributed to Robert Frost, although he apparently never wrote as much in print) that "poetry is what is lost in translation," I have given the original text as well as Faulkes's literal prose rendering of the stanza:

Aura stendr fyrir orum
eik fagrbúin leiki.

(The fairly adorned coin-oak stands in the way of our pleasure.)

Meiðr er morgum oeðri
morðteins i dyn fleina.
Hjorr far hildiborrum
hjarl Sigurði jarli.

(Beam of the killing-twig is better than many in spear-din; the sword wins
land for the battle-keen earl Sigurðr.)

Askþollum stendr Ullar
austr at miklu trausti
roekilundr hinn ríki
randfárs brumaðr hári.

(The powerful shield-danger-wielding grove with hair for foliage provides
Ullr's ash firs in the east with great security.)[39]

Although I've identified the person-as-tree kenning as something of a blind
motif, these three examples still produce startling hybrids. In the first,
a woman becomes *fagrbúin eik aura* (beautifully adorned [female] oak of
coins)—there are both masculine and feminine words for "oak" in Old Norse;
this is the latter—as she intervenes between the poet and (presumably) the
object of his sexual desire. Oaks have symbolic resonances as large, sturdy,
enduring trees, but here the transformation of the woman into the tree seems
much more than symbolic: it/she is an actual and actant obstacle—she has the
same physical agency *as a tree.*

The second half stanza, which Snorri attributes to Kormákr Ogmundar-
son, extends the metaphor by making a sword into a *morðtein*—a "murder-
twig." The warrior is a *meiðr* ("pole" or "beam") of "murder-twigs." *Meiðr* is
an interesting choice of base word (by no means uncommon) for a man-tree
kenning, since this word is never applied to a living tree, only to wood that
has been worked in some way.[40] Here, the denatured tree seems to reassert
its woody identity by sprouting deadly twigs that allow it to defeat its enemies
in battle. In this kenning, the warrior's humanity is entirely subsumed into his
treeishness—a fusion between man and plant takes place. A similar extension

of the trope occurs in the last of these examples, which Snorri states was composed by Hallfreðr vandræðaskáld (his splendid nickname means "troublesome poet"). This stanza is remarkably arboreal. Both (grammatical) subject and (grammatical) object of the sentence are replaced by man-tree kennings, and both kennings are expanded beyond the basic "tree equals man" conceit. First, we have *rœkilundr randfárs*—the "cultivating-grove of shield-danger." "Shield-danger" is a sword, or possibly battle, and the grove (or tree—this collective noun is singular and is used as a substitution for singular referents) who cultivates or cares for the danger of shields is a warrior. The idea of a tree or forest being able to "cultivate" is intriguing and suggests a new type of nonhuman actancy: perhaps nonhumans are capable of care or stewardship. The "cultivating-grove of shield danger" is also *brumaðr hári* (budded with hair): where a tree has foliage, this hybrid has hair—it seems as though we are watching an entirely real, physical transformation between man and tree taking place before our eyes. Finally, Hallfreðr—who is clearly having tremendous fun with this stanza—uses two more tree words in his kenning *askþollar Ullar*. Most literally, this construction means "ash-firs of Ullr," with firs presumably being "men" while *askr Ullar* is a kenning for "shield" that works by making *askr* a metonym for "ship." "Ullr's ship" is a conventional shield kenning for which no explanatory narrative survives. Shields are ships; ships are trees; trees are people. We are all made of the same wood.

Lamenting the Loss of Trees

Skaldic poetry was composed throughout the medieval period and across the whole Old Norse–Icelandic world. Over the course of the tenth and eleventh centuries, Icelanders became particularly renowned for their versifying, with many poets making the journey from Iceland to the courts of rulers in Norway, Denmark, and the British Isles. Others stayed at home and composed verse in a land that was becoming increasingly treeless. I have suggested that the centrality of Yggdrasill to Norse mythology indicates that the world-tree myth probably originated outside Iceland, where it is hard to imagine people conceiving of a religious worldview centered on trees; the same is probably true of Norse skálds' fascination with blending the human and the arboreal in their kenning images.[41] But Icelandic skálds, fully immersed in these traditions, continued to think about trees, even when composing far away from Norway's dense forests.

No surviving literature from medieval Iceland addresses the psychic or emotional impact of the island's deforestation directly, yet we know it happened. It is also clear that trees occupied a place close to the center of the pagan Norse worldview. One final case study will provide an example of the naturecultural context against which the deforestation took place: the greatest poetic elegy in Old Norse, Egill Skallagrímsson's *Sonatorrek*. This poem is a lament for two men—the poet's sons, who had both died shortly before its composition, or so *Egils saga* tells us.[42] *Sonatorrek* is an exceptionally powerful exploration of grief and human impotence in the face of hostile fate. It is also a poem that engages with the nonhuman world in almost every stanza. Although an ecocritical reading of the whole poem would be productive, here I wish to focus on three stanzas that specifically mention trees.

Egill's father, Skalla-Grímr, was a settler in one of the first waves of Iceland's colonization; his land-taking was one of the most extravagant in the nation's history. The huge swathes of land that he claimed included some woodlands. Although *Egils saga* does not dwell on Skalla-Grímr's activities in these woods, it does describe his building several farms and searching out grazing for his flocks, and it mentions his prowess as a shipwright.[43] Despite his ownership of wooded land, the saga emphasizes that driftwood was already an important resource, even so soon after the first settlers' arrival: his third farmstead was built at Mýrar, which was particularly well placed for the collection of driftwood. As the saga describes it, Egill's upbringing took place in an already sparsely forested environment. But, as a poet, he had to work in a tradition that was founded in a mythical natureculture in which trees and people were consubstantial and in which the whole universe was structured around an arboreal figure. The occasional verses that the saga attributes to Egill include kennings like *lauka lind* (linden of herbs) for a woman and *lagar mána þollar* (firs of moon of the sea) for men, with "moon of the sea" being a kenning for gold.[44] But when we get to *Sonatorrek,* his greatest and most heartfelt composition, we find that his use of tree imagery goes deeper than merely providing base words for people kennings.[45]

In the opening part of the poem, Egill explains how hard it is for him to express his grief, but also the necessity of his doing so. The fourth stanza runs

> Because my lineage is at an end
> like hewn-down trees of the forest;
> it is not a glad man who carries the
> body of a relative from the house.[46]

We can read Egill's reference to *hræbarnir hlynir* ("hewn-down trees": *hlynr* probably refers to a member of the maple family) as a simile, if we wish: his family line has been chopped down, cut off from the roots that gave it life, just as a maple might be cut down in the forest. But this line also works as an indicative statement: my lineage has come to an end *because* the trees have been chopped down. Egill's two sons are the trees, harvested prematurely. Their corpses become a copse.

Next, Egill thinks of what he must do to honor the young men's memory, and the productive potential of a dead tree—its capacity to transcend death—provides the stanza's key image:

> Yet I must first speak of the death
> of my mother and father;
> I carry out of the temple of words
> the timber of praise, leaved with words.[47]

Here, Egill's parents, the trunk of the genealogy of which he is a branch, are implicitly figured as trees, since their deaths provide the raw material for his "timber of praise" (*timbr mærðar*), the poem he must fashion. His memorial is to become a tangible object, a cultural manifestation of the natural process of death. Wood is the perfect choice of material to compare his poetry to, since it is always both natural and cultural: when the tree is alive, its potential cultural uses lie latent; upon its death and conversion into an object of cultural worth, its natural substance remains and becomes preserved. A plank remains part of the tree from which it was carved, retains its treeishness, though the tree is long dead. Egill's parents will live on in his memorial poem in much the same way: their natural death has become reified through its shaping into a cultural artifact.

Much later in *Sonatorrek*, Egill resumes his use of tree imagery as he turns on Óðinn, his own patron god, whom he has come to blame for the death of his elder son, Gunnarr. As Michael Bintley points out, stanza 21 seems to partake of *Vǫluspá*'s image of the human Askr's creation, when Óðinn raised up a piece of driftwood and gave it life. The prose of *Egils saga* also tells us that Egill's son Bǫðvarr had been washed ashore, lifeless, where Egill found the body and carried it away for burial.[48] The discovery of Bǫðvarr's corpse reads like an ironic inversion of the Askr and Embla myth: people are no more than driftwood without life to animate them.[49] But now Óðinn has taken up a second ash tree, Gunnarr, and deprived him of life:

> I still remember when Óðinn raised up
> to the world of the gods
> the ash-tree of my lineage
> which sprouted from me and the family branch of my wife.[50]

Once again, a conventional reading of this stanza suggests that Egill's conventional use of *askr ættar* (ash of family) to refer to his son is metaphorical. Gunnarr was not a tree, but he can be compared to a tree on the basis of the audience's understanding of trees and men being in some sense comparable, especially combined with the image of the family tree and of the natural generation of offspring with which Egill concludes the verse. In other words, this is a cultural appropriation of an image drawn from nature that is effective precisely because a man is *not* a tree. It is the artificiality of the idea that places it in an elevated poetic register. But I would prefer to dwell on the seeming *naturalness* of this image, for if men and trees are kindred beings, if they are ultimately made of the same substance and have a common origin, then this is a perfectly naturalistic representation of reality as the poet perceives it, except that the very idea of "naturalness" is determined by our own cultural preconceptions.

Egill represents his family as a tree and his family members as individual trees. This is a cultural appropriation of a nonhuman phenomenon to explain an aspect of human life. But more than this, from the perspective of Old Norse mythopoesis, each member of his family *is* actually a tree. They all share in the fundamental treeishness of the universe, a treeishness that is always simultaneously natural and cultivated, real and imagined. *Sonatorrek* is, in part, a naturecultural attempt to come to terms with deforestation. When a loved one dies, a new clearing appears in one's family forest, leaving only a small store of timber out of which to create something than can transcend his or her death; and when we chop down a tree, however necessary that action is, we should be aware that we are losing one of our own. In the next chapter, however, we will see that these feelings of identity and solidarity with members of the plant kingdom, which seem to have such deep roots in Norse culture, did not stop the early settlers of Iceland from chopping down the island's woodlands in a remarkably short space of time—only to replace it in their literature with an artificial paradise of fake trees, a simulacrum or parody of what they had destroyed. As we will see, this vision of an Icelandic earthly paradise is just as unsustainable as its tree-filled landscape had been in reality.

5   Trees, Vines, and the Golden Age of Settlement

DURING HER FOUR TERMS in office, Vigdís Finnbogadót-
tir, president of Iceland between 1980 and 1996, was an enthusiastic planter
of trees and a proponent of the nation's reforestation. Some indication of the
scale of the task that faced her is provided by a record of a comment made
by the British monarch during a state visit. Upon being shown Vinskógur, the
"friendship forest" established in Þingvellir national park where foreign dig-
nitaries are encouraged to plant a tree in the name of international peace and
fraternity, Queen Elizabeth apparently said, "Yes, but where is the forest?"[1]
Although trees are returning to Iceland—the total area of forest has increased
by about 20 percent per decade since the 1970s—they grow slowly.[2] Iceland's
contemporary landscape remains notable (to most European observers, at
least) for its treelessness as much as for its volcanoes and hot bubbling mud.
Karen Oslund quotes a story of a young Icelander arriving in Scotland in 1811,
having "never seen a tree" before.[3] Although this tale is presumably apocry-
phal, or at least exaggerated, it is not completely implausible: in 1950 less than
1 percent of Iceland was wooded, and that situation had remained fairly stable
since at least the eighteenth century.[4]

When Iceland was settled, circa 870 CE, however, nobody needed to ask,
"Where is the forest?" The trees, as one approached Iceland at the end of
the long voyage from Norway or Faroe or the British Isles, were right there.
As the earliest vernacular history of Iceland, Ari Þorgilsson's *Íslendingabók*,
tells it,

> There was a Norwegian man named Ingolfr, of whom it is truly said that he
> first came from there to Iceland when Haraldr the fine-haired was sixteen
> years old; he came back for a second time a few winters later. He dwelled
> in the south, in Reykjarvík. The place to the east of Minþakseyrr where
> he came ashore is called Ingolfshǫfði, and the place to the west of Ǫlfossá

which he later took possession of is called Ingolfsfell. At that time, Iceland was grown over with trees between the mountains and the shore.[5]

Writing in the twelfth century, over two hundred years after the settlement, Ari makes it clear that the Icelandic forest is already a thing of the past: "*At that time,* Iceland was grown over with trees" suggests that the situation might be different now. And in Iceland's case, this postarboreal era began rather soon after the arrival of people. By Ari's day, deforestation was not total in Iceland, but it was well under way. Some time ago, Ian Ashwell and Edgar Jackson suggested that "the major destruction of the forests took place in the years from A.D. 880 to about 1200 under the initial impact of human settlement in Iceland."[6] Subsequent research has tended to support this hypothesis.[7] Ari's statement about the forests of Iceland in days of yore was thus written in the shadow of an environmental catastrophe—but probably not in the shade of a tree.

"Forests from Fell to Foreshore"

The lush and capacious Icelandic forest that Ari evokes is a literary construct: a trope forming part of an origin myth that explains Iceland's attractions to the settlers in environmental terms. It is a product of the mind—a trope-ical brain forest, if you will forgive me. In reality, Iceland was covered in a sparse layer of scrub birch and willow that in many areas never reached full maturity, owing to the poor soil, harsh weather, and short growing season.[8] In the sagas, on the other hand, the Icelandic woodlands work alongside descriptions of fjords full of fish and seals, of lush green pastures and a relatively temperate climate, to create a vision of the golden age of a virgin territory, which is blessedly free of humans yet exists in anticipation of the new settlers and their needs. *Egils saga* provides a second iteration of this motif: "Then Skalla-Grímr explored the land and there was a large amount of moorland and broad woodlands; it was a long way between the fells and the foreshore and there was plenty of seal hunting and excellent fishing."[9]

Landnámabók (*The Book of Settlements*), meanwhile, has some fun at the expense of the early explorers while retaining the idea of Iceland as a natural paradise (of sorts). A Norwegian named Flóki—by repute the man who gave the island its present name—was allegedly the first person to stay in Iceland over the winter. As *Landnámabók* has it, the waters of Vatnsfjǫrðr teemed with so many fish that Flóki's men completely neglected their normal diligence as farmers. They failed to make hay while the sun shone in Iceland's short summer, and all their domestic livestock perished when the weather turned bad. After this unhappy experience, Flóki and his companions returned to Norway, where they gave differing accounts of Iceland's *landskostir* (a useful Old Norse noun that means "qualities of land" and that generally refers to the potential of an uninhabited area for settlement or economic exploitation): "They sailed to Norway the summer after, and when men enquired of them about the land, Flóki spoke ill of it, and Herjólfr told both the good and the bad of the land. But Þórólfr said that butter dropped from every blade of grass in the land which they had discovered, and therefore he was called Þórólfr Butter."[10] Þórólfr's buttery blades of grass resonate with the idea of Iceland as a land of milk, if not necessarily honey. Although *Landnámabók* is equivocal about the country's claims to being an earthly paradise, it is still recognizably part of this tradition of the golden age of pre-settlement Iceland.

As the sagas tell the story, Iceland held two major attractions for the Norwegian settlers. On a cultural level, the empty land was attractive because of its emptiness: lacking a king or any centralized authority, it was devoid (actually and symbolically) of those aspects of "civilization" that some of the Norwegian chieftains were beginning to find oppressive under the rule of King Haraldr hárfagri (fine-hair). The new Icelanders were presented with a blank space that they could fill with a new type of society. At the same time, their new home seemed to offer them the natural resources that could be converted into the necessities of cultural life. Iceland's mythical golden age of pristine Nature, we should note, lasted only as long as there were no inhabitants around to enjoy its gifts. And these natural gifts included trees: trees cut down for homes and ships and shields and spear shafts; trees burned for cooking and heating; trees made into charcoal or cleared for grazing.

As Gillian Rudd observes, the golden age tradition "creates a notion of an idyllic past long gone while also relying on the common knowledge that such a past never existed."[11] It seems likely that Ari and the saga authors were aware that Iceland's golden age was an illusion, even as they set it up as a way of explaining the superficially inexplicable choice of Iceland as a place to build a civilization. Even if they really did believe in this notion of Iceland as an (ar)boreal Eden, they were aware that the golden age lasted for only a moment. The settlers had to see Iceland, in order to recognize its *landskostir* and declare them good, but as soon as they began to make use of the resources on offer, the environment was never pristine again. As with all golden age narratives, we are dealing here with a story of decline; from earthly paradise to a hostile, cold, treeless, and horribly eroded land that in places hardly looks earthly and that never again would resemble Eden. Writing in the twelfth through fourteenth centuries, these authors could see the signs of Iceland's fall from grace all too clearly. By 1200 Iceland had lost huge swathes of woodland; in 1262, following a bitter civil war, the Icelanders pledged their allegiance to the king of Norway, losing their cherished status as an independent people. Deforestation contributed to soil erosion, as did overgrazing, which diminished Iceland's already precarious ability to grow its own food supply.[12] Coupled with a worsening climate, these changes to the land meant that the Icelanders lost much of their self-sufficiency over succeeding centuries. While an ever-greater share of Icelandic fish and wool production began to be exported, the Iceland-ers themselves depended increasingly upon imports, which came to be closely controlled by the Danish crown after it had absorbed Norway and its territories during the fifteenth century. Sigurður Gylfi Magnússon identifies the period between about 1400 and 1700 as a "Dark Age" in Iceland, with the darkness covering "both the state of the country under foreign rule and the literature, which is sparser and generally considered inferior in value and quality to that of the earlier age," especially the sagas.[13] Orri Vésteinsson and his coauthors, meanwhile, explicitly relate the decline in Iceland's economic fortunes to the early settlers' exploitation of the land's resources: "The choices of the *landnám* (lit. 'land taking') generation thus had resonance for good or ill throughout all the subsequent history of political, economic, and environmental interactions in both islands. Over the succeeding 1100 years, these interactions proved intense and often disastrous."[14]

The trajectory of Icelandic cultural history is aligned with its political his-tory, which is aligned with its environmental history. In all three spheres of life, the Icelanders perceived themselves to be falling from a state of grace they had enjoyed during the Saga Age. Their initial state upon quitting Nor-way for Iceland seemed triply blessed: they lived in a time and place of abun-dant natural resources; they ruled themselves; their literature flourished and produced some of medieval Europe's most original and remarkable works in both prose and poetry. But the golden age transmuted—in a sort of reverse alchemy of cultural entropy and ecological degradation—into an age of lead.

Nostalgia—a key and constant mood in much "Nature writing" and a fre-quent source of anxiety for ecocritical scholarship—is tacitly endemic to the sagas. Each successive composition or copy of a narrative set in the Icelandic golden age is performed in a world that is ever further removed from the golden age. Susan Stewart writes that "the prevailing motif of nostalgia is the erasure of the gap between nature and culture, and hence a return to the utopia of biology and symbol reunited within the walled city of the maternal."[15] When medieval saga writers reimagine pre-settlement and early post-settlement

Iceland as an earthly paradise, there is undoubtedly an element of this uto-
pian eco-nostalgia at play. (As we will see, a very similar scenario is found in
mythologized form in *Vǫluspá*'s own golden age of the Æsir.) There are dangers that attend such nostalgia. Morton warns us that the "constant elegy for a
lost unalienated state" produced by critique that embraces nostalgia as a mode
of ecocritical thinking "is like scratching an itch that doesn't exist—thereby
bringing it into existence."[16] The sagas' valorization of independent, Commonwealth Iceland did not prevent the loss of that independence in thirteenth
century, the period at which saga composition was at its height in Iceland,
any more than imagining the quondam Icelandic forest stretching down to
the shore will provide enough wood to build you a new ship. Recalling a time
when the fjords were thick with fish and the hillsides covered with trees does
nothing in itself to halt or reverse ecological degradation or to improve living
standards in the here and now.

The rapid deforestation of Iceland, which had serious ecological consequences, can easily be read as an example of the struggle between Nature and
Culture in the telling of which the ecocritic tries to speak for Nature. In the
sagas' accounts of the settlement, we are presented with a highly mediated
but nonetheless true-seeming image of a pristine, virgin landscape that is
quickly overwhelmed by the colonizers' need and desire for the raw materials
of production. Culture relies on the physical world for its survival but can
only operate by turning Nature into Culture, by cultivation, by de-naturing.
We could see the death of Iceland's forests in these terms as an example of
a universal process in which (to quote Rudd once again) "this is simply what
happens to trees; they exist in order to be incorporated into the human economy."[17] What is happening to the tropical rainforests today, what happened
to the great woodlands around the Mediterranean in the days of the Roman
Empire, also happened to Iceland's trees. This is the first and most obvious
eco-reading of the Icelandic settlement narrative: it suggests to us the inevitability of environmental degradation in the face of what we now call "development." Culture triumphs over Nature, but it is a pyrrhic and extremely
short-lived victory.

Ecomyths of Norse America

The settlement of Iceland was not the only example of Norse *landnám* in the
medieval North Atlantic—nor the only example to end in a social collapse that
can be linked to environmental change. In stories of the Norse discovery and
settlement of both Greenland and North America we see similar golden age

mythologies in development. In both these cases, the golden age seems more artificial, more illusory, and more clearly the product of wishful thinking than even the master narrative of Icelandic settlement, which presumably provides something of a model for subsequent accounts of colonization.

Two of the *Íslenginga sögur* are devoted specifically to the Norse discovery of Greenland (which took place in the 980s), and what they called Vínland (probably "Wineland," though the etymology is disputed: *Vinland* or "Meadowland" may have been the original form of the name)[18]—a stretch of Newfoundland coastline the precise extent of which is unknown. The discovery of Vínland is traditionally dated to the year 1000 CE. The sagas of the Greenlanders (*Grœnlendinga saga*) and of Eiríkr the Red (*Eiríks saga rauða*) postdate the events they narrate by more than two hundred years—they both originate in the great age of saga composition of the thirteenth century.[19]

Greenland owes its name to a fairly blatant case of "greenwashing"—a marketing strategy that plays up the "green" credentials of an organization (or, here, a landmass) to change public perception about the environmental impact of its activities. Greenland has never really been a very green land—not even in the slightly warmer climate of the tenth century. The first thing that Eiríkr the Red saw when he arrived was a glacier. The name "Iceland" already being taken, Eiríkr called the new land Greenland, "as he said people would be attracted there if it had a favourable name."[20] The sagas do not comment directly about the efficacy of this public relations initiative, but migrants began to arrive in Greenland fast on Eiríkr's heels.

Neither of the Vínland sagas describes Greenland in particularly glowing terms, however.[21] *Grœnlendinga saga* begins by telling the story of Bjarni Herjólfsson, an Icelander who decides to follow his father, one of Eiríkr's men, to the new settlement despite not being at all clear about how to get there. As with the stories of Iceland's initial discovery, chance or fate always plays some role in bringing Norse mariners into contact with the new territories. Bjarni and his crew are lost in fog and buffeted by unfavorable winds for days before they first spy land, which Bjarni quickly decides is not Greenland. They sail in closer to take a look and "soon saw that the land was not mountainous but did have small hills, and was covered with forests."[22] The men know enough of Greenland to know that they are searching for a more rugged landscape, although the crew does attempt to go ashore in search of "both timber and water" at their second landfall, which is "flat and wooded" (*slétt land ok viði vaxit*). Bjarni says to them: "You have no shortage of those provisions" (*at engu eru þér því óbirgir*), which may have sounded a bit rich to people who had left behind a largely treeless land in which timber was an extremely scarce and valuable resource. So, they press on until they see mountains and glaciers—which is apparently all Greenland has to offer.

But Greenland is ironically not the landscape that the *Grœnlendinga saga* really evokes. Rather, it is the settlement of what becomes known as "Vínland" that is mythologized in this text. Leifr "the Lucky," son of Eiríkr the Red, discovers the new continent in a manner strongly reminiscent of the accounts of Iceland and Greenland's discovery. Leifr is motivated to seek out the lands that Bjarni had observed on his way to Greenland; he makes successive stops at places that he deems unsuitable for habitation, and he gives names to places on the basis of the land's qualities. First, he reaches a place he calls Helluland (Stone-slab land), which appears to be a single flat expanse of rock, with no grass anywhere to be seen, echoing the creation myths' account of the primordial void as being defined by its lack of vegetation prior to Ymir's dismembering into the physical world's elemental building blocks. Although Leifr's party do better than Bjarni by at least landing here, the saga tells us that "this land seemed to them of little use" (*sýndisk þeim þat land vera gœðalaust*) and the explorers go on their way.[23]

The second location on Leifr's tripartite itinerary is much more promising, since the land is gently sloping, well forested, and with white sandy beaches—this, presumably, is the place where Bjarni's crew members wanted to stop to replenish their supplies of water and timber. Leifr says that this new land will be named according to its qualities, and called Markland (Forest-land).[24] Like Iceland, newly discovered landmasses farther into the North Atlantic are classified according to their *landskostir*, and these "qualities," as we saw in *Landnámabók*'s accounts of Flóki's original land-taking in Iceland, are related to the new lands' ability to sustain human communities. Markland should be a prime candidate for land-taking, since forests from mountain to foreshore are so regularly praised in descriptions of Iceland's pre-settlement landscape. For settlers leaving Iceland's by now almost treeless ecosystem, timber was a pressing need. It is surprising that nobody decides to settle Markland and exploit this abundance. But perhaps Markland is excessively forested: we know that densely wooded areas could be a source of anxiety for Norse people, as well as a resource. With nothing but forests, Markland only partly meets the explorers' needs. There is better still to come.

The shores of North America, when Leifr and his companions see them, surpass even Iceland in their natural bounty, their obvious suitability to the needs of people. Two days' journey from Markland, they reach an island to the north of the mainland. Upon putting ashore, they discover that the dew on the grass tastes ambrosial—sweeter than anything they had ever experienced before.[25] Finally, the Norsemen set foot in the New World, whose *landskostir* surpass anything produced by the *landnám* imagination:

> When the incoming tide floated the ship again, they took the boat and rowed to the ship and moved it up into the river and from there into the lake, where they cast anchor. They carried their sleeping-sacks ashore and built booths. Later they decided to spend the winter there and built large houses. There was no lack of salmon both in the lake and river, and this salmon was larger than they had ever seen before.
>
> It seemed to them the land was so good that livestock would need no fodder during the winter. The temperature never dropped below freezing, and the grass only withered very slightly. The days and nights were much more equal in length than in Greenland or Iceland. In the depth of winter the sun was aloft by mid-morning and still visible at mid-afternoon.[26]

This new land corrects some of the "faults" that some of its discoverers had found with Iceland. Iceland's fjords had abounded with fish—but these fish are bigger. Iceland's grazing lands certainly would not support livestock outside during the winter—but this new settlement must be far enough south that grass grows almost all year round in climatic conditions that seem temperate by comparison with those that afflicted the other northern colonies. Once again, *Vǫluspá*'s initial vision of the absence of grass in the primordial void comes to mind. Light and vegetation are inextricably linked in these various mythologized landscapes just as they are in life, and their centrality to Old Norse–Icelandic settlement narratives is entirely congruent with the lived experience of far northern latitudes.

But Vínland only truly gains its mythical status when it is given a name. Even if the name the settlers actually gave to the new territory was "Meadowland," by the time the sagas were written down, the alternate spelling and interpretation of the name were both established. In *Grœnlendinga saga*, the wine of "Wine-land" is the most remarkable and impressive of the region's *landskostir,* and unambiguously the source of its name.

The saga tells us that among Leifr's crew was a German named Tyrkir—whose name means, essentially, "guy from the south"—who discovers vines and grapes after becoming separated from the rest of the party.[27] It is important that a non-Scandinavian is present in this story, since Tyrkir is able to say that he knows all about vines from his youth on the European mainland. The effect his discovery has on Tyrkir is striking:

Leifr then asked him, "Why were you so late returning, foster-father, and how did you come to be separated from the rest?"

For a long time Tyrkir spoke only in German, with his eyes darting in all directions and his face contorted. The others understood nothing of what he was saying.

After a while he spoke in Norse: "I had gone only a bit farther than the rest of you. But I have news to tell you: I found grapevines and grapes."

"Are you really sure of this, foster-father?" Leifr said.

"I'm absolutely sure," he replied, "because where I was born there was no lack of grapevines and grapes."[28]

Readers have sometimes found this part of the story comic. The saga may be making a sort of joke about the Norsemen's unworldliness: coming from the frigid north, these explorers would have no firsthand knowledge of viticulture, and little enough of wine. It is therefore necessary for them to have a foreigner in their company to identify the produce from which comes the product that gives the new land its name. A broader sense of humor might be tickled by the suggestion that Tyrkir's strange behavior—"his eyes darting in all directions and his face contorted"—is a result of inebriation. It is certainly a curious image, and earlier critics sometimes claimed that it demonstrates the saga author's naïveté about wine, since eating grapes will not make you drunk. In this interpretation, we get to laugh at both authors and characters for their lack of sophistication, as well as enjoying Tyrkir's bizarre simulation of possible, if implausible, drunkenness.[29] (Perhaps Tyrkir's chattering in German and strange face-pulling merely indicates his excitement at discovering Vínland's bounty, which reminds him of home.)

Whatever we should make of the character of Tyrkir, his function in the Vínland narrative is to offer technical expertise that enables the conversion of a resource into an economically useful commodity. The great benefit of vines that grow uncultivated—like the "self-sown wheat" that grows in Vínland, according to *Eiríks saga rauða*—is that they represent a potential source of cheap calories or potential profit; more so in the case of vines, since wine was a quintessential luxury product in Scandinavian markets of the time. The sagas do not describe whether the North American *vignoble* produces a vintage that was ever drunk beyond its shores, but *Grœnlendinga* makes it clear that the opportunity to exploit these resources by exporting them to elsewhere in the Norse world was immediately on Leifr's mind. The day after Tyrkir's discovery, Leifr tells his men: "We'll divide our time between two tasks . . . picking grapes or cutting vines and felling the trees to make a load for the ship."[30]

Although the vines of Vínland give the new colony its name in this account, we also see the settlers' rapacious desire for lumber having an immediate impact on the previously apparently pristine environment. The goal of exploration is exploitation, and Vínland is represented as ripe and ready for the taking.

In *Eiríks saga rauða,* however, the colonization of Vínland is more problematic and the land less welcoming than in *Grœnlendinga saga.* Lucky Leifr Eiríksson has a much smaller role in his father's saga. He is credited with the first discovery of the new land west in the sea, which he finds by chance and explores only briefly, noting that "there were fields of self-sown wheat there and growing vines. There were also trees known as *mǫsurr.* They took samples of all these things."[31] Here, Leifr and his men sound more like disinterested naturalists or awestruck tourists than rapacious capitalists or land-hungry colonizers. The scientific interest of this terra incognita is apparent in the saga's unusual specificity in naming the trees as *mǫsurr,* which readers have most often interpreted as referring to some kind of maple, giving the narrative a touch of Canadian local color.[32] (Near the end of *Grœnlendinga saga,* Karlsefni sells a decorated object, the nature of which is uncertain, to a different German for half a mark of gold. The saga specifies that this object was made out of *mǫsurr* wood from Vínland.)[33]

The real Vínland pioneers in *Eiríks saga* are Karlsefni and Snorri, two of Eiríkr's neighbors in Greenland. Karlsefni and Snorri give the land names in *Eiríks saga:* Helluland, Markland, Bjarney (Bear-island), and the Furðustrandir (Wonder-beaches), named for their surprising length. There are, once again, foreigners in the landing party who play an important role in exploring and establishing the *landskostir,* but this time two Scots take on the role that Tyrkir has in *Grœnlendinga:* "When they had sailed the length of Furðustrandir, they put ashore the Scottish people and told them to run south into the land to explore its *landskostir* and come back before three days had passed. . . . And when they came back, one had grape-stalks in his hand and the other had self-sown wheat."[34] Grapes and vines make much less of an impression on these explorers than on their counterparts in *Grœnlendinga saga.* Scottish people would presumably have not much idea of what to do with grapes, and we never even hear about the naming of Vínland in *Eiríks saga.* By the time Karlsefni and Snorri set off in search of the land Leifr discovered, they already know the name of what they are looking for, but of the origin of that name we learn nothing.

But if grapes fail to excite these settlers to the extent they do their counterparts in *Grœnlendinga saga,* the new version of the new world still emphasizes the almost fantastical bounty of Vínland. First, they land on an island where there are so many seabirds that one can hardly walk along the shore without stepping on their eggs. One manuscript of the text notes that "the grass was tall"—and the whole scene is summarized as a *fagrt landsleg*, a "beautiful lie of land," which suggests a possible aesthetic appreciation of what we would call landscape, though in Norse usage it is hard to differentiate this term firmly from *landskostir*. The way the land lies is related to its qualities, and both are assessed as good or bad from the point of view of the people who would use it. Karlsefni and the others initially imitate the example of Floki in his abortive attempt to live in newly discovered Iceland: their only concern at first is to explore their new space (*þeir gáðu einskis, útan at kanna landit*), and they fail to prepare for the winter, which is harder than *Grœnlendinga saga* would prepare us to expect. Their catches fail, and food becomes scarce.[35]

It turns out, however, that the explorers have not yet reached the true Vínland. The narrative of *Eiríks saga* is a little confusing at this point, but it takes more sailing southward before Karlsefni and Snorri find the place they are looking for—and so we might wonder where it was that their Scottish companions found their grapevines, if the initial landing place suffered such hard winters. They do much better farther south: "They found self-sown wheatfields in the hollows there, and grapevines all over the hills. Every stream was full of fish. They dug pits at the point where the land and the water met, and when the sea ebbed away, there were holy fishes in the pits. There was a great number of animals of all kinds in the forest. They were there for half a month and enjoyed themselves and feared nothing. They had their livestock with them."[36] This passage marks the zenith of the North Atlantic golden age trope in Old Norse literature. Pre-settlement Iceland was a paradise, but a marginal one, always at risk of being lost through deforestation or volcanic eruptions. Greenland was the result of a successful marketing campaign that covered up the land's actual shortcomings as a place to live. Successive iterations of the discovery of Vínland narrative represent the newest and most distant Norse colony as an earthly Eden that surpasses Iceland in its natural bounty, its suitability for human habitation and exploitation. Its *landskostir* are unlike those of the other territories. They are exotic, with their grapes and maples; they are superabundant; they are accessible. But only in this passage from *Eiríks saga,* and only for a brief period of time, do we see the Norse colonists of North America actually living in the Arcadia that these descriptions evoke. In *Grœnlendinga saga,* Leifr's first trip results in plundered timber to take back to Greenland, and the saga says that after that Vínland voyages "seemed to bring men both wealth and renown."[37] But in *Eiríks saga*'s golden age of Vínland, the settlers do not need to work. Everything is laid out before them; all their needs are met by the *oikos*. The landscape is varied but gentle, and each type of terrain provides a different source of food. They have meat and fish for protein, wheat for carbohydrates, grapes for some vitamins and the prospect of wine. They have wood for building, and they have their livestock with them, which will provide them both with dairy products and with a familiar sort of cultural capital. The Old Norse word for livestock, *fé*, is also used to refer to money or movable wealth of any sort. Karlsefni's community seems rich beyond measure in comparison to those scrabbling to sustain life and enhance prestige in the harsher environments of Greenland and Iceland. Here, the Norse Americans can actually enjoy themselves (*skemmta sér*). Their golden age is an age of leisure. It lasts for two weeks.

Paradise Lost in Vínland

There is no need to doubt that Norse explorers landed on the North American continent around the year 1000. It is also certainly possible that the sagas written about these events preserve traces of an "environmental memory," of accurate information about the land, its climate and ecology, passed down from the Norse pioneers through generations until it reached the ears of the authors who would compose the texts. But the presence of *mǫsurr* trees in Vínland—if they are indeed maples—is perhaps the only example of truly region-specific ecological information in the sagas' descriptions, although the image of grapevines is so pervasive across the tradition as to suggest that Vínland's name has its basis in botanical observations. The presence of "wine-berries" in the North Atlantic would have seemed a most remarkable—and therefore memorable—feature of this environment. But we should always bear in mind that while the sagas always assert that places were named for their *landskostir*—"Bear-island" is named after the bear they saw there; "Forest-land" is a land with forests—there are no Norse place-names in North America against which we can check the sagas' namings.[38] We have also seen, in the famous case of Greenland, that places could be given names that mislead people about the *landskostir* they might expect to find there.

It does not much matter whether the Vínland sagas accurately represent the environment of Newfoundland around the turn of the first millennium as the explorers would have experienced it, however. Vínland is an extension of the ecomythologizing strategy that saw Iceland figured as an earthly paradise and saw the real environmental conditions of Greenland camouflaged beneath its misleadingly promising name. Vínland is a mythologized *oikos*, an earthly paradise, Iceland perfected. The settlement narratives produced for all the

Norse Atlantic territories are acts of literary colonization.[39] They assert that the virgin lands the Scandinavian explorers encountered were perfectly suited to the needs of settlers—indeed, that the ecological features of these landmasses mesh perfectly with and therefore exist to meet the needs of the colonizers and thus are ripe for the taking. When there are problems with a territory—Greenland's climate, Iceland's volcanoes—these natural "flaws" can be airbrushed out. Or, as in literary reimaginings of Iceland's abundant forests, the landscape can be retroactively modified to correct these ecological infelicities.

I have suggested that Iceland's ecological golden age, as invented and promulgated by later historians and saga authors, is a response to the slowly worsening conditions—environmental, economic, and social—that gave and give the impression that Iceland's fortunes had been in decline almost from the very beginning. Vínland, on the other hand, is a dream of an earthly paradise that no historical reality can dispel because in this case paradise was literally lost. Although there is some evidence that Norse Greenlanders continued to visit the shores of Newfoundland to gather resources—timber, inevitably, being first among them—until the Greenland colony itself began to collapse in the fifteenth century, Norse colonization of Vínland was aborted after a handful of years. There was no connection between the *oikos* of Vínland and the life experience of the authors and audiences of the Vínland sagas. They knew nothing of what it was like to try to make a home there, because Norse people had stopped trying to make a home there. So, even if the Vínland sagas are based on information from contemporary witnesses that was transmitted with perfect accuracy down to the time of the texts' composition, their conjuring of Vínland is necessarily illusory. Norse Vínland has to be seen with the eye of imagination because there are no longer any settlers to see it with their own eyes. The absence of a continuing lived engagement with the land permits a much more fantastical rendering of Vínland's environment than would be possible when writing about Iceland. It also means that we may view the Vínland sagas primarily as mythical narratives—narratives that signify on the basis of their timeless cultural concerns rather than their particular historical resonances. I do not wish to claim for a moment that the sagas have no value for historians of the North Atlantic colonies, or even that they are "untrue." Rather, the Vínland sagas show how easily and productively historical fact can be mythologized as part of a colonialist outlook on the world, especially when examined from an ecocritical perspective.

The very notion of assessing, naming, and thereby "taking" land and its "resources" according to its "qualities," implicit in all the sagas' descriptions of *landskostir,* is ecologically problematic. As a totality, Vínland can be read as a perfect instantiation of the Heideggerian *Bestand*—Nature as "standing resource."[40] This is a common colonialist move. As Todd Borlik shows, the same impulse motivates some of the earliest descriptions of North America's ecosystems after its rediscovery by Europeans in the sixteenth century. The first part of Thomas Harriot's *A Briefe and True Report of the New Found Land of Virginia* (1588), for example, is "nothing more than an inventory of the abundant 'marchantable commodities' of the New World that await only the hand of an intrepid entrepreneur to be converted into a handsome profit," and trees have pride of place in Harriot's catalogue for the wide variety of marketable products that are just waiting to be chiseled out of them.[41] In *Grœnlendinga saga,* Leifr Eiríksson represents the type of merchant adventurer who opportunistically converts a new standing resource into movable forms of capital. It is doubtful whether Leifr ever has it in mind to found a permanent settlement in Vínland on the model of Greenland. Although he and his companions do build houses and overwinter in the new land, Leifr's impulse is to load his ship with timber and export it back to Greenland, another largely treeless area where this commodity is in great demand.

Karlsefni, however, hopes for both wealth and a new and prosperous home: "Karlsefni and his crew made an agreement that anything of value they obtained would be divided equally among them. They took all sorts of livestock with them, for they intended to settle the country if they could."[42] As we saw, *Eiríks saga* also emphasizes that Karlsefni has his animals with him when he settles on Vínland's paradisiacal shores. But in this account, mention of the colonists' cattle prefigures the first indication that there may be a snake in this particular Eden—that Vínland may be too good to be true.

The problem with Vínland, which otherwise appears to be the perfection of colonizable land, in marked contrast to Iceland and Greenland, is that the territory is already inhabited. The sagas represent encounters with indigenous people as the most important cause of anxiety and conflict for the Norse incomers, and suggest that the difficulty of living alongside another population was a reason for the ultimate failure of settlement in the area. Called *skrælingar* in the Old Norse texts, the aboriginal inhabitants of Newfoundland are represented as profoundly Other to the settlers, in line with many similar colonialist discourses from other periods in history.[43] The sagas stress the *skrælingar*'s physical alterity: *Eiríks saga* describes Karlsefni's party experiencing a sense of "wonder" at the sight of their new neighbors, but this "wondering" is pretty much the standard subalternating gaze of the colonist. "They were black men and ugly," says the saga, "and had bad hair on their head; they had great big eyes and were broad in the cheek."[44] Even if *Eiríks saga*'s use of *svartir menn* does not encode quite the same racial conceptions that underlie later deployments of "black" or "negro," darkness of skin is regularly associated with inferiority of culture or morals in Old Norse literature.[45] On one famous occasion, a *skræling* is even represented as a member of a monstrous race. *Eiríks saga* has an *einfœtingr* ("single-footed creature" or "uniped") assassinate Þorvaldr Eiríksson, the unlucky brother of Leifr, with an arrow. Despite the widespread occurrence of unipeds in medieval literary accounts of exotic locales and their monstrous inhabitants, even the *einfœtingr* has at times been treated by scholars as possibly representing an authentic memory of something that really happened in Vínland.[46]

The *skrælingar*'s unworldliness, lack of cultural and technological sophistication, and, above all, Otherness are frequently signaled in the course of their dealings with their new Norse neighbors. The sagas make a not altogether funny comedy of misunderstanding out of the first contact between natives and explorers. Although the difference established between the two groups of people rests largely on cultural distinctions, some of these have ecocritical implications, as they relate to the different ways the two groups interact with the nonhuman world. It is too simplistic to say that the *skrælingar* are more "in tune" with their environment, or that they live "closer to Nature" than the Norse do—to do so would be to pander to another form of eco-colonialist rhetoric.[47] Nonetheless, the fact that the two populations come from very different naturecultural backgrounds has an important effect on their interactions with each other.

The first time indigenous people are spotted in *Grœnlendinga saga*, they appear to be part of the landscape. The summer after Leifr's first voyage, his brother Þorvaldr returns to Vínland and finds a sheltered cove: "This is an attractive spot," says Þorvaldr, "and here I would like to build my farm."[48] He assesses the *landskostir* and decides they merit *landnám*. But Þorvaldr soon realizes that there is something strange in this alluring landscape. He sees three "hillocks" on the beach, which turn out to be upturned boats, made from animal skins, under each of which three *skrælingar* are hiding. The inferiority of local boatbuilding methods to those of the Vikings is obvious, but these craft are well adapted to the naturecultural situation that has produced them. The *skrælingar* use these canoes (or coracles) in shallow, coastal waters; they make use of a by-product of this hunting community's staple food gathering practices; they are portable and can be used as temporary shelters. And, in sufficient numbers, they are capable of being useful in a fight. After Þorvaldr and his men execute all but one of the men they find on the beach, a flotilla of skin boats pursues the Norsemen as they try to flee on their ship.

Þorvaldr Eiríksson does not die at the hand of a uniped in this version of the story, but he nonetheless perishes from the wound made by a *skræling*'s arrow. He tells his men that he wants to be buried on the headland that had looked so suitable a site for his farmstead.

Subsequently, trouble with the *skrælingar* is what puts an end to Karlsefni's briefly idyllic habitation in Vínland. This time, differences in farming and trading practices are implicated in the almost immediate breakdown of relations between the Norse and the *skrælingar*, who do not, it must be emphasized, arrive with hostile intentions. In *Grœnlendinga*, Norse pastoralism seems to cause particular problems with the country's prior inhabitants, who presumably had no familiarity with this type of agriculture: "After the winter passed and summer came, they became aware of natives. A large group of men came out of the woods close to where the cattle were pastured. The bull began bellowing and snorting very loudly. This frightened the natives, who ran off with their burdens, which included fur pelts and sables and all kind of skins."[49] We should note that the *skrælingar* come out of the woods (*ór skógi*)—out of a feature of the landscape that, in the Norse imagination, is aligned with the natural rather than the cultural, a place designated for outlaws and criminals. While the Norse explorers are delighted to exploit forested land by chopping its trees down for conversion into houses and ships and other objects of cultural value, it is impossible to imagine them inhabiting this sort of space, of living in among the trees.

Karlsefni and his people barricade themselves indoors, misreading the fear and confusion of the *skrælingar* as belligerence. Soon, however, despite not understanding their language, it becomes clear to the Scandinavians that the natives wish to trade with them, offering their (highly desirable) animal skins in exchange for items of Norse manufacture, preferably weapons. But Karlsefni forbids his companions from arming the *skrælingar* in this way: "He sought a solution by having the women bring out milk and milk products. Once they saw these products the natives wished to purchase them and nothing else. The trading products with the natives resulted in them bearing off their purchases in their stomachs, leaving their packs and skins with Karlsefni and his companions."[50] To the *skrælingar*, the fruits of pastoral farming are as enticing as its technology—in the form of the bellowing bull—is perplexing. Annette Kolodny speculates that the natives would have been attracted to the high fat content of the Norse women's milk and cheese, even though "these milk-based (rather than animal fat-based) delicacies would soon cause painful cramps and other digestive system discomforts in the lactose-intolerant Indians."[51] Perhaps the increasing bellicosity of the *skrælingar* from this point in the story onward reflects their irritability as they suffer the consequences of their creamy bingeing. More likely, however, their perhaps excessive fondness for what was a quotidian staple of the Norse colonists' diet is to be interpreted as another way of figuring the difference between the two communities in a way that underscores the natives' "primitivism" in contrast to Eurocentric norms of food production and consumption. Moreover, I agree with Jerold Frakes in regarding this scene as showing that the *skrælingar* lack the profit motive that characterizes the Norse side of these trading exchanges. Frakes argues that exchanging valuable pelts for milk (or, in the analogous part of *Eiríks saga,* demanding the same price for ever smaller strips of woolen cloth) represents a "systematic defrauding of the 'natives' . . . all too familiar to us from later explorer narratives," even if the sagas indicate that the *skrælingar* were pleased with the goods they received in this bartering.[52]

In *Eiríks saga,* dairy products are nowhere mentioned, although Karlsefni's bull puts in another appearance, scaring away the *skrælingar* and bringing an end to their market. Three weeks later the natives return in great numbers and with hostile intent, putting the Norsemen to flight. The *skrælingar*'s advance is only halted when—in one of the most famous and strangest scenes in all saga literature—a pregnant woman named Freydís, daughter of Eiríkr the Red, bares her breast and smacks it against the flat of a sword. Why this particular gesture should be so effective at scaring away North American Indians has never been explained, though plenty of people have tried.[53] Whatever the origin—historical or literary—of this scene, Frakes argues that "the Americans' panic at the sight of Freydis demonstrates that from a Eurocentric perspective, they are indeed 'primitives.'"[54] When someone is frightened of something you know not to be frightening, it becomes an easy source of condescension. It can work both ways: when the *skrælingar* return in *Eiríks saga,* they terrify the Norsemen by hoisting a round object, dark in color and the size of a sheep's stomach, to the top of a pole. When whirled around overhead and thrown toward Karlsefni's men, it makes a threatening noise (*lét illiliga við*) upon landing, sufficient to strike great fear into people who do not understand the nature of this object.[55]

But in the Vínland sagas, the clearest manifestation of the difference between indigenous people and newcomers lies in the former's attitude toward tools, and specifically the ax. The ax is an alien thing for the *skrælingar,* who appear—in common with other, more assuredly historical North American communities prior to European colonial activity—to have no experience with metalworking. When a couple of warriors take an ax from a dead Norseman's body, they are unfamiliar with the substance from which the blade is made. They are also unsure about the ax's function—is it a weapon or a tool? In either case, how does it work? In *Grœnlendinga*, the discovery of the ax is the final encounter between the *skrælingar* and Karlsefni's men: "one of the natives then picked up an axe, peered at it awhile and then aimed at one of his companions and struck him."[56] The *skræling* is so surprised when he kills his friend with this blow that he straightaway throws the object as far as he can out to sea.

The version of the story told in *Eiríks saga* is different. Here, the natives have a different inkling about the purpose of the ax: "The natives also found a dead man, an axe lay beside him. One of them took up the axe and chopped at a tree, and then each took his turn at it. They thought this to be a treasure and to bite well. Then one of them struck a stone so that the axe broke. Then it seemed to them that a thing which could not withstand stone was of little worth, and they threw it down."[57] In our complacency about the inevitable superiority of the colonists' technology over that of the colonized, Eurocentric readers can find the natives' behavior quaint and amusing—look at how close they are to working out what to do with an ax! But they expect to be able to cut stone with it![58] The *skrælingar*'s rejection of the ax, however, has an ecological resonance that should not be ignored. As they intuit, a tree is the ax's natural prey. Although axes were an important weapon for Norse people—less expensive than a sword, less cumbersome than a spear—the ax owes its presence in Vínland at least as much to its usefulness in chopping down trees, of creating lumber, of converting the *Bestand* of the forests into movable capital. It was axes like this that did for the Icelandic forest. It would be similar iron tools that would clear the forests of North America to provide room for European settlers and pasture for their livestock in the next colonization of the continent, five centuries later. In casting the ax out of their world, the *skrælingar* symbolically (if unwittingly) reject the Norsemen's way of life—their pastoralism, their dairy products, their deep-keeled wooden ships. All these things are the products of a type of ecological exploitation that these *skrælingar* do not seem to understand. Perhaps they desire it; they are at least curious about the manufactured goods the settlers carry with them, and they clearly have a notion of the mechanics of trade. But in this small, sad, comical act of petulance, the *skræling* who throws away the ax because he thinks it ought to be able to cut through stone prevents further Norse expansion in North America. Immediately after this act is completed, *Eiríks saga* tells us that "Karlsefni and his companions now realized that, although the *landskostir* were good, there would always be trouble and enmity coming from the people who lived there previously."[59] Pausing only to slaughter another group of *skrælingar* they find eating blood and deer marrow—on the assumption, nowhere explained, that these men must be "outlaws"—Karlsefni and his crew prepare their ship for the journey back to Greenland.

All Good Things Come to an End

The Vínland sagas thus represent the "failure" of the Norse settlement of North America as a consequence of actual and threatened conflict with the indigenous population. The Norse colonization of the outlying North Atlantic territories had hitherto been remarkably straightforward because each new land was almost entirely empty of people. The Faroes were empty; Iceland was empty, discounting a few Irish hermits who possibly were on the island before the Norsemen arrived; the sagas do not talk about an Inuit presence in Greenland.[60] Norse *landnám* is not a question of taking land *from somebody else*, but of appropriating inchoate space and making out of it a coherent naturecultural entity for the benefit of the colonists. But it turns out that Vínland is more than the sum of its natural *landskostir*—it is already a natureculture, and one that the Norsemen do not properly comprehend and certainly cannot adapt to. *Landnám* in North America following the Icelandic model is for this reason impossible. We see this, for example, in the problems caused by the settlers' attempts to introduce their conventional forms of pastoral agriculture to an unfamiliar and probably unsuitable ecosystem. Lacking the resources of manpower and technology needed to convert the land into the right type of landscape for their desired way of life in the face of the *skrælingar*'s competition, and lacking the ability to reconfigure their own naturecultural expectations and aptitudes in a way that would allow them to cohabit with these "natives," the Norse explorers abandon their hopes of living in a new utopia.

If the Vínland sagas are the first surviving written account of America they are also the earliest surviving example of an American Dream—a colonizer's vision of the virgin land as a realm of unlimited possibility. That this particular dream was unlivable in practice does not diminish its importance: the idea of the earthly paradise is as imaginatively sustaining as it is unsustainable in reality.

The Vínland myths are tied to three particular strands of ecomythologizing that are important elsewhere in the corpus. First, their attitude toward the use and exploitation of the *landskostir* of a new (and empty) space—the way they convert it, imaginatively, into a place for habitation—is an extension of the *landnám* myths that the sagas tell about Iceland and, to a lesser extent, Greenland. To settle a new land, one first needs to reduce it to *landskostir*—a set of qualities, resources, opportunities for people. These *landskostir* are inscribed onto the land by naming each new place on the basis of what it can provide; in both instances, trees and woodlands are represented as one of the land's most important resources, ripe for the taking. In accounts of the Icelandic *landnám,* the island's emptiness facilitates this conversion. But Vínland is already taken, already under a successful naturecultural regime, and the failure of the colony rests on the Norse settlers' inability to convert the *skrælingar* into a "quality of the land" that can be objectified, exploited, or displaced in the way that later colonists of North American did with such brutal efficiency. These myths of *landnám* have a correlative in the Norse creation myths, and especially in the conversion of Ymir's body into the physical spaces that become demarcated as the dwelling places of the gods and other classes of being. And, as we saw in chapter 3, these acts of land-taking also recall the treatment of Jǫrð, the feminized personification of the land, who becomes the passive object, and frequently victim, of the desire of men to possess and control the physical world. The virgin territory is prized for its virginity, which the colonists can't wait to take away, to deflower.[61]

Encounters between the explorers and the *skrælingar* in Vínland also instantiate a second fundamental aspect of Norse mythology: the deeply destabilizing anxiety about the Other that the Æsir experience throughout the myths. As discussed in chapter 2, Norse cosmology is entirely predicated around the need to provide a safe space for the In-group that is clearly demarcated from the world of the outsiders. The border between the two realms of existence must be defended at all costs. As we will see in the remaining parts of this book, however, the Norse gods cannot keep the giants and other hostile forces away: the boundaries they create are porous. They are indefensible. During the settlement of Iceland, the human Other was absent, and the first Icelanders had space and time to construct their dwelling places in the manner they preferred: with the farmstead at the center and concentric circles of increasing wildness and threat reaching out from this central point into the wilderness. But the explorers of Vínland never get the chance to construct a bounded habitation that is sufficiently robust to keep the *skrælingar* out even in the short term. The two communities are deeply implicated in each other's place in Vínland for as long as the Norse people remain.

Finally, I see in the Vínland narratives an arc that mirrors the most important strand of the master myth of the Norse pagan world. The tendency of the pagan universe is for things to fall apart, for things to get worse the longer they go on. This is a story that is familiar to us from many mythologies across the world, presumably because it always feels intuitively true to time-bound mortals. We are accelerating toward an end of the world, and the gods are right there with us. But things have not always been so bad: once upon a time, there was a golden age, when we lived in Eden, when the world was ours for the taking. In the imagination of the saga authors, the vision of Iceland with forests stretching down to the shore and fish teeming in the rivers is one such Eden, and the settlement period a golden age of plenty and potential. Vínland is an even more powerful image of golden age living—a land of milk and honey (or trees and vines) whose exoticism heightens its paradisiacal atmosphere.

But as we have seen, the promise of paradise that Vínland offers is ephemeral, evanescent. We see the golden promise of this new age in a new world tarnish before our eyes. The Vínland sagas look back nostalgically from a position long after the expulsion from this particular Eden had taken place. The sagas of Icelanders and *Landnámabók* re-create the golden age of Iceland's independence and surprising natural fecundity from a perspective that has to take into account that this golden age is also over, or ending, or about to begin ending. Luckily for the Icelanders, despite the increasingly severe depredations they had to endure over the course of the late medieval and early modern periods, their civilization did not collapse completely in the way that the Norse settlements of Vínland and Greenland did.[62] But the golden age myth has to be written in a period of decline. Inhabitants of Arcadia have no need of such stories.

Like their human counterparts scattered around the North Atlantic, the Norse gods also find and create the conditions that produce a brief but glorious golden age. Like the other golden ages discussed here, a succession of problems and calamities begin to beset the gods. Despite their best efforts, their most cunning strategies, and the expenditure of an enormous amount of their power, the Æsir cannot prevent things falling apart. They cannot hold the center. They cannot sustain their desired way of life in the face of challenges both social and ecological. In the next two chapters, we will see that the gods' decline and fall, culminating in the great universal catastrophe of Ragnarǫk, mirrors some of the concerns we have seen being played out in the Old Norse–Icelandic myths of settlement. It will also become apparent, however, that Ragnarǫk gives us a chilling foretaste of our own apocalyptic experiences in the face of global warming and the myths we tell ourselves to explain (and, often, to try to escape) our fate. Readers are warned: none of this is going to end well.

6   The Æsir and the Anthropocene

THE VÍNLAND SAGAS hold out the possibility of a perfect naturecultural existence in the North Atlantic that turns out to be an illusion, an impossibility, a paradise that may never be regained. They conform, therefore, to one of the master paradigms of Western mythology—the story of the Fall, of mankind's decline from a state of grace or even divinity in which Nature served our needs unbidden. The Norse myths proper adhere to very similar narrative patterns. The trajectory of the pagan cosmos traces a steeply declining arc from an always already lost state of perfection to an apocalypse in which all existing structures of human society are swept away in the expectation that a new and improved world will become possible in the wake of the old world's death. A better world will rise, phoenixlike, from the ashes of our worn out, moribund, sinful civilizations. These apocalypticisms have clear resonances with ideas about the anthropogenic ecological collapse that threatens to bring about the end of all our casual and complacent conceptions of what human society is or can be in the twenty-first century. Many of us believe that we are on the edge of a precipice right now, that the end of the world, of our world, is imminent, and that it is the business of ecocriticism to help us prevent or simply survive the catastrophe. In this chapter and the one that follows, I discuss how the Norse gods, upon finding themselves in precisely the same type of crisis that we are in, are constitutionally incapable of taking any action that prevents Ragnarǫk, the "fate of the divine powers," or "doom of the gods," as the Norse apocalypse is called. The gods' fate is to repeat and amplify the mistakes that create the conditions in which the world inevitably will end. Trapped in a hole of their own design, the gods keep digging. The gods, I will argue, are strikingly modern in the futility of their response to naturecultural collapse: the worse things become in the world, the more tightly the Æsir cling to the structures that have caused this collapse; the more they invest in propping up their old way of life, the more impossible becomes the task of preventing its bloody and fiery demise. The myth of Ragnarǫk is, in effect, the myth of modernity, of human progress, of the Anthropocene.

Just as J. L. Schatz suggests they must, ecocritics and environmental activists frequently deploy ideas and images of apocalypse in their work: "We cannot motivate people to change the ecological conditions that give rise to thoughts of theorization without reference to the concrete environmental destruction ongoing in reality. This means that, even when our images of apocalypse aren't fully accurate, our use of elements of scientifically-established reality reconstructs the surrounding power structures in beneficial ways."[1] A critical movement inspired by crisis mobilizes the rhetoric of the ultimate crisis in an attempt to effect the changes that may, in fact, prevent the crisis from ever fully coming to pass. As Lawrence Buell famously put it, apocalypse is "the single most powerful master metaphor that the contemporary environmental imagination has at its disposal."[2] Apocalypticism's appeal to the imagination—as manifest in so many thousands of artworks in all periods and genres—makes it a uniquely important way of convincing people of the fact of ecological breakdown and the urgent need to do something to attempt to forestall it.

These rhetorics of annihilation have a long pedigree, of course. Sometime before 1016 CE, for example, the English archbishop Wulfstan of York began his most famous sermon with the ringing phrase "this world is in haste, and it nears its end. And it is always this in the world: the longer things go on, the worse they get."[3] Wulfstan was not concerned with the collapse of ecosystems. His deployment of apocalyptic tropes addressed moral concerns about contemporary society: he believed that unless the English abandoned sin and embraced goodness and the rule of law, their world would be destroyed by the Viking armies, who had, he claimed, brought God's wrath with them on their mission to plunder and despoil the realm of King Æthelræd (the "Unready"). These Vikings had their own apocalypse to worry about: it seems likely that Vǫluspá, the fullest and grimmest vision of the Norse apocalypse Ragnarǫk, existed in some form in the early eleventh century, and the myths it draws upon are presumably older.[4] Vǫluspá narrates in full and in detail the end of a version of the universe that the pagan gods, the Æsir, ruled or had ruled. It is thus most commonly read as a document that reveals the social and religious anxieties surrounding the conversion of Scandinavia to Christianity: the feeling that the old gods were doomed, and with them the traditional way of life of their followers, is characteristic of this cultural situation. But the myths of Ragnarǫk told in Vǫluspá and other sources do not merely speak of the doom of the gods, they speak of the destruction of everything in the physical universe, divine and earthly, human and nonhuman, natural and cultural. Even if their point of origin lies in cultural concerns, these myths are myths of the collapse of the *oikos*—in Old Norse the *heimr*—from a nurturing home into an inhospitable wilderness and thence into nothing: a return to the void. All apocalypses are ecological, even if their causes are entirely human, and Ragnarǫk is far from an exception to this rule.

Ages of Men: *Verǫld* and Anthropocene

In the final two chapters of this book, therefore, I read *Vǫluspá* as a document of ecological catastrophe and Ragnarǫk as a situation analogous to the one we currently find ourselves in with respect to global warming. Our ability to be at home in the world has been traduced by our movement into the age of men in which we live. There is an uncanny kinship, both etymological and conceptual, between the Old Norse term *ver-ǫld* (man-age) and the Anthropocene, the epoch of people.

"Anthropocene" is a recent coinage that reflects a growing consensus among geologists, botanists, and climate scientists that human impact on the Earth has decisively altered the planet's lithosphere.[5] In geological terms, the changes that have occurred in the Anthropocene are vastly disproportionate with the time frame over which they have taken place. The Holocene, the most recent "official" geological epoch, is conceived of as lasting from the end of the last Ice Age to the present—some twelve thousand years. Many advocates of the term "Anthropocene" believe, on the other hand, that mankind's planet-altering behavior has taken place over just the past two or three centuries—and indeed that the most decisive period, the so-called Great Acceleration, is a phenomenon of the latter half of the twentieth century, coterminous with the atomic age and the baby boom in the West.[6] We can blame the Industrial Revolution, the steam engine, asymmetrical population growth; technology has enabled the unprecedentedly efficient conversion of natural resources into carbon dioxide; deforestation has diminished the planet's ability to absorb greenhouse gases; the population explosion has been fueled by and demanded huge changes in agriculture.[7]

Other scientists place the origins of the Anthropocene much earlier: humanity's intervention in the carbon cycle, with all its ramifications for global temperature change, may have begun as early as seven thousand years ago.[8] In this scenario, the domestication of animals and establishment of arable farming—which entailed the first widespread deforestation of human-inhabited regions and an enormous increase in methane output—can be regarded as the first and most decisive anthropogenic change to the world's climate.[9] As William Ruddiman—one of the main proponents of the early Anthropocene theory—is careful to point out, however, industrialized societies do not escape responsibility simply because early humanity had already left its mark on the planet.[10] The postindustrial acceleration is real, even if the Anthropocene was already in motion long before.

It is hard to know which option to be more dispirited by. We are accustomed to laying the blame for ecological degradation at the feet of industry, in both its free market and statist flavors. Is it worse or better to realize that our distant ancestors, far from living in perfect harmony with their environment, began the rot as soon as they started clearing land for crops and domesticating livestock for milk and meat? The possibility arises that there was no golden age of human-earth interactions: that social development means climate change. Changing our living conditions through technological advances will leave a trace in the Earth. If we think of global warming, of a modified carbon cycle, of deforestation and land erosion, of changes in the oceans' acidity, as damage—and of course we do, and we should—then humans have been damaging the planet for as long as we can identify their actions as human ones. This is what an ecological world history would reveal. An early onset to the Anthropocene would indicate that there has never been a "natural world" for as long as there has been a "social world" to speak of. The Industrial Revolution just enabled us to warm the atmosphere more efficiently in the same way that it allows us to make clothes or motive power or battleships more efficiently. It was a continuation of a work in progress.

We cannot go back to a pre-Anthropocene era. There never was a time when humanity lived in harmony with Nature. (Because, naturally, there was never any such Nature in the first place.) Certainly, the longer things have gone on, the worse they've become. Our particular problems are the result of our particular techno-historical situation. But recognizing the possibility of an early-onset Anthropocene is a specific against too much ecological nostalgia: the age of men has always already been in progress, shaping the Earth according to men's needs. There's no point in wishing to return to Eden: when Adam delved and Eve span, their primitive attempts at agriculture and manufacturing at once disrupted the pre-Anthropocene tranquility by transforming the Earth into a "resource," the Heideggerian *Bestand*. There is no pre-Anthropocene past. There will be no post-Anthropocene future for us, at least not on this planet. Yet myriad potential futures are possible within the Anthropocene, which is an emergent phenomenon, still undelineated and up for negotiation.

At this point, we return to *Vǫluspá*. *Vǫluspá*'s *ver-ǫld*, or "age of men," comes to an end. This epoch passes, and with it one particular version or vision of the

world perishes. Something new takes its place. The gods meet their doom—
Ragnarǫk means "fate of the divine powers"—but the universe survives and
comes to be inhabited again. The world that ends is a temporal world, a phase
we were going through, as well as a physical entity and a geographic schema.
In Timothy Morton's thinking, the Anthropocene is apocalyptic in a similar
way: "The end of the world is correlated with the Anthropocene, its Global
Warming and subsequent drastic climate change, whose precise scope remains
uncertain while its reality is verified beyond question."[11]

Morton places the origin of the Anthropocene very precisely at the start of
the Industrial Revolution: "It was April 1784, when James Watt patented the
steam engine, an act that commenced the depositing of carbon in the Earth."
(We can forgive Morton the hyperbole—Watt's stroll to the patent office presumably did not itself deposit any carbon in the Earth's crust.)

The beginning of what we might call modernity is the end of the world,
by this view. But Morton does not mean that an earlier, more ecologically
integrated, less damaging world that actually pertained before 1784 came to
an end in that year. That would be another temptation toward nostalgia. No,
the end of "the world" *tout court* really did happen just then. And it has happened again between then and now: "Since for something to happen it often
needs to happen twice, the world also ended in 1945, in Trinity, New Mexico,
where the Manhattan Project tested the Gadget, the first of the atom bombs,
and later that year when two nuclear bombs were dropped on Hiroshima
and Nagasaki. These ideas mark the logarithmic increase in the actions of
humans as a geophysical force."[12] Since I am sitting here typing these words
and perhaps one day you might find yourself reading them, Morton's claim
is counterintuitive. How can the world have ended if I am still here? Ignoring such solipsism, Morton and *Vǫluspá* both reveal that it is the *concept* of
"world" that is at stake, not the physical existence of the planet or the cosmos—specifically, it is the historical *verǫld* world that has ended.[13] Or perhaps
it is ending now, or will end soon: "The worry is not whether the world will
end, as in the old model of the *dis-astron,* but whether the end of the world
is already happening, or whether perhaps it might already have taken place.
A deep shuddering of temporality occurs."[14]

This "deep shuddering of temporality" recalls the crucial line in *Vǫluspá*
45: *áðr verǫld steypisk* (before the *verǫld* tumbles/falls/collapses). It is at this
point in time that the whole concept of *verǫld* becomes unsustainable in the
cosmos. The emergence of the Anthropocene does the same for our idea that
the world exists as a sort of stage on which the lives of human subject-actors
play out, a background to our foreground, or as a standing reserve of "natural

resources" for us to exploit for our gain. If the Anthropocene began seven thousand years ago with humanity's first forays into land husbandry, all we can say is that this concept of world was over before it ever got going. No mode of human society has been sustainable, since the sum of seven thousand years of technological development and economic growth is our current ecological situation. Global warming is unsustainable for people—we will not be able to sustain our idea of what the world is to us in the face of the changing climate. But the planet will persist; humans will continue to live on the Earth. They will have to live differently in the later Anthropocene, however, if they do not wish their worlds to keep ending, over and over again, in more and more painful and horrifying ways.

Vǫluspá presents us with an analogous situation. The cosmos does not cease to be just because Ragnarǫk happens. The Norse apocalypse is specifically the doom of the gods—the end of their lives and their way of life. But life itself goes on after Ragnarǫk, just as life will go on beyond the catastrophe of global warming. What sort of life will it be? Who will be left, and under what conditions? If, as Morton argues, the end of the world has already happened; if it is already too late (always already too late) to right the sinking ship, then what should the survivors do when they struggle to the shore and survey the wreckage? The ethical dimension of the apocalypse comes into a new focus: it becomes a question not of avoiding a disaster but of preparing for its consequences. Ragnarǫk cannot be prevented. There is no hope for this world save that the next world may be a better one—a world that can sustain and be sustained by all its inhabitants in a way that we suspect that is no longer possible in our world.

Ragnarǫk is, by this reading, an ecological catastrophe. It represents the failure of interactions between the gods and the nondivine world. In an ecocritical reading of *Vǫluspá*, the Norse gods occupy the subject position that humans assert for themselves in modernity, as we saw clearly in our reading of the creation myths; *Vǫluspá* is not much concerned with the actions of men and women on Earth as we would recognize it. The poem is set in an indistinct geography that conforms to no real-world environment, though it sometimes resembles one. Notionally immortal, the gods conceive of space and time on a scale radically different from our own. Yet the predicament that they find themselves in as they hurtle toward Ragnarǫk has uncanny and chilling resonances with modern humanity's experience of global warming and its struggle to come to terms with a crisis of its own making.

The reading of *Vǫluspá* that follows is self-consciously anachronistic. Although some scholars have made plausible connections between the myths of Ragnarǫk and extreme climactic and geophysical events in pre-Viking Scandinavia, my reading does not depend on a historical context to explain the myths.[15] Rather, I make use of the myths' timelessness, their unmooring from the "real world," as a way to interrogate eco-catastrophic experiences in their universal dimensions. Ragnarǫk is not, or not merely, a metaphor for our own experiences in the High Anthropocene. In an ecocritical reading, I believe that these myths assert the transhistorical immanence of anthropogenic ecological breakdown, which is the price we pay for a few decades (or centuries, or even millennia) of fooling ourselves into thinking that we have had mastery over Nature. As Aidan Davison puts it: "The price paid for humanity's epochal power is forms of earthly flux that endanger human endeavour (including the endeavour of saving nature) and social forces seemingly beyond human control. The terrible paradox of this Anthropocene is that its stewards face the task of saving the Earth from no less than themselves so as to also save themselves."[16] The Norse gods—who had a hand in creating the universe, who are immortal (up to a point), and who have supernatural dominion over all things—cannot prevent Ragnarǫk; they *cannot prevent themselves from causing Ragnarǫk,* even when preventing Ragnarǫk is the only way they can save themselves.

The Æsir as Moderns: Reading *Vǫluspá* with Bruno Latour

Reading *Vǫluspá* in the Anthropocene as a document of the Anthropocene requires us to place the Æsir in our position as moderns. In this exercise, I am guided by Bruno Latour's brilliant exposé of the contradictions of modernity, *We Have Never Been Modern.* In Latour's analysis, at the heart of the modern condition is a belief in, and a determination to enforce, the separation of Nature from Society. The "modern constitution" guarantees that "Nature and Society must remain absolutely distinct" by ensuring that Nature (a human social construction) is made to appear transcendently nonhuman, while Society (for Latour, an immanent network of networks constituted by a wide variety of human and nonhuman actants) pretends to be made only by and for humans.[17] This separation is achieved by what Latour calls the practice of "purification": the division of the world into two separate "ontological zones: that of human beings on the one hand; that of nonhumans on the other." At the same time, however, moderns constantly and promiscuously engage in works of "translation," by which they create "mixtures between entirely new types of beings, hybrids of nature and culture," networks that always comprise human and nonhuman participants.[18] While modernity privileges the work of purification, of establishing strict borders between humans and the world, this position is only tenable because works of translation and hybridization are happening somewhere all the time. Scientists studying Nature with the intent of establishing its laws as they exist beyond human society, for example, do so only by translating the nonhuman through networks of human knowledge and social practice. The Nature that we wish to believe is separate from Society is ironically a construction of that same Society, but according to Latour we moderns are willfully blind to this fact: the twin projects of purification and hybridization must be kept apart from one another if we are to continue to be modern.

In *Vǫluspá*, the gods are modern in the Latourian sense because they are constantly engaged in both purification—the creation and maintenance of false dichotomies in the world—and the production of hybrids. It is often these hybrids which then go on to challenge and thwart the Æsir's efforts at purification, which only strengthens the urgency with which the Æsir work to enforce the boundaries they have set up. Sometimes these boundaries result from attempts at social purification: the conflict between the gods and their ancestral enemies, the giants, is fundamental to Norse mythology, as I discussed in chapter 2. But since the giants are always figured as the Other in these myths, they also gain associations with Nature as opposed to the Æsir's Society. The giants are associated with mountainous, almost uninhabitable regions, with wilderness and the wild; their lands in Jǫtunheimar are located in Útgarðr, the "outer-yard" on the fringes of the world; they are often portrayed as tricky, or deceitful, or stupid, or lascivious, or all of these things at once.[19] They are always the enemy. The whole fabric, the very structure, of both cosmic geography and mythological history depends on the gods and giants being and remaining separate from one another.

But in reality, the project of purification that the gods embark on is impossible to maintain. The Æsir have to work ceaselessly to keep themselves apart from their foes, but they also over and over again transgress their own boundaries. It would be impossible not to transgress them, for at a fundamental level there is no dichotomy between the giants and all they represent and the gods and all *they* represent. The gods' first creative acts are a form of purification through demarcation: whereas the great void Ginnungagap was amorphous and chaotic, the created universe will be neatly divided into land and sea and made fertile by the Æsir's actions. (In stanzas 5 and 6 of *Vǫluspá*, the gods also establish the positions of the heavenly bodies and instigate the passage of time.) The most important act of purification, however, may be the Æsir's decision to kill Ymir, even though this episode is barely alluded to in *Vǫluspá*. The primary creative act in Norse cosmology—the one that creates the form of the world as its inhabitants know it—is an act of god-on-giant violence. This dramatic act of purification clears the way for the Æsir—and the Æsir alone, or so they might expect—to occupy and enjoy the world they have just created. But they may have sown the seeds of their own destruction in the process.

The Golden Age and the End of the Beginning

The beatific vision of an unblemished "natural" world—not, in fact, "natural," since the Æsir have just created it—that *Vǫluspá* 4 presents, with its lush vegetation warmed by the sun shining out of the south, gives way to a brief glimpse of a correspondingly pristine social world in stanzas 7 and 8:

> The Æsir met on Iðavǫllr plain,
> high they built altars and temples;
> they set up their forges, smithed precious things,
> shaped tongs and made tools. (*Vǫluspá* [K] 7)[20]

Here, the Æsir begin to exploit the world they have created through their deployment of technology. Their forges and tools mark them as belonging to a sphere separate from the nonhuman environment: the poem speaks not of living trees but of trees-as-timber, which exist in order for the gods to make temples (*hátimbruðu hof*), presumably in veneration of themselves. This stanza records a small-scale industrial revolution, the beginning of an Anthropocene, even the origins of a form of capitalism. The Æsir are not merely crafting life's necessities, they are now wealth producers, entrepreneurs: the likely etymology of the name Iðavǫllr, a combination of *vǫllr*, "field," with a word relating to *iðja* (activity, business),[21] neatly encapsulates the land's newly productive function within an economy that is devoted to producing *auð*. *Auð* means "wealth," although Larrington's translation of line 7 as "they smithed precious things" neatly captures the aura of luxury that suddenly surrounds the gods. In the first half of the next stanza, we learn that they have succeeded in creating a surplus, and even that they have become something approaching a leisure society: "They played chequers in the meadow, they were merry, they did not lack for gold at all . . ."[22]

Snorri expands on *Vǫluspá*'s terse narrative here, making this period in the world's history into a true golden age: "The next thing they did was lay forges and for them they made hammer and tongs and anvil, and with these they made all other tools. After that they made metal and stone and wood, using so copiously the metal known as gold that they had all their furniture and utensils of gold, and that age is known as the golden age."[23] There is certainly a hint of decadence in Snorri's description of the Æsir's golden chairs and utensils: conspicuous consumption arrives early in the world, it seems. Because the Æsir relax *í túni* (in a meadow), this golden age also resembles a pastoral or pseudo-pastoral Arcadia: the *tún* was a Scandinavian farmstead's best grass-land, surrounding the house and often enclosed by a turf wall.[24] This is not a pastoral of hardworking shepherds, however. Here, the meadow has been transformed into an enclave of moneyed leisure, a literal playground for the nouveau riche gods.

The Æsir's golden age, therefore, is a product first of technological advance. Without their ability to master the use of tools, to obtain and refine gold, the wealth that defines this epoch would be unavailable to them. Once the gods have produced a surplus of wealth, they appropriate the landscape of pastoral husbandry in which to pursue their leisure interests—industrial barons enjoy-ing the gardens of their country homes, safe from the rabble behind high walls and strong gates. This moment, I suggest, is the point of origin for an epoch in Norse mythology analogous to the Anthropocene in our own history: the life-style that the gods create for themselves rests on their exploitation of technol-ogy and "natural resources"—all that gold has to come from somewhere—and it is unsustainable from the start. For if we know anything about golden ages, it is that they do not last. In fact, the Arcadian scene lasts for no more than half a stanza in *Vǫluspá*, which brings the golden age to an abrupt and inexplicable end: ". . . until three ogre-girls came, all-powerful women, out of Giant-land."[25]

This verse is strange. The identities of the three figures mentioned are unclear, though their gender and place of origin are both clearly important. These giant women are never mentioned again, and we never learn what it was about them that had the power to end the Æsir's idyll. For once, Snorri either doesn't know the explanation for this stanza or is not inclined to invent one: he simply agrees that the golden age was "spoiled by the women's arrival" (*en spiltisk af tilkvámu kvennanna*).[26] Lars Lönnroth suggests that the arrival of these three giant women reminds us of "the demonic qualities of gold," though it is hard to see how. Lönnroth goes on to say, "The three women rep-resent something evil that threatens the order and well-being of creation—this much is quite clear. Throughout the entire poem the giants symbolize chaos and evil; this applies equally to Ymir and the giants who oppose the gods in the Ragnarǫk section. At the same time, however, the giants are in possession of great wisdom and magical abilities which often makes it necessary to win their friendship."[27] This reading fails to explain stanza 8 satisfactorily, however, because it reveals neither the giantesses' motivation in leaving Jǫtunheimar and entering the world of the gods nor the cause of what we assume to be the gods' discomfort. How can three women bring the gods' golden age to an end simply by their turning up, even if they are *ámátakr* (very powerful)? Ursula Dronke suggests that the giantesses have come to challenge the gods to a game of *tafl* in order to "get control of the mechanism of the gods' prosperity," which seems a plausible aim for them to hold, even if the specific connection between the Æsir's board games and the mechanism of their prosperity is tenuous.[28] For Dronke, the giantesses' hostility toward the gods can be taken as a given.

In the Latourian mode of reading that I am attempting here, the three giant women do not need to be manifestations of evil: we can, indeed, imagine that their intentions are entirely benign, if we wish. The problem for the Æsir is that for the first time—the first of many—their project of purification reveals itself to be doomed to failure. The great fortification of Miðgarðr, built, according to Snorri, on account of the enmity of the giants, fails its first test; the boundary between the separate zones of existence that the gods have tried to establish is porous from the outset. Whatever the gods need the giants to represent—evil, Nature, a barbaric, primitive subaltern Other—it cannot be kept separate from what the gods symbolize for themselves. For Latour, the "Great Divide" of modernity is the partition between Nature and Society, which is unique to moderns. From the point of view of moderns, premoderns are those who do not distinguish between Nature and Society, who do not insist on enforcing a clear ontological gap between signs and things. For the Æsir, who are taking the place of modern humans in this experiment, the giants represent Nature in its "ahuman, sometimes inhuman, always extra-human" dimensions.[29] We never inquire what the gods represent for the giants, because from the modern perspective they are assigned the premodern worldview, in which "Nature and Society, signs and things, are virtually coextensive."[30] By their very nature, structuralist readings enforce Latour's Great Divide by asserting its transcendence when it is in fact a technology of purification, a tool for constructing and reconstructing itself. Miðgarðr is a physical instantiation of modernity's preoccupation with purification; its failure to keep the giants out is a foreshadowing of modernity's failure, in spite of constant vigilance, to keep Nature and Society, the world and mankind, Them and Us apart, restricted to separate spheres of existence.

The purification that Miðgarðr is supposed to ensure has important political dimensions, too. Its purpose is to keep the hostile giants out, not to prevent the Æsir from leaving their home. As twenty-first century debates about human migration continually remind us, the ingress of Them into Our territories is viewed as problematic, often undesirable, and at least requiring strict regulation, while We believe strongly that We should have complete freedom of movement into Their territory if We desire it for the purposes of commerce or leisure or the maintenance of hegemonies. Similarly, stories of the Æsir voyaging into Jǫtunheimar to obtain magical items or numinous knowledge, or to marry, abduct, or rape giant women, or simply to put some giants to the sword or hammer—to exploit the giants' resources and to oppress them to the extent necessary to exploit them—are legion in Norse mythology.[31] The giants are notionally always in the object position relative to the gods' subject position. But three giantesses arriving at the home of the gods is enough to throw the whole world into chaos. It is not so much the porousness of their border that shocks the gods, but the fact that this porousness is bidirectional. Miðgarðr is also unable to enforce desired-for gender boundaries. To this point in Vǫluspá's narrative, no goddesses have been present in the cosmos: in its pristine golden age, the Æsir's world is an entirely homosocial society of men.[32] The giantesses' coming is transgressive on multiple levels: they transgress spatial, social, and gender boundaries which are perfectly acceptable for Us to transgress—this is a mythology in which Þórr dresses in drag to take part in a sham wedding and Loki turns into a mare to seduce a stallion, after all—but which the Other is supposed to observe.

The Æsir's response to the first failure of their project of purification, of maintaining separation from the giants on their own terms, could be regarded as the production of a new sort of hybrid—an act of mediation between natural and social worlds. Characteristically, the gods respond to the apparent crisis of the giantesses' incursion by holding a meeting:

> Then all the Powers went to the thrones of fate,
> the sacrosanct gods, and considered this:
> who should create the lord of the dwarfs
> out of Brimir's blood and from Bláinn's limbs? (Vǫluspá [K] 9)[33]

This is the second such meeting in Vǫluspá signaled by the formulaic refrain (þá gengu regin ǫll . . .) in the first half of the stanza. In their previous council (stanza 6), the gods had proclaimed a set of boundaries of a different sort, by naming, and thereby enforcing, divisions between day and night, morning and afternoon, so that the years may be counted—in effect, the gods' first summit meeting marks the formal introduction of time (as conceived by humans) into the cosmos. The subject and outcome of the discussion that the gods hold in stanza 9, however, is much more ambiguous. Assuming that this verse represents an attempt to respond to the giantesses' arrival in stanza 8, how does the creation of the race of dwarfs represent such a response?

To hypothesize the purpose of the Æsir's apparently capricious decision—and while keeping in mind the fact that caprice is a perfectly likely motive for many of their actions—we need to examine more closely the nature and function of the dwarfs in the Old Norse mythological universe. *Vǫluspá* is extremely interested in dwarfs: as the poem stands, stanzas 11 through 16 preserve a lengthy list of dwarfs' names that is presumably an interpolation triggered by their mention in the main narrative sequence of stanzas 9 and 10.[34] But the narrator of *Vǫluspá* knows more than she tells about this topic, as with so much else in this poem. The dwarfs' creation is important for some reason: the modal auxiliary verb *skyldi* implies a sense of obligation or inevitability; but it is not clear to the gods which of them has to undertake this task of creation. The Æsir understand the composition of dwarfish bodies: dwarfs are made from "Brimir's blood" and "Bláinn's limbs." Brimir and Bláinn are probably both alternative names for Ymir, the primal giant killed by the gods and from whose dismembered corpse the cosmos is constructed. Presumably, his blood and limbs are respectively water and earth—*Vǫluspá* 10 also specifies that the dwarfs were made *ór jǫrðu* (out of earth). The dwarfs are thus elemental creatures that moderns would not hesitate to assign to the realm of Nature, like the giants, even though they are created in the service of (the gods') Society. In fact, they are hybrids, as Snorri Sturluson shows in his elaboration of *Vǫluspá* 9–10: "Next the gods took their places on their thrones and instituted their courts and discussed where the dwarfs had been generated from in the soil and down in the earth like maggots in flesh. The dwarfs had taken shape first and acquired life in the flesh of Ymir and were then maggots, but by decision of the gods they became conscious with intelligence and had the shape of men though they live in the earth and in rocks."[35] Even more clearly than his source poem, Snorri's account of the dwarfs' creation emphasizes their Nature-Culture hybridity by assigning to them a primarily bestial mode of existence, which requires the intervention of the forces of Culture to tame and humanize—to de-Nature.

Latour claims that such acts of hybridization are possible for moderns precisely because of the moderns' constant policing of these categories: "To undertake hybridization, it is always necessary to believe that it has no serious consequences for the constitutional order. There are two ways of taking this precaution. The first consists in thoroughly thinking through the close connections between the social and the natural order so that no dangerous hybrid will be introduced carelessly. The second one consists in bracketing off entirely the work of hybridization on the one hand and the dual social and natural order on the other."[36] In the case of the dwarfs, the gods' decision to create a class of creature that belongs neither to Nature-as-Other nor to Society-as-Ourselves reveals their naïveté or complacency about the security of their ontological borders. They believe that their constant vigilance in maintaining the purity of their distinction between Us and Them, between the "primitive" and the "civilized," can accommodate and control and exploit hybrids of their own creation. As we will see, the gods are manifestly deluded in their subscription to a Latourian modern constitution. As they progress toward their doom, they will constantly conjure up hybrids in attempts to enforce their notions of purification, and they will quickly lose control of these hybrids.

Understanding the dwarfs' hybrid nature does not help us understand the gods' motivation in producing this hybrid or how this act is in any sense a solution to the problem that seems to have provoked this act. John Lindow suggests that the reference in *Vǫluspá* 10 to the dwarfs receiving "human likenesses" (*mannlíkǫn*) may reveal the end product of the gods' mediation between the earthly and divine to be human beings, some of whom will fight with the gods against the giants and other "forces of chaos."[37] In this reading, which follows Snorri's conception of the matter, the bestial maggoty dwarfs preexist their transformation into rational, cultural beings that can be of use to the Æsir. They never get to share in the Æsir's subject position, never become part of their In-group. Rather they become an exploited underclass—their substatus reflected in their subterranean dwelling places—whose service has an economic rather than military value to the gods.

The dwarfs' main role in Norse mythology is the production of precious objects, and especially those numinous or magical items on which the Æsir most specially depend. Dwarfs create the mead of poetry that Óðinn steals and shares with the other gods and with favored humans; dwarfs make the best weapons, including Óðinn's spear Gungnir and Þórr's hammer Mjǫllnir; dwarfs make a ship for Freyr that can be folded up and carried in one's pocket; they fashion the ring Draupnir, which spontaneously gives birth to other golden rings—an endless source of wealth. Bearing in mind the dwarfs' pre-dominant function as crafters of precious objects, I propose that we read their creation not only as the gods' response to the giant women's transgression of their zone of purity but also a direct response to the end of the golden age that accompanies it. Whereas the gods had previously created wealth for themselves by their own labor, from this point on, manufacture will be outsourced to the dwarfs. And the dwarfs, like the giants, will be expected to do business with the gods only on the gods' terms. Any attempt on the dwarfs' part to reverse the flow of goods and services between them and the Æsir is doomed to failure. When Alvíss, the protagonist of *Alvíssmál,* wishes to marry Þórr's daughter, for example, his presumption earns him an early death.

As Lois Bragg and Lotte Motz have argued, the dwarfs are also figured in negative ways throughout the mythology. Like the *Skrælingar* of Vínland, they are portrayed as dark, ugly, and misshapen, both recalling their bestial origins and suggesting their alignment with other Out-groups such as the "African" or the "crippled."[38] They are a subaltern group whose place, in both the geographical and social senses of the word, is defined for them by the gods and whose function is to serve their creator-masters by producing luxury objects for scant reward and with no prospect of emancipation. There are suggestive parallels between the representation of dwarfs in Norse mythology and discourses surrounding "the Negro" in colonial America: both groups are valued primarily for their labor and the servitude of both can be justified on the grounds of a claimed fundamental, ontological divide between slaves and masters, which is manifest in, among other things, physical appearance and intellectual abilities.[39] The subordination of Out-groups like these is often supported by aligning them with Nature as opposed to Society, with the premodern as opposed to the modern, but such attempts at purification necessarily entail hybridization. To exploit the subaltern requires the notionally distinct halves of the modern constitution to come together. This is why moderns invest so much rhetorical energy in attempting to assert that this hybridization does not invalidate their conception of the moderns as separate from and superior to the nonmoderns. The "primitive" may be exploited by the "civilized," the African by the European, or the dwarfs by the gods because the categories of Nature and Society, modern and premodern, and Us and Them are ineluctable, implies Latour's schema. But the Out-groups' service of the In-group depends upon the boundaries between the two groups being permeable.

After an interlude in which human beings are created (*Vǫluspá* 18) and the arrival of three more mysterious women, the Norns, introduces the mechanism of fate into the cosmos (*Vǫluspá* 19–21), the gods' next source of anxiety is "the first war between peoples in the world." Stanza 21, which narrates the first part of this conflict, is unfortunately one of the most obscure in the whole poem:

She remembers the first war in the world,
when they stuck Gullveig with spears
and in the High-One's hall they burned her;
three times they burned her, three times she was reborn,
over and over, yet she lives still. (*Vǫluspá* [K] 21; 22 in Larrington)[40]

We do not know who this Gullveig is or why she has been treated so dreadfully, but we should note at once that she is another female figure who has either penetrated a space that is gendered male—Óðinn's hall—and must be punished for it, or been brought thither in order to be penetrated by spears, a Freudian interpretation of which seems justified in this instance. Two stanzas later, we learn that the Æsir's antagonists are the Vanir, a rival group of deities who have come to be associated with fertility, though their origins and significance in pagan Norse culture are uncertain. Gullveig is presumably one of these Vanir, perhaps even the goddess Freyja in disguise.[41] Her name means something like "gold-drink" or "gold-drunk," which led Karl Müllenhoff to view this stanza as providing another feminine symbolization of gold's intoxicating, corrupting influence on men.[42] Gullveig's repeated burning, which she survives, would in this reading evoke gold's ability to be melted down and take on new forms over and over again. The parallels between Gullveig's coming to the world of the Æsir and the giantesses' arrival in stanza 8 are important. In both cases women who are doubly Other on account of their gender and their belonging to an Out-group threaten the gods, or the gods' modern constitution, by entering the gods' space. According to Zoe Borovsky, Gullveig's treatment at the hands of the Æsir is an example of how the gods "project blame onto those with the most contact with the outside and label them as mixed, contaminated, or tainted with that outside evil and often ruthlessly expel them."[43] In other words, transgression of boundaries is an offense for which the punishment can be labeling the perpetrator as a hybrid and thereby ensuring that they lose their place in the settled hierarchy of the Æsir's constitution, even as it is precisely their hybridity that makes the transgression possible in the first place.

The gods' response to Gullveig's incursion and their failure to destroy her is, as it was before, to hold a meeting. Stanza 23 makes it clear that the gods are not sure what is happening to them, since they are unable to decide whether they owe compensation—presumably to the Vanir for their treatment of Gullveig—or are owed it, presumably from the Vanir, though for what it is impossible to say:[44]

Then all the powers went to the thrones of fate,
the sacrosanct gods, and considered this:
whether the Æsir should yield the tribute
or whether all the gods should receive payment.[45] (*Vǫluspá* [K] 23;
   24 in Larrington)

The following stanza reveals the outcome of the gods' discussion: Óðinn throws his spear—presumably, the product of a dwarfish sweatshop—over the host, and the first war begins in earnest. Soon, however, the poem reveals that the gods cannot rely on their military might to fend off their enemies: ". . . the wooden rampart of the Æsir's stronghold was wrecked; the Vanir, with a war-spell, kept on trampling the plain."[46] The Vanir possess special abilities that enable them to withstand the Æsir's assaults; the Æsir's zone of purity is once again penetrated as their physical barriers fail to hold.

Time for another meeting. The Æsir retreat to their thrones and attempt to apportion blame for what appears to have been a disastrous war with the Vanir:

Then all the powers went to the thrones of fate,
the sacrosanct gods, and considered this:
who had troubled the air with treachery,
or given Óðr's girl to the giant race. (*Vǫluspá* [K] 25; 26 in Larrington)[47]

Stanza 25 appears to refer obliquely to a narrative preserved in full in *Snorra Edda*. Known as the Giant Builder myth, this story reveals once again both the gods' desperate desire to secure their borders and their helpless reliance on the Other that they wish to segregate themselves from:

It was right at the beginning of the gods' settlement, when the gods had established Miðgarðr and built Valhǫll, there came there a certain builder and offered to build them a fortification in three seasons so good that it would be reliable and secure against mountain-giants and frost-giants even though they should come in over Miðgarðr. And he stipulated as his payment that he should get Freyja as his wife, and he wished to have the sun and the moon. Then the Æsir went into discussion and held a conference, and this bargain was made with the builder that he should get what he demanded if he managed to build the fortification in one winter, but on the first day of summer if there was anything unfinished in the fortification then he should forfeit his payment.[48]

So anxious are the Æsir about Miðgarðr's failure to prevent the ingress of the giants that they are prepared to employ one of their enemies to fortify their defenses, and to pay an extremely unfavorable price for the work. (Freyja had presumably only just been accepted into the Æsir's company, as part of the peace settlement between the two groups of gods. The Vanir were soon absorbed by the Æsir, producing a hybrid community of gods under the name of the latter.) While the gods are enthusiastic despoilers, and occasional husbands, of giantesses, the threat of a giant gaining access to one of the Æsir's women is anathema. As it becomes clear that the giant builder will fulfill his end of the bargain, it becomes imperative for the gods to act to preserve the boundaries that the completion of their new fortification is ironically about to cause to collapse. They hold another meeting, at which Loki is made the scapegoat—it was apparently his idea to promise Freyja to the giant—and given responsibility for clearing up the mess, at pain of death. Loki's first appearance in the narrative, though he is not named in Vǫluspá at this point, marks an important turning point in the progression of the cosmos toward Ragnarǫk.

Loki: Weapon of Mass Destruction

Loki is the most modern of the Æsir, in Latourian terms. It is therefore unsurprising that he is the figure most directly responsible for the end of the world, even if to make him the sole instigator of Ragnarǫk is to ignore the Æsir's ongoing mendacity and complacency. Loki is himself the product of a work of hybridization: although seen constantly at the heart of the Æsir's society, plans, and actions, Loki is not quite a god, although Snorri says he is considered as one of them:

> That one is also reckoned among the Æsir whom some call the Æsir's calumniator and originator of deceits and the disgrace of all gods and men. His name is Loki or Loptr, son of the giant Farbauti. Laufey or Nál is his mother. Loki is pleasing and handsome in appearance, evil in character, very capricious in behavior. He possessed to a greater degree than others the kind of learning that is called cunning, and tricks for every purpose. He was always getting the Æsir into a complete fix and often got them out of it by trickery.[49]

Loki's father is a giant, and his mother Laufey (or Nál) is of an unknown lineage. He is not bound to the Æsir with the same direct bonds of kinship that link most of the pantheon. Loki is capable of moving freely between the many worlds of the cosmos: his main role in many of the extant myths is to transgress spatial and social boundaries—like those represented by Miðgarðr—in order to further the gods' agenda or rescue them from the catastrophic consequences of their failures, which often result from Loki's own malice or capriciousness. The Giant Builder myth is a good example of the type. The gods wish to engage in a work of purification that reinforces the Nature/Society boundary they have erected between themselves and the giants, but to do so they must engage in a work of double hybridization: they must allow a giant into their zone of purity, and they must offer as payment the prospect of further hybridization in the shape of Freyja's betrothal to the mason, with its attendant risks of miscegenation. The gods are always happy to make giantesses pregnant, but they are not sanguine about the prospect of a male giant returning the favor to one of their women—this pattern is of course familiar from almost all systems of colonialist oppression.

It is likely that Loki instigated the plan for the giant builder's work and his payment, either out of complacency, if he cannot imagine that the mason will be able to complete the work on time, and thus Freyja is safe, or malice, if he knows full well that the deal will have to be consummated and wishes for his own amusement to see Freyja the bride of a giant. The gods are incapable of seeing the irony in their situation, but they are alive to its threat. They force Loki to cheat the mason out of his payment by distracting the giant's remarkable stallion from his work before the fortification is complete. Loki achieves this goal by transforming himself into a mare—his own hybridity encompasses the ability to shift between species identities as well as between genders—and mating with the giant's stallion. The gods' failure to enforce the cordon sanitaire between themselves and the Other can only be mitigated by a shamefully messy act of fraternization across the boundaries whose maintenance is the goal of the whole scheme. The outcome of Loki's equine tryst is a further hybrid: the mutant, eight-legged horse Sleipnir, who becomes Óðinn's steed and constant companion. In the meantime, Þórr turns up and enacts the Æsir's alternative strategy of purification—hitting the giant with an enormous hammer until he is dead.

Sleipnir is not the only hybrid that Loki produces. According to *Snorra Edda,* Loki is the father of three of the gods' most dangerous antagonists through his adulterous sexual relationship with a giantess named Angrboða:

And Loki had other offspring too. There was a giantess Angrboða in Giantland. With her Loki had three children. One was Fenrisúlfr, the second Jǫrmungandr (i.e. the Miðgarðr-serpent), the third is Hel. And when the gods realized that these three siblings were being brought up in Giantland, and when the gods traced prophecies stating that from these siblings great mischief and disaster would arise for them, then they all felt evil was to be expected from them, to begin with because of their mother's nature, but still worse because of their father's.[50]

Although their birth finds no place in *Vǫluspá*'s narrative, Loki's monstrous offspring will be essential players in the drama of Ragnarǫk. All three are weapons of mass destruction, doomsday devices. Once they have been created, they have to be suppressed, monitored, encompassed, kept under control for eternity, as their freedom to do the job for which they are destined will result in the apocalypse. In Snorri's account, the gods make a further attempt at purification by casting Loki's children out, by placing them in high-security facilities that will contain them and render them unthreatening. Hel is placed in the underworld and given dominion over the (nonheroic) dead. The Miðgarðr serpent, Jǫrmungandr, is thrown into the ocean, growing so large that it eventually circumscribes the inhabitable world. The great wolf Fenrir, meanwhile, requires more active management: he has to be bound with fetters made (by the dwarfs) from six impossible things—the sound of a cat's footfall, a woman's beard, and so on—and in order to get Fenrir to submit to being bound, the god Týr has to offer his hand as surety. When the Æsir trick Fenrir into allowing them to put the deceptively flimsy bonds on him, the wolf bites off Týr's hand, giving a foretaste of his god-killing actions at the end of the world.

Loki's monstrous children resemble another feature of Anthropocene modernity and its contradictions. Whether read as waste or weapons, there is an eerie correspondence between the gods' treatment of Fenrir, Jǫrmungandr, and Hel and our modern predicament with regard to nuclear and other toxic materials. The development of nuclear weapons and their almost equally problematic civilian progeny in the 1940s is another decisive marker of the advent of the High Anthropocene, an important accelerant of the Great Acceleration. Their entry into the world was also accompanied by a new strain of apocalypticism, a feeling that the end could once more be nigh: like the Æsir when faced with Loki's children, we can see only mischief and disaster arising from them at some unknown, later point in time. Their threat is "futural," to use Morton's term, in the way that radioactivity is futural. The half-life of plutonium is incomprehensibly long on the scale of a human lifespan, or even human history, yet our present actions with regard to these to-us-immortal "hyperobjects" will have repercussions for life on earth millennia into the future, "scoop[ing] out the objectified now of the present moment into a shifting uncertainty."[51] By binding Fenrir, banishing Hel, and throwing the serpent into the sea, the Æsir are trying to prevent disaster. But we know—or will soon discover—that the disaster cannot be deferred indefinitely, because it is always already upon us. The end of the world has already happened, as we have seen Morton claim. Or, as Maurice Blanchot puts it: "We are on the edge of disaster without being able to situate it in the future: it is rather always already past, and yet we are on the edge or under the threat, all formulations which would imply the future—that which is yet to come—if the disaster were not that which does not come, that which has put a stop to every arrival."[52]

The Æsir believe that they can control the agents of their destruction by consigning them to a separate realm, both spatial and ontological, in which they can safely be ignored, in the same way that we bury nuclear waste deep beneath mountains or dream up plans to sequester carbon dioxide in basalt structures. But as Morton has argued repeatedly, we delude ourselves in these endeavors because "there is no *away* to which we can meaningfully sweep the radioactive dust. Nowhere is far enough or long-lasting enough."[53] Loki's monstrous brood can no more be contained permanently than global warming can be reversed within a chronology scaled to the lives of individual humans or nuclear waste "made safe." The Miðgarðr serpent, in particular, resembles a Mortonian "hyperobject" in that it is massively distributed— larger, in fact, than the whole world that it comes to encircle and define, to the point where everything exists within the ambit of the snake, rather than vice versa. It is impossible for a human-scale observer to view all of it at once. The finite immortality of all three creatures—a sort of half-life in which they are inactive but by no means neutralized, their toxicity neither quite active nor altogether latent—chimes with Morton's insistence that hyperobjects like nuclear waste or Styrofoam are also massively distributed in time, belonging to no now of which we can speak. And for Morton, hyperobjects are directly implicated in the end of the world,[54] just as we (and presumably the gods) always already have a feeling that Hel, Fenrir, and Jǫrmungandr will be among the prime agents of destruction at Ragnarǫk. The refrain of the last part of *Vǫluspá* (beginning with stanza 43 in the Konungsbók text) is categorical about the matter: *festr mun slitna, / en freki renna.* The bond will break, and the wolf will run.

The same fate awaits Loki. Eventually, the gods will have him bound, gruesomely, in the entrails of his son, until Doomsday. His freeing then precipitates the earth-shattering events of the final stages of Ragnarǫk. His crime—the incident that is most commonly regarded as the tipping point at which Ragnarǫk becomes inevitable—is to instigate the murder of the beloved god Baldr. This heinous act is conventionally regarded as a breakdown of the social order, a transgression of taboos against killing within the kin group, and indeed that is what it is.[55] But it is also another example of the Æsir's failure to impose artificial dichotomies onto the world, the great crisis of their modernity.

Loki's motivations seem as capricious as ever in this episode, despite the seriousness of the offense. *Vǫluspá* is once again allusive and elusive at this point in its narrative: stanzas 31 through 34 tell how Baldr's blind brother, Hǫðr, shoots Baldr with a shaft of mistletoe and how Óðinn takes vengeance on Hǫðr by begetting another son who kills Baldr's killer within hours of being born. Then, the narrative focus switches to the scene of Loki's binding, although there is no direct causal connection between this event and its narrative precedents. *Snorra Edda* gives us a much fuller version of the myth, as usual. Here, Snorri records that Baldr's death follows a sequence of events that runs thus: Baldr experiences dreams that forebode his death. The Æsir, concerned to protect their beloved brother from all harm, demand that the whole of creation promise never to hurt Baldr: "Frigg received solemn promises so that Baldr should not be harmed by fire and water, iron and all kinds of metal, stones, the earth, diseases, the animals, the birds, poisons, snakes."[56] This is perhaps the Æsir's most ambitious work of purification. It enacts a quite unambiguous Nature/Culture dichotomy, with all nonhuman entities expected to subordinate themselves to the requirements of the culture. As it turns out, the gods would have been better off directing their attention to the tensions within the In-group than reinforcing their ontological barriers against the threats they perceive to be offered by the rest of creation. They get assurances from objects they perceive to be potential instruments of disaster, but they pay no attention to the cultural forces that will instigate the use of these instruments.

The Æsir are renewed in their complacency by the apparent success of their imposition of cultural dominion over the "natural" world. In the second great ludic interlude in their history, trying to harm Baldr becomes a favorite game of the Æsir: "And when this was done and confirmed, then it became an entertainment for Baldr and the Æsir that he should stand up at assemblies and all the others should either shoot at him or strike at him or throw stones at him. But whatever they did he was unharmed, and they all thought this a great glory."[57] Loki is displeased that Baldr is unharmed by this display of the gods' apparent mastery of the physical world, although we learn nothing of why he is displeased. Presumably, he is jealous of Baldr's insider status, resentful of the favor Baldr enjoys among the Æsir despite his negligible contribution to the gods' community: in the myths that survive to us, Baldr is either absent or entirely passive, and as far as we know this god had no function in the religious practice of any historical Norse paganism.

Almost uniquely among the Æsir, Baldr has a pristine, unmixed bloodline as the son of the chief god and his official consort; his hands, and his conscience, are clean, largely because he has apparently lived an existence of absolute leisure. He has done none of the gods' dirty work. Rather, he has been hermetically sealed off from the Other: "Óðinn's second son is Baldr, and there is good to be told of him. He is best and all praise him. He is so fair in appearance and so bright that light shines from him, and there is a plant so white that it is called after Baldr's eyelash, and from this you can tell his beauty both of hair and body. [. . .] He lives in a place called Breiðablik. This is in heaven. No unclean thing is permitted to be there."[58] Exceptional whiteness is associated with moral purity in Old Norse sources—with all the troubling resonances that this idea produces for twenty-first-century sensibilities—and Snorri's description probably draws on the image of *Hvítr-Kristr,* the "White-Christ" of Norse Christian parlance.[59] Baldr's purity extends to his dwelling place, to which no "unclean thing" is permitted—another zone of purification that is doomed to collapse. Snorri says that "it is one of his characteristics that none of his decisions can ever be fulfilled."[60] For all that Baldr seems the most aloofly discriminating of the gods, his discrimination has no force. Loki, the symbol, manifestation, and agent of all the messy works of hybridization that the gods' society constantly requires for the maintenance and defense of the (illusion of) purity, of separateness from the rest of the cosmos that Baldr represents, wishes to see Baldr brought low, whether out of spite or envy, or simply on account of the nihilistic fondness for chaos that trickster figures—of which Loki is a prime example—always display.[61] In my Latourian reading, Baldr is a symbol not of purity but of purification, an instantiation of the modern temperament's desire to cleave the cultural subject from its "natural" environment.

The Æsir's command over the "natural" world briefly seems complete, and for a moment it seems as though they may be able to enjoy a second golden age: their antics with the invulnerable Baldr recall the atmosphere of the days when the world was fresh and new and they happily played games in the meadow. But Loki—after once again demonstrating the fluidity of his gender identity by taking on the form of an old woman—gets Frigg to admit that a single actant, the mistletoe, had not made the same pledge as the rest of creation. The mistletoe, Frigg says, had seemed too young to need to swear the oath not to harm Baldr. Loki at once fashions a dart from a spring of mistletoe, convinces blind Hǫðr that it would be fun for him to join in the other gods' games, and guides Hǫðr's hand in the fatal shot. Baldr is dead; Ragnarǫk is inevitable, or so it is often assumed.

But why is Baldr's murder, despicable as it is, enough to trigger a chain of consequences that will lead to the end of the world? Why should a social catastrophe—if that is really what Baldr's death is, considering his negligible role in the gods' earlier doings—result in a physical cataclysm? From its earliest stages, the complex of events that coalesce into Ragnarǫk disrupts all prevailing norms and structures in the cosmos—temporal, spatial, meteorological, geological, as well as social. As we will see in the final chapter, the difficulty of untangling causes from effects in this narrative sequence, and the constant blurring of Nature/Society dichotomies in the period between Baldr's death and the gods' final battle with their enemies, provide an anticipatory echo of our own slow-motion apocalypse, with its causal feedback loops between anthropogenic activity and "natural" disasters, between climatic upheaval, ecological degradation, and social turmoil.

7   Reading Ragnarǫk at the End of the World

AFTER THE ÆSIR HAVE SLAKED their thirst for vengeance by binding Loki—an act which takes some guts—*Vǫluspá*'s pacing changes. In the Codex Regius version of the poem, the narrative voice provides us with a series of vignettes of different locations in the cosmos, all of which have, or have now taken on, sinister import: a hall with a roof made out of serpents' spines at a place called "Corpse-Beach" (*Vǫluspá* 37: *á Nástrǫndu*); an infernal landscape in which murderers and perjurers must "wade heavy streams," while a monster called Níðhǫggr (Hateful-striker) tears into human corpses (38). In stanza 39, we see an old woman sitting in a place called Járnviðr (Iron-wood), where she tends (or possibly gives birth to) "Fenrir's kindred," presumably the wolves who will run alongside the chief of their breed when Fenrir finally breaks out of his bonds:

> In the east sat the old woman in Iron-wood
> and nourishes there Fenrir's offspring;
> one of them in trollish shape
> shall be snatcher of the moon. (*Vǫluspá* [K] 39)[1]

We never learn the identity of the woman, or in whose service she nurtures these wolves—one of which will take on the "form of a troll" and eventually grab the moon out of the sky—who she is working for, or to what ends. But this wolf nursery is undoubtedly sinister; it sounds like a secret research lab turning out genetically modified organisms or biological warfare agents. The animal world is being pressed into service by the machinations of a diabolical military-industrial complex, perhaps. Wolves, animals that normally represent the antithesis of domestication, are brought into husbandry. Even the name "Iron-wood" conjures a perverse and grotesque hybridization of the vegetable and mineral, that which lives as trees and that which deprives trees of life. The comforting structures and hierarchies of being that we apply to the world—out of which we create a world—are already crumbling.

And in the following stanza, we have the clearest indication that Ragnarǫk is an apocalypse of climate change, just as ours is:

It [i.e., the wolf] gluts itself on doomed men's lives,
reddens the gods' dwellings with crimson blood;
sunshine becomes black all the next summers,
weather all vicious. Do you know yet—or what? (Vǫluspá [K] 40)[2]

The second half of this verse, as I mentioned in the prologue, is often interpreted as describing a volcanic eruption or ash cloud—a distinctively Icelandic disaster, if so. But the notion that the sun will turn black also resonates with modern anxieties about, for example, the prospect of nuclear winter in the aftermath of an atomic explosion. And the phrase veðr ǫll válynd (weather all vicious) is eerily prescient of our experience of the weather in the Anthropocene: Old Norse vá is cognate with "woe" in English and connotes danger as well as grief or sadness.

Snorri's narration expands this reference into a full-fledged account of what he calls Fimbulvetr (great or terrible winter), and here the climatic triggers (and consequences) of Ragnarǫk are described in more detail:

Then spoke Gangleri: "What information is there to be given about Ragnarǫk? I have not heard tell of this before."

High said: "There are many important things to be told about it. First of all that a winter will come called *fimbul*-winter. Then snow will drift from all directions. There will then be great frosts and keen winds. The sun will do no good. There will be three of these winters together and no summer between. But before that there will come three other winters during which there will be great battles throughout the world.[3]

The myth of Fimbulvetr is not widely attested outside *Snorra Edda*, and its currency or antiquity in Norse mythological traditions is uncertain.[4] But Snorri's account of this catastrophe, regardless of its point of ultimate origin, is clearly a variety of eco-apocalypse, which is to say that it is a breakdown of the norms that people expect or even demand from the natural world—the idea that the physical world exists as our *oikos* and should continue to do so indefinitely. Climate change is uncomfortable not merely in its physical effects, chilling though they are; it also challenges our deepest notions of environmental propriety, the idea that the planet exists to be a home for us. The anxiety encoded in the Fimbulvetr myth surrounds global cooling rather than global warming, but at heart this aspect of Ragnarǫk is identical with our current dominant apocalyptic mythos: all that we have taken for granted in the world-outside-ourselves can no longer be assumed to be operative.

In *Vǫluspá* and *Snorra Edda* the cause of the new Ice Age is not made specifically anthropogenic. But the gods and all other beings in the world are implicated and caught up in these developments. Snorri has Fimbulvetr marking the start of Ragnarǫk proper, although his chronology is not unambiguous: the three years of social unrest that precede Fimbulvetr with their "great battles" suggest that one of the "human" contributions to this emergency—the collapse of social order—comes before the breakdown of climatic norms, even if it is not the direct cause of the dire winters. *Vǫluspá* 40 suggests the same priority for society's misdeeds: before the sun turns black and the weather becomes woeful, doomed beings have already begun to spill each other's blood. The Ragnarǫk myth returns to the breakdown of familial and communal bonds and norms of behavior in stanza 44, after the climatic crisis has begun:

> Brother will fight brother and be his slayer,
> sister's sons will violate the kinship-bond;
> hard it is in the world, whoredom abounds,
> axe-age, sword-age, shields are cleft asunder,
> wind-age, wolf-age, before the world plunges headlong;
> no man will spare another. (*Vǫluspá* [K] 44)[5]

This stanza evokes the promiscuous hybridity and absolute interdependence that link social and physical worlds in a time of such crisis. This stanza describes a situation of utter moral collapse, of violence, faithlessness, and upheaval, but it is impossible to unlink these cultural disturbances from what is happening in the physical world: it is not merely an ax age and a sword age but also an age of winds and wolves. Changes to the environment neither directly cause nor are caused by the breakdown of the cultural world, but they cannot be kept apart from it, either.

The global climatic crisis of Snorri's Fimbulvetr, and the social turmoil and carnage of *Vǫluspá* 44, both possess considerable prophetic force with regard to the Anthropocene's ongoing apocalypse. Our own experiences of global warming—of which we are only at the beginning—are enmeshed with future-focused fears about the economic and social ramifications of living with a radically changed climatic system. It has become a commonplace to predict that global warming will act as a trigger of future conflicts, especially in the context of a still rapidly growing world population and the increasing demands on resources required by development. The strains placed on social institutions by very high levels of climatological stress have been shown to lead to significant upheaval. In a 2013 meta-analysis of sixty previous studies, for example, Solomon Hsiang and his coauthors determined that both interpersonal and intercommunity conflicts are more likely to occur, and more likely to escalate into violence, when climatic conditions deviate from their historic norms: "Future anthropogenic climate change could worsen conflict outcomes across the globe in comparison to a future with no climatic changes," they conclude.[6] Although links between climate change and human conflict are still uncertain in the eyes of many scholars—as yet, a methodology that securely accounts for a necessarily vast range of variables on both the climatological and social sides of the question has not been established[7]—it is becoming increasingly clear that though the precise nature of their relationship might be undefined, conflict and sociopolitical disturbances are likely to be an increasingly important aspect of the twenty-first century's experience of global warming.

The Old Norse Ragnarǫk mythos thus bespeaks a familiar anxiety about the social consequences of ecological disaster, whether or not they arise out of a real-world situation of climatic catastrophe. Bo Gräslund and Neil Price believe that they have found such a historical correlative to the Fimbulvetr portion of Ragnarǫk in the form of the so-called dust-veil event of 536 CE.[8] Historical climatologists have identified a period of as long as fifteen years in which global temperatures dropped markedly—by as much as 3–4 degrees Celsius in northern Sweden, for example. The cause of this anomaly has been attributed, on the basis of contemporary written accounts originating in the late Roman Empire, to a period in which the sun was abnormally dim for a period of almost two years. This dimming may have been produced by some kind of massive shroud of dust produced by either a supermassive volcanic eruption or the impact with the Earth of a large extraterrestrial object, although no firm cause has so far been established. Gräslund and Price propose that the extant myth of Fimbulvetr encodes a cultural memory of this dust-veil event and a catastrophic series of cold summers that seems to have had a significantly negative impact on agriculture and social cohesion in parts of Scandinavia in the mid-sixth century. They also use this historical event to explain a mysterious alternative spelling of Ragnarǫk that appears in manuscripts of *Snorra Edda:* in opposition to *Vǫluspá*, Snorri calls the apocalypse *Ragna-røkkr,* which means "twilight (or "darkening") of the divine powers," as opposed to their "fate," which is what *rǫk* connotes, and which is the word that *Vǫluspá* uses in stanza 43 of the Codex

Regius text.[9] For Gräslund and Price, the existence of this alternate form is another sign of the Ragnarǫk mythos's connection to the global dimming of the mysterious dust-veil event that they identify with Fimbulvetr.

The approach that Gräslund and Price take to this myth is an eco-historicist one, and it is a valuable reminder that mythology can be a repository of sublimated ecological experiences. Although their interpretation risks creating a hermeneutic circle—events that predate the texts in question by at least four centuries are used to explain the Ragnarǫk myths, which are used to illuminate the cultural impact of the sixth-century dust-veil event—it has the benefit of revealing the ways in which the effects of climate change in the distant past could have long-lasting cultural afterlives. Our ancestors have had to experience and process climate change just as we have to experience and mentally and imaginatively process global warming. Mythmaking is an important part of this process.

Ragnarǫk's Great Acceleration and the End of the End

Stanza 44 of *Vǫluspá* marks a decisive turning point in the affairs of the gods and all other beings in the cosmos. The *verǫld*, the "age of men," is crumbling: we are at the end of history. What will come in its place?

First of all, there will be a further loosening of all bonds, even greater chaos in both the social and physical realms: in stanza 43, "the wolf" (presumably Loki's child, Fenrir) gets loose; in stanza 45, the Æsir finally seem to realize the seriousness of their predicament as Heimdallr blows his horn and Óðinn embarks on one last, fruitless quest for information about the end of the world, consulting on this occasion with the severed head of the famously wise giant (or perhaps god) Mímir.[10] Whatever Óðinn learns from Mímir is insufficient to prevent the next stage of the catastrophe, which occurs in stanza 46, when the world-tree Yggdrasill shakes and groans, and the "giant becomes free": "The standing ash-tree, Yggdrasill, shudders; / the old tree groans and the giant gets free" (*Vǫluspá* [K] 46; 45, lines 5–6 in Larrington).[11] I have already discussed (in chap. 4) how *Vǫluspá* 46 is one of a cluster of verses in the *Poetic Edda* that grant absolute actancy, and indeed considerable agency, to Yggdrasill. The great ash has survived every cataclysm in cosmic history so far: it is still standing. But now the events of Ragnarǫk become so damaging or distressing to the world-tree that it can no longer remain passive. Yggdrasill shakes, groaning as it does so, and I am inclined to read this action as deliberate on Yggdrasill's part: it is as if the physical world is attempting to shrug off the cultural world that clings to it, that depends on it. Yggdrasill—standing here for the whole biosphere in a manner reminiscent of Lovelock's image of Gaia rejecting humanity as a form of self-defense—is itself turning against the organisms that have been responsible for making the *heimr* effectively uninhabitable (for themselves, as well as for their nondivine/nonhuman Others). Yggdrasill's great shuddering can represent the final collapse of the Æsir's hard-won edifice of purification that kept them separate from the rest of the world. When the "giant becomes free" in the last line of the stanza, we are presumably to understand its referent to be either Loki or (less likely) the wolf Fenrir—both of whom have previously been bound by the Æsir, both of whom are hybrid beings, both of whom are profoundly Other at this point of the narrative, precisely because the Æsir have made them so and worked to keep them so. But once these hybrids are roaming the earth, once the Other is no longer suppressed, the gods' idea of a world structured according to the modern constitution becomes untenable. The hybrids they have produced in the act of performing their work of purification now overrun the world, destroying all the boundaries that the gods were relying on them to enforce. The absolute collapse of the Æsir's world and their worldview follows quickly.

Thus, Ragnarǫk is an example of Kate Rigby's idea that "Apocalypse . . . is not necessarily synonymous with the real or imagined end of *the* world; it can imply, rather, the end of *a* world, which is to say the end of a particular practice, or set of practices, of world-making. As an unveiling, moreover, 'the apocalyptic event,' as James Berger defines it, 'must in its destructive moment clarify and illuminate the true nature of what has been brought to an end.' Potentially, this unveiling can become a trigger for transformation."[12] Since what is left in *Vǫluspá*'s Ragnarǫk narrative is a sequence of fights that does not conclude until all the gods, all their monstrous opponents, and apparently almost every other being in the universe is dead, the prospects for a transformative outcome to Ragnarǫk at first seem bleak. Stanza 55 brings the curtain down on the world and a definitive end to the Æsir's history with a striking image of geological, meteorological, and even astronomical flux, suggesting a return to the chaos out of which the cosmos was created in the first place:

> The sun turns black, land sinks into the sea,
> the bright stars vanish from the sky;
> steam rises up in the conflagration,
> hot flame plays high against heaven itself.
> (*Vǫluspá* [K] 55; 54 in Larrington)[13]

Entropy has done its thing. Things have fallen apart. The End.

The Postapocalyptic Pastoral and Its Problems

But it is not the end. The narrator of *Vǫluspá* takes stock for a moment, repeating the stanza that has served as a refrain for the Ragnarǫk section of the poem and that concludes with the claim that she "sees further forward into the fate of the powers, the doom of the victory-gods."[14] Then, the image of the earth sinking into the sea is reversed and a new world is born:

> She sees, coming up a second time,
> earth from the ocean, eternally green;
> the waterfalls plunge, an eagle soars above them,
> over the mountain hunting fish.
> (*Vǫluspá* [K] 57; 56 in Larrington)[15]

This stanza, to my mind one of the most beautiful in all Old Norse poetry, presents us with a beguiling, almost Romantic vision of a pristine world of Nature unsullied by human activity. The new world is *iðjagrœnn*—probably this word means "green forever," although the element *iðja-* is related to a verb and a noun that connote activity, business, prosperity; the Middle English cognate *i-the* is glossed as "to thrive." In a "green" reading of *Vǫluspá,* therefore, the new world that the *vǫlva* describes would be viewed with an approving eye. If Ragnarǫk has come about because of the failure of the Æsir's plan for the management of the "natural world," then this vision of a postdivine future suggests that, absent the deleterious effects of the gods' modernistic culture, there is the possibility that the rest of creation will get a chance to thrive, to live according to their natures in harmony with Nature. No longer does the eagle have to worry that the fish it pursues may turn out to be a trickster deity in disguise: from now on, a fish will just be a fish. We are accustomed as ecocritics to seek out textual passages that give us glimpses of a world-beyond-us or world-without-us, to view these accounts of Nature with an approving eye and to take pleasure in them. If *Vǫluspá* ended with its evocation of the green world, we might then read the whole poem as an ecological fable with a "happy" ending. The gods—standing in for humans—have an unhealthy, unsustainable relationship with Nature which eventually proves their undoing. But in the end, Nature is triumphant: the "natural" order of things is restored, and the nonhuman world enjoys its day in the sun.

Once more, however, *Vǫluspá* confounds these expectations by not ending on this note of ecological hopefulness. For, though we believed them all to have perished at Ragnarǫk, it turns out that some of the gods have survived to return and repopulate the world:

The Æsir find one another on Iðavǫllr
and they converse about the mighty Earth-girdler [Jǫrmungandr]
and Fimbultýr's ancient runes.
  (Vǫluspá [K] 58; 57 in Larrington)[16]

We do not learn who these Æsir are until stanzas 60 and 61—they are Baldr
and Hǫðr, the two arguably blameless gods whose deaths preceded Ragnarǫk
proper, and Hœnir, about whom we know very little—but we do learn immediately something of the nature of the world that they will inhabit:

There will be found again in the grass
the wonderful golden chequers,
those which they possessed in the bygone days.

Without sowing the fields will grow,
all evil will be healed, Baldr will come;
Hǫðr and Baldr will settle down in Hroptr's victory-homesteads,
the slain gods are well—do you know yet, or what?
  (Vǫluspá [K] 59–60; 58–59 in Larrington)[17]

It seems that the new gods will begin their habitation of the new world in
much the same manner that the old gods occupied the old world: the symbolically pregnant discovery in the grass of the golden chess pieces that they had
owned in the past predicts the advent of a new golden age of leisure for the
chosen few. Fields will grow crops without cultivation, recalling the narratives
that figure Vínland as an earthly paradise, a land of grapes and self-sown wheat.
The new world will provide, and these worthy gods will be free to enjoy leisure,
to reflect on past deeds, and to dwell in peace and considerable comfort:

A hall she sees standing, fairer than the sun,
thatches with gold, at Gimlé;
there the noble fighting-bands will dwell
and enjoy the days of their lives in pleasure.
  (Vǫluspá [K] 62; 61 in Larrington)[18]

The gods will inhabit a golden house; they will have dominion; they will "enjoy
the days of their lives in pleasure." These vignettes very much resemble the
ersatz pastoral of the golden age in stanzas 7 through 9 of the poem, even down
to the formulaic opening *Hittusk æsir / á Iðavelli* shared between stanzas 7

and 58. Clearly, the renewal of the world also brings about a quick renewal of living standards for those who have for whatever reason been allowed a second chance at world-building.

In *Vafþrúðnismál,* but not in *Vǫluspá,* the tally of Ragnarǫk survivors includes two humans who will repopulate the mortal world. Their names are Líf and Lífþrasir ("life" and something like "life-striver"), and they seem to be content with a simpler, more ecological mode of existence than the reborn Æsir:

> Líf and Lífþrasir [will survive], and they will hide
> in Hoddmímir's wood;
> they will have the morning dew for food;
> from them generations will spring. (*Vafþrúðnismál* 45)[19]

Líf has the distinction of being apparently the only woman to survive the apocalypse. Her relations with Lífþrasir, their sylvan dwelling place, and their basic diet are all strikingly "natural" by comparison to the Æsir's rebooted civilization. Perhaps Líf and Lífþrasir embody the possibility of a hopeful, and sustainable, post-Ragnarǫk future for humans. Their names certainly suggest that there is a life force beyond the gods' dominion that cannot be extinguished even by the end of the world. Nothing else is known about these figures, however: even Snorri can do no better than repeat the information that *Vafþrúðnismál* gives about them.[20] The narrator of *Vǫluspá* makes no attempt to integrate the renewal of human life into her account of a second golden age for the Æsir.

As discussed above, the golden age myth complex necessarily carries with it the knowledge that the golden age will end: it is always a trope of nostalgia and a way of signaling the inadequacy of the present in the face of an idealized past. In this instance, it reminds me of Latour's comments on the moderns' inability to conceive of "their future," which "has never been contemplated face to face, since it has always been the future of someone fleeing their past looking *backward,* not *forward.*"[21] The *vǫlva*'s description of the second golden age of the Norse gods is a peculiar brand of nostalgic futurity. Her tone is somehow elegiac even as she indicates that the reborn Æsir will lead lives of pleasure: presumably our sense of unease is triggered by our memory of the first golden age, its end, and its aftermath. We expect the golden age to end, and so it is no surprise to read *Vǫluspá*'s final stanza, in which the gods' prospects are made out to be a good deal less rosy than they previously seemed:

There comes the shadow-dark dragon flying,
the gleaming serpent, up from Dark-of-moon Hills;
Níðhǫggr flies over the plain, in his pinions
he carries corpses; now she [i.e., the vǫlva] will sink down.
    (Vǫluspá [K] 63; 62 in Larrington)[22]

The last image that Vǫluspá offers is not of the Æsir enjoying a new integrated ecological existence in a world cleansed of all sins; it does not even
leave us with a picture of their privileged, aristocratic existence in a hall
made of gold. Rather, the poem ends with the sight of a monstrous Other,
the serpentine dragon Níðhǫggr, carrying corpses in his talons, flying across
the vǫllr—the same tamed and bounded landscape as the one in which the
Æsir are accustomed to meet and perform their works of culture. This symbol of bestial evil at the end of the poem suggests that the promise of eternal
happiness offered by the second golden age is illusory: evil is still present
in the world—we recall that Níðhǫggr was last seen tearing apart the bodies of humans in stanza 38. Although Ragnarǫk and its aftermath give the
impression of offering catharsis, the chance of a fresh start in a world that has
been wiped clean of the Æsir's misdeeds, there is nothing to suggest that the
returning gods' mode of life will be any more "ecological" or "sustainable"
than it had been before. They are still interested in superimposing themselves
onto a natural world that serves as a resource to be exploited in furtherance of
their economic and social interests. They still very much like shiny things that
evoke the earlier golden age's luxury and decadence. And the ominous sound
of Níðhǫggr's wings beating across the sky fills the audience's ears as the vǫlva
takes her leave of us. We do not anticipate a happy ending for Baldr, Hǫðr,
and the gang any more than we anticipated the old gods surviving Ragnarǫk
or look forward to sudden salvation from the horrors of anthropogenic global
warming in our own future.

In Hauksbók's version of Vǫluspá, however, the prospect of such salvation
is held out briefly by a short stanza that the Codex Regius text lacks, and that
many scholars believe is a late addition to the poem's narrative material—an
addition at the hands of a poet-scribe with an explicitly Christian agenda:
"Then the powerful one comes in mighty judgment, / strong from above, the
one who rules everything" (Vǫluspá [H] 57).[23] As I discussed in chapter 2,
Vǫluspá's religious status has long been controversial: it is the fullest and most
detailed account of pagan cosmology in the Poetic Edda, yet it also seems
to bear the clearest traces of having absorbed some tenets and images from

Christian eschatology. *Hauksbók*'s "mighty one," who comes down from the sky to rule the whole world after the pagan cosmos has been obliterated, has normally been interpreted as a Christ figure. If so, this reference is much more explicitly Christian than the other echoes of the newer religion's teachings that we find in the poem, and it has important ramifications for our interpretation of its concluding section. It takes a mighty one, somebody strong in judgment, powerful—the insistent emphasis of Christ's power makes him sound somewhat dictatorial—to rule the world that the old gods failed to rule adequately, as proven by the simple fact that their mode of existence is no more. The advent of *inn ríki*'s sole rule provides an alternate sociopolitical paradigm for the new world to employ. The poem seems to suggest that the Christian model of stewardship or dominion over Nature—an authoritarian, hierarchical, patriarchal, singular power structure—should replace the old, failed model of authoritarian, hierarchical, patriarchal, but diversified power structure that the Æsir employed. The pagan cosmos was finite. A Christian cosmos with Christ as its ruler, *Hauksbók* suggests, offers the one thing that paganism cannot provide: the hope of permanence, of everything being all right forever.

But even that promise is an illusion. *Hauksbók*'s Christ stanza is not the end of the poem, either. Níðhǫggr returns here just as in the Codex Regius text. The dragon will come back to haunt a Christ-centered cosmos just as it will to one ruled by the pantheon of the Æsir. Nothing has changed. The Æsir have fallen into the trap of what Latour calls the "strong, ever so modernist, temptation to exclaim: 'Let's flee as before and *have our past future back*' instead of saying: 'Let's stop fleeing, break for good with our future, turn our back, finally, to our past, and explore our new prospects.'"[24] The Æsir's future offers only the prospect of more of the same. And everybody else in the cosmos is dead.

What Ragnarǫk Tells Us about the Anthropocene and Vice Versa

The goal of this chapter and the one that preceded it has been to read the Ragnarǫk myths as myths of an anthropogenic apocalypse analogous to the environmental catastrophe that attends the Anthropocene and that is accelerating exponentially in the era of global warming, the by-products of nuclear technology, overpopulation, and mass extinctions. I identify six key factors that link Ragnarǫk to our own experience of the Anthropocene and its slow apocalypse.

1. The Ragnarǫk myths attempt to make sense of and impose
order on a massively complex set of phenomena.

Adam Trexler asks of modern and contemporary literary works that treat aspects of the Anthropocene: "How can a global process, spanning millennia, be made comprehensible to human imagination, with its limited sense of place and time?"[25] I suggest that *Vǫluspá,* in particular, makes a very good attempt at this project. Myth is a form of discourse that deals with universals rather than specifics and that uses timeless narratives to explore temporally bounded concerns. In Mircea Eliade's terms, myth deals with the *illud tempus,* now-and-always time, although in their telling myths are also always interacting with their tellers and audiences in the here and now.[26] Thus, *Vǫluspá*'s remarkable manipulation of scale effects—its ability to zoom in and zoom out, to tell the whole history of the cosmos from a viewpoint that is both microscopic and macroscopic, to keep both now and always in its sight—offers considerable narrative advantages over (for example) realist prose fiction and other nonmythic forms.

Ragnarǫk is an enormously complex system of causes and effects in which a huge array of actants—divine, human, monstrous, geological and meteorological, animal, vegetable, and mineral—are implicated. Just as we cannot consider the technological advances of the Industrial Revolution in isolation from the social and political situation of eighteenth- and nineteenth-century Britain, or the technical development of the atomic bomb without considering contemporary American foreign policy, and as both of these trajectories of the Anthropocene intersect with the trajectories of countless individuals and groups, their choices and decisions, so Ragnarǫk blurs distinctions between individual and collective responsibility, accident and design, where events end and where they begin.

Just as Stephen Hartman and his coauthors write of our own environmental predicament, Ragnarǫk is "not primarily an ecological crisis, though its ramifications are far reaching within ecological systems; rather it is a crisis of culture. . . . The processes by which societies negotiate environmental challenges and respond to threats are neither natural nor a matter of scientific understanding in the classic sense. They are cultural transactions explicable via modes of inquiry traditionally encompassed within the social sciences and humanities."[27] The destruction of the physical world at Ragnarǫk is not a "natural disaster." Ragnarǫk shows, rather, that cultural causes produce effects in and upon the nonhuman world that feed back into further cultural responses to what become perceived or figured as natural phenomena.

It is the quality of these responses that determines whether environmental conditions improve or worsen and whether the progress toward disaster is hastened or retarded.

2. There is no tipping point: we do not know when Ragnarǫk begins.

One of the questions that my analysis of the Ragnarǫk myths has failed to answer is "when does Ragnarǫk begin?" I have suggested that it is impossible to find a single tipping point in the sequence of events that can be identified as the origin of Ragnarǫk, the true beginning of the end. The most commonly offered "solution"—that it is the murder of Baldr that precipitates Ragnarǫk—does not, in my view, hold up: something either caused Loki to arrange Baldr's downfall or at least set the conditions in which this act could take place. And what would have happened if the Æsir had not sought vengeance on Loki by killing his son and using his son's entrails to bind him in agony? It is possible to see the loosing of Loki's bonds as the start of Ragnarǫk proper, the point at which there is no possibility of averting the catastrophe—so the act of binding is an essential precondition for Ragnarǫk to take place, and it is the Æsir's choice to impose this punishment on him.

These events are important, but we can identify some seeds of the Æsir's downfall as belonging to the very earliest periods of their inhabiting the newly created world. In reading the golden age and its unexplained collapse as a document of the Æsir's attempt to impose a modern constitution on the world, of enforcing a separation between Nature and Society and between themselves and an Other that is always figured as hostile, something to be controlled, exploited, and dominated by the gods, I propose that we find another root cause of Ragnarǫk. The gods' antagonism of the giants explains why the giants will fight against the gods—and this antagonism is not innate, but rather absolutely the construction of the Æsir's desire to ring-fence their own mode of existence from the rest of creation. At the same time, we cannot say that the progression we see in the narrative from golden age to apocalypse is directly causal. We simply do not know when Ragnarǫk begins, because it has always already been unfolding.

Likewise, the quest to identify the origins of the Anthropocene in a particular era or even moment in time looks increasingly like the wrong question to pursue. Humanity has always already been having an impact on the planetary environment far in disproportion to the number of individuals belonging to the species—at least as far back as the beginnings of agriculture. Rather than seeing the Anthropocene as a static phenomenon with a single point of origin and a single trajectory, we should acknowledge instead the Anthropocene as the totality of a succession of points of origin, of different human projects of world-making—agriculture, Christianity, the Enlightenment, consumer capitalism, nuclear technology, among many other possible culprits—coalescing and collapsing into one another, giving birth to new modes of existence, none of which has halted the Anthropocene's slow apocalypse. "As the contingent emergent sum of innumerable and probably incalculable processes happening across the earth at divergent timescales," writes Timothy Clark, "a 'tipping point' per se is neither unitary nor representable in any one, sufficient image."[28] The end of the world is a process rather than an event.

Ragnarǫk is conventionally imagined as a sudden and singular cataclysm—and of course on one level it is: the land does indeed collapse into the sea; the gods are all killed in a climactic battle with their enemies. But an ecocritical reading of these myths suggests that the fast apocalypse of the very final moments of the universe is only part of a much longer, slower history—one that we only identify as an apocalypse when it is far too late. It is always already far too late, for the Norse gods and for us. Ragnarǫk is the totality of the gods' past, present, and future, as the Anthropocene is ours. As Andrew McMurry puts it,

> Ours may be understood as an apocalypse without origin or destination. It
> may have begun to unpack with the advent of the junk bond, the A-bomb, the
> concentration camp, the internal combustion engine, the corporation, or even
> the scientific method; and it may cease only when most of those things are no
> more. So then: is this apocalypse I have described really an apocalypse, or just
> the motion of history itself? For the multitudes who have died, are dying, and
> will die under modern history's heavy feet there is no significant difference.
> Perhaps it is time to ask ourselves the questions we have foolishly assumed
> this same history has already settled. Who says the human presence on this
> earth was ever sustainable? Why do we continue to believe so strongly in our
> competency to manage the risks we compound daily? Where is this secret
> heart of history we trust has been beating? What precisely leads us to believe
> our world is not perishing? Why isn't this the Apocalypse?[29]

3. We do not know where we stand in relation to the chronology of Ragnarǫk/the Anthropocene.

Following on from the idea that a slow apocalypse has a destabilizing effect on our conceptions of past, present, and future is the question of where the gods are located in the chronology of the cosmos—what is the mythic now from which we learn about Ragnarǫk in Vǫluspá. Vǫluspá's weird and bewitching narrative structure owes much to the poem's manipulation of tenses.[30] In the now of the poem, Óðinn has sought out the *vǫlva,* presumably as part of his futile quest to learn information about the end of the world that will be sufficient for him to prevent it. In several framing stanzas, the *vǫlva* speaks directly to Óðinn in the present of their meeting. Much of the Æsir's history has already taken place: the creation of the world, the first golden age, the war with the Vanir—all the events that have occurred in the first half of the poem are in the *vǫlva*'s memory of what has come before. Baldr's death and its aftermath are similarly narrated in the past tense. Stanza 40—the verse in which the sun turns black and the weather becomes disastrous—switches to the present tense, suggesting that these developments might be concurrent with the scenario of Óðinn's encounter with the seeress. Thereafter, *Vǫluspá*'s narrative oscillates between present and future tenses: we find it impossible to pin down what is happening now and what is yet to come. It seems probable that Óðinn has come to the *vǫlva* in the wake of Baldr's death, but beyond that, it is hard to place the episode of the narration of *Vǫluspá* into any conventional chronology. Óðinn learns a great deal about the end of the world; but he cannot know when it will happen. The *vǫlva* takes some delight in taunting Óðinn about his ignorance: seven times in the Codex Regius poem she utters the refrain *vituð er enn—eða hvat?* (Do you know yet—or what?).[31] She challenges Óðinn to admit the limitations of his knowledge; he always needs more information than he has or she will give him. At the same time, Óðinn always already knows the truth, the fact of Ragnarǫk's coming. He does not need to ask, but he cannot stop himself from asking.

Óðinn's predicament calls to mind Morton's claim that one of the main disorienting effects of consciously living in the Anthropocene is a "deep shuddering of temporality," the necessity of questioning of "whether the end of the world is already happening, or whether perhaps it might already have taken place."[32] This is precisely the question for which Óðinn seeks an answer in his interview with the *vǫlva*. It is probably the wrong question. If the Anthropocene (or Ragnarǫk) has always been immanent, its imminence becomes a moot point. We should be asking: since the world has ended—is ending—will end, what shall we do? How do we live under these conditions? What is the best life still available to us?

4. The modern constitution is implicated in both Ragnarǫk and the Anthropocene.

"Modernity's 'promise' now appears threatening and unsustainable," writes Paul Alberts of the Anthropocene.[33] This promise was a myth, one of history's many golden ages which, as the Æsir learn too well, exist only in retrospect. Regarding the pagan Norse gods as moderns—participants in what Latour defines as the quintessentially modern project of "guarantee[ing] Nature its transcendent dimension from the fabric of Society"—is an act of against-the-grain reading that may seem perverse to some. It should certainly be anachronistic, since we usually believe that premodern cultures, like that of the pagan Norse people, should, again in Latour's terms, depend on "the continuous connection between the natural order and the social order . . . which . . . kept the premoderns from being able to modify the one without modifying the other."[34] The gods' mode of existence is however predicated on a clean and clear (if always fallible) separation of the cosmos into their social order and the natural order to which they attempt to confine the Other. This Other is most importantly personified as the giants, and the Æsir's construction of Miðgarðr and banishment of their antagonists to the far beyond constitutes an ongoing act of purification, the failure of which is a key aspect of Ragnarǫk. The gods' reliance on Loki—a profoundly hybrid figure—to enforce their standards of purity, or to put things right when they go wrong, is also problematic: they end up attempting to deal with the negative aspects of Loki's hybridity by segregating him and his monstrous children from their world of culture, to sequester him and thus neutralize his malignant powers.

Loki and his offspring are the products of a hybridity that is an affront to the gods' notions of purity. They transcend conventional norms of time and space—the world serpent Jǫrmungandr, who circles the whole world and thus is in all places at once but may never be seen in his totality from a viewpoint in the same dimension, is the clearest example of this. Loki's ability to move between worlds, to adopt different identities that confound norms of gender and even species, is another. The gods try to contain these hybrid hypermonsters, but they can only be contained up to the point when they can no longer be contained, and that point is Ragnarǫk. Loki, Fenrir, and Jǫrmungandr cannot be "made safe" by confining them to geographically remote areas or by enacting technologically advanced security measures. In this way, they resemble nuclear waste, that quintessential output of modernity: the byproducts of atomic fission are the products of human ingenuity whose being far exceeds their original point of manufacture or intended use. Nuclear waste is massively distributed in time and space—no matter where, when, and how the material is stored, its radioactivity is always nonlocal and immensely long lasting: its half-life measured in millennia, nuclear waste is not going "away" any time soon. It may well be the only truly enduring legacy of modernity.

5. We do not know whom to blame,
but we want someone to blame.

The concept of the Anthropocene is founded in the notion of blame: something has gone wrong with the world, and responsibility for this wrongness rests not with God, an impersonal fate, or a blindly disinterested Nature but with human beings, whether conceived of as a whole species or subdivided into more or less culpable parties. Peter Rudiak-Gould gives four propositions—by no means mutually exclusive—that account for the possible rhetorics of blame in the face of anthropogenic climate change.[35] First, climate change invites ubiquitous blame. *Everyone* is to blame, because none of us—from the richest to the poorest, from the most pious ecowarrior to the most nefarious climate-change denier—contributes nothing to carbon dioxide emissions. We are the problem—it's in our nature. Likewise, we could place blame for Ragnarǫk indiscriminately at the feet of all its actors. The dualistic system that operates in the god-ordained cosmos is maintained by all who participate in it: the giants are faithless, violent, and acquisitive, just like the gods. The goddesses are implicated in Ragnarǫk by their passivity and helplessness just as much as the male gods' futile activity renders them unable to stop the avalanche of Ragnarǫk once it has been set in motion.

But Rudiak-Gould's second proposition proposes that climate change also invites ubiquitous *blamelessness.* He cites Cass Sunstein, who writes that "warmer temperatures are a product not of an identifiable perpetrator or any human face, but of the interaction between nature and countless decisions by countless actors. . . . There are no obvious devils or demons here—no human beings who actually intend to produce the harms associated with climate change."[36] We could say that Ragnarǫk happens because it was always going to happen; perhaps the end of a world is a precondition of world-building in the first place. The apocalypse may simply be an effect of entropy in the universe. Physical events and processes in the cosmos may be kept separate from the actions of the gods and their adversaries in the cultural sphere. But this proposition is counterintuitive in the case of Norse mythology, in which we do have an obvious "devil"—or at least an obvious scapegoat—in the person of Loki. Loki's treatment in the Ragnarǫk myths suggests that Rudiak-Gould's third proposition—that climate change invites selective blame—is in operation. Since we know that Loki's actions are malicious, capricious, and destructive by design—since he knows what he's doing—we can assign him the perpetrator role in the Ragnarǫk narrative, and make the Æsir into his victims. But in my analysis of the myths, I have tended to place blame on the Æsir as a group, since it is they who most obviously benefit from the conditions out of which Ragnarǫk develops, resembling the remarkably small "clique of white men" in the nineteenth century who Malm and Hornborg suggest may be uniquely and directly responsible for founding a carbon-based capitalistic society.[37] But placing blame on Loki as an individual remains a valid interpretation, even at the risk of scapegoating a single character for the sins of a collective—or, better, for the flaws and illogic of a particular mode of existence. As Rudiak-Gould puts it in his final proposition, "Climate change can make whatever and whoever we want blameworthy. Bias feeds on ambiguity, and given the material and moral complexity of climate change, there is more than enough ambiguity to go around."[38] It is convenient for the gods to blame Loki for Ragnarǫk, just as it is convenient for some to blame nineteenth-century industrialists, or car drivers, or meat eaters for global warming. It serves their purpose, but like climate change, Ragnarǫk is too complicated and ambiguous a system to be reduced to a singular point of origin or blamed on any one of the many individuals or groups who are implicated in it. As Roy Scranton writes of the Anthropocene, placing blame on any one entity or group is merely an exercise in buck-passing: "The enemy isn't *out there* somewhere—the enemy is ourselves. Not as individuals, but as a collective. A system. A hive."[39]

6. Ragnarǫk and the Anthropocene are both gendered phenomena.

The actors in the Ragnarǫk-mythos are predominantly male, especially in the story told in *Vǫluspá*.[40] The female figures we encounter—with the important exception of the narrator herself—are few, passive, and often objectified: there is the mysterious Gullveig whom the Æsir burn three times, though she still lives (*Vǫluspá* 21); Freyja, named only by reference to her husband (she is referred to as *Óðs mey*, "Óðr's girl," in stanza 25), is mentioned as the price of the gods' bargain with the giant builder. Frigg, wife of Óðinn and mother of Baldr, is defined by these relationships to men, and appears first as an active but impotent advocate for Baldr's safety and then as a passively grieving figure after his and Óðinn's deaths (stanzas 33 and 52). The three women from giant-land who appear as a somewhat inexplicable threat to the Æsir's peace of mind or way of life in stanza 8 are doubly Other by dint of both their gender and their ethnicity, while another woman, the crone who nurtures the race of wolves during Ragnarǫk, is similarly aligned with the gods' monstrous adversaries (stanza 39). The three Norns, who appear in the twentieth verse of *Vǫluspá*, are perhaps the most active female characters in the poem, as they have the important task of assigning fates to mortals, potentially disrupting the linear chronology from creation to destruction that the male Æsir oversee.

The goddesses are nowhere to be found in either the first or second golden age of the Æsir. Ragnarǫk is a process that is attributable solely to the actions of male figures. The Æsir's patriarchy is, moreover, one that has significant, though indistinct, problems with women, and these problems can manifest themselves in gendered violence. The Æsir's constitution assigns the feminine to the sphere of the Other; Loki's ability to transgress gender boundaries is yet another sign of the hybridity that the gods both fear and need in him.

It seems intuitively accurate and politically important to regard the *anthropos* of Anthropocene as gendered male beyond its neutral designation as "human being." The Anthropocene has not been an age of people in general; it is an age of *men.* Although individual women may have contributed in many ways to humanity's deleterious impact on the Earth, they have overwhelmingly done so in patriarchal contexts. Certainly, the Enlightenment, the Industrial Revolution, the rise of the corporation, and the advent of the atomic bomb are all developments in which men are implicated to a surpassing degree and from which women have been largely marginalized. We might adopt another new coinage, the *Androcene,* as yet another variant on the concept of Anthropocene, one that confidently asserts that the end of the world is the work of men and signals our rejection—as Claire Colebrook and Jami Weinstein suggest we must—of the homogenous, heroicized, patriarchal "'anthropos' of a pre-postmodern, prefeminist, critique."[41]

How to Prevent Ragnarǫk

Ragnarǫk and the Anthropocene both arise from what Plumwood has called "hyper-separation" and Latour "hyper-incommensurability"[42]—the logical endpoint of the dualistic thinking that results in a hierarchical power dynamic between men (or people, though men have historically been the main problem) and a reified Nature-as-Other/Other-as-Nature complex, from which we develop an "illusory sense of autonomy."[43] The central thread that runs through the Norse myths is the conflict between the Æsir—the In-group dwelling at the center of the cosmos, enjoying the trappings of civilization—and the giants, who are figured only as the gods' antagonists, banished to the peripheries and the hostile wilderness, perennially occupying the object position relative to the gods' subject position. They are a hostile Other who must be kept separate at all costs from the Æsir's central places, unless they have something—a woman, a certain magic object, some numinous knowledge—that the gods wish to possess or exploit. But the separation between gods and giants, between In-group and Out-group, and between the Society and Nature that they represent is not an innate, intrinsic, or natural aspect of the cosmos. Good and Evil, Nature and Society, Us and Them—these structures are all constructions, all of which need constant maintenance if they are to remain standing. The Æsir's great fortification, Miðgarðr, is a superb symbol for the hyperseparation that the gods believe is the best way to maintain themselves in their mode of existence, to ensure that their golden age of purification will endure.

Yet there never was any real ontological separation between the gods and the giants. These two groups are kin with each other, enmeshed in a complex web of naturecultural relationships that simultaneously obscure and reveal the fact that gods and giants are of the same nature. This recalls Nikolas Kompridis's assertion that ecological modes of living demand of us first that we recognize the world as "my kin, my twin. [Acknowledging] the world as one's 'kin' and 'twin' is to see that a change in one's condition is coextensive with a change in the condition of the world."[44] For Donna Haraway, "kin" means "something other/more than entities tied by ancestry or genealogy. . . . Kin-making is making persons, not necessarily as individuals or humans."[45] Although gods, giants, and the rest of the cosmos—down to the very mountains that were fashioned out of Ymir's bones—are indeed related to each other genealogically in Norse myth, the project of kin-making in the Anthropocene demands us to pay special attention to those things that seem furthest from our mode of existence, seem on the surface least like family to us.

Let us propose, therefore, that the first step in preventing Ragnarǫk would have been not to build Miðgarðr to keep the giants out of the gods' green home, but instead to establish a mode of existence that embraced what had previously been rejected as Other as an intrinsic aspect of the self. Going even further back in time, the Æsir could have refrained from killing Ymir, whose death seems to be an ultimate cause for the giants' hostility—but in that case, would the universe have come into being at all? Perhaps not in the form that it appears in the current cosmology, but life had already quickened in the void and presumably something would have come of it. At any rate, this act of primal violence establishes the preconditions for the separation of, and hostility between, gods and giants, and the first act of purification that asserted the Æsir's control over the world-beyond-the-Æsir, their first act of domination of a Nature of their own creation, the first transferal of the world from the ontological realm of being to that of resource. It arguably would have been better to leave the world unmade than to make it in the form that produces Ragnarǫk.

To prevent Ragnarǫk, then, the gods would have needed to pay attention to the questions that the feminist economic critics who write as J. K. Gibson-Graham pose with regard to regional development in the Anthropocene: "How [do] we (that is all the human/nonhuman participants in the becoming world) organize our lives (or how [does] life [organize] us) to thrive in porously bounded spaces in which there is some degree of interconnection, a distinctively diverse economy and ecologies, multiple path-dependent trajectories of transformation and inherited forms of rule[?]"[46] The boundaries—spatial, ethnic, and ideological—between the Æsir and their antagonists were always porous, which the gods viewed not as an opportunity for the enacting of new, heterarchical practices of living and being together in the world but as an affront to their sense of hyperincommensurability with their Others. (And, it should be noted, the giants do not necessarily practice more ecological modes of existence: their constant figuring as the gods' Out-group, their alignment with the nonhuman, and their object status in the narratives distorts our impression of the giants, tempting us to identify them with Nature against their will.)

Aidan Davison proposes that our goal in the Anthropocene must be "to enact human life as a political distribution and differentiation of agency within human-other-than-human wholes . . . to open up ontologies of intermingling, interagency, and co-production that can guide us past modernity's mirrored horizons, and the reckless narcissism they cultivate."[47] But as ardent modernists, the Æsir are far from prepared or equipped to undertake such experiments in living: their whole mode of existence is predicated on the maintenance—the maintenance at all costs, up to and including the end of the world—of the subject/object binary, of jealously guarding everything that allows them to pretend that there is a world which can revolve around them. They are not up to the task that Latour sets us: "Far from trying to 'reconcile' or 'combine' nature and society, the task, the crucial political task, is on the contrary to distribute agency as far and in as differentiated a way as possible—until, that is, we have thoroughly lost any relation between those two concepts of object and subject."[48]

The gods need to abandon their entwined projects of wall-building and category maintenance, their obsessive fear of contamination by the Other, and their protocapitalist pursuit of surplus wealth. In a more tentative, experimental mode of existence, founded in the principles of mutual belonging, not separation, and openness rather than reticence in the face of the world-beyond-them, the Æsir might have found Loki gave them fewer problems. Loki's role in the myths is continually problematic because he always crosses the boundaries that the gods wish to create and troubles the categories that these boundaries are supposed to enforce. He is both god and giant, man and animal, man and woman; queer, rather than straight or gay or bi. Or, rather, he is constantly oscillating within and between these categories, bringing their validity, utility, the very fact of their existence, into question. No reading of the Ragnarǫk mythos can ignore the fact that Loki's role in the death of Baldr is an act of pure malice or that, in general, his ethics are at best questionable. Nonetheless, another way to avoid Ragnarǫk might to be embrace—rather than simultaneously to suppress and destroy, as the Æsir do—the hybridity, diversity, and belonging-potential that Loki represents, since he is the only one of their number who can move with true freedom across the ontological zones they are so determined to uphold. The gods believe that they can neuter Loki's threat by binding him; I argue that they would have been more successful in preventing Ragnarǫk if they had let him run free, if they had been able to find a way to accommodate themselves to Loki's existence and the hybridity that he represents, rather than seeking to confine and repress it.

Finally, Ragnarǫk might be prevented if the gods' society were reconfigured on more gender-equitable lines. Without giving any credence to the essentializing idea that women are somehow closer to or more in touch with Nature than men are, the absence of the goddesses from positions of responsibility or influence, their consistent lack of agency, is an important component of the Æsir's failure to prevent the end of the world. Patriarchy and its attendant modes of existence—monotheistic religions, monarchy, capitalism, communism, and so on—have proven over millennia to be incapable of providing the conditions in which humanity can flourish on an equitable footing with its nonhuman cohabitants. The (male) gods' problems with gender—manifest in their strange, freaked-out reaction to the arrival of three giant women near the beginning of *Vǫluspá,* among other episodes—are yet another effect of their paralyzing dependence on the binary structures of their constructed, and jealously protected, worldview. In Snorri's version of the myth, we should remember, it is only the goddess Frigg who attempts to take proactive, positive measures to protect Baldr and bring him back from the dead—and she does so by engaging with the whole nonhuman/nondivine world. The male gods think first of vengeance, and it is their vengeance on Loki that will trigger the final stages of Ragnarǫk. We do not know in what ways a Gynocene—an epoch in which women's activities determined the fate of the planet—would differ from the Androcene; nor do we know how a matriarchal pantheon might have avoided the apocalypse. But in either case, putting women in charge would hardly have produced a *worse* result.

It is too late for us to prevent the advent of the Anthropocene, just as it has always already been too late for the gods to prevent Ragnarǫk. However, *Vǫluspá* shows us that the end of the world—the end of the practices of world-making or the very idea of a world that can no longer be sustained as much as a particular physical environment—can lead to the beginning of a new world. It is on this new world, a world created within and out of the Anthropocene, that our attention should now be focused. The Earth still exists; we are still here. Yet worlds keep ending, and will keep ending for as long as we maintain our delusions about the nature of this world and the possibility of our mastery of it. The second coming of the Æsir does not bring with it a revised constitution that shows the gods have learned from their mistakes and are determined not to repeat them; rather, every indication suggests that they will model their new world on the society of their ancestors, the same mode of existence that resulted in their deaths, and the death and suffering of countless others, the first time around. The revived gods remain backward-looking rather than forward-looking, appealing to tradition rather than looking for innovative new modes of life. Women are absent from their society; Nature is once again a passive backdrop onto which the gods project their desires for dominion. The gods' new world is the old one with fewer people in it: fewer people, but still the dreadful death-dragon, Níðhǫggr. There is no sign that the apocalyptic cycle has been broken. Nothing has changed. Anthropocene humanity must do better than the Norse gods, or we will share their fate.

Conclusion

NEAR THE START OF THIS BOOK, I found inspiration in Vin Nardizzi's assertion that "medieval and Renaissance ecocriticisms can help to imagine for our world a range of futures unfolding from banned, censored and forgotten pasts."[1] Norse mythology seemed like it might offer signposts toward a particularly rich or unusual set of such retrofutures, I thought, because it originates prior to the major fracture points of Western culture that have most frequently been blamed for the anthropogenic ecological catastrophes of the twentieth and twenty-first centuries. It predates the Industrial Revolution, the Enlightenment, the troubled birth of modernity wherever one places that event. We could say as much, of course, for any body of medieval literature. But Old Norse–Icelandic literature is also the product of a geographical periphery with a unique sociopolitical heritage: while always connected to Scandinavia and the wider world by strong cultural bonds, Iceland was a brand-new polity formed in a brand-new physical environment, and its identity and worldviews coalesced at a significant remove from the grand narratives of Western European history across the medieval period. Crucially, the roots of Norse mythology tap into centuries—if not millennia—of pre-Christian culture, giving us the hope of being able to interrogate early European ecological worldviews beyond the influence of Judeo-Christian traditions. In most regions of medieval Europe, paganism was so thoroughly censored or erased upon conversion to Christianity as to be effectively inaccessible to us. In Scandinavia, however, and especially in Iceland, we have a relatively full and relatively authentic record of pagan mythology that can help us to (re)construct an alternative ecopoetical trajectory for northwestern European religious culture. My starting point for this investigation was the idea that the ecological alterity of pagan Norse culture—its position on the "banned, censored and forgotten" periphery of our historical consciousnesses—might teach us something about variant ways of ecological existence from which we could learn something that might help us prepare for a less frightful future than we currently anticipate in the era of global ecological crisis. Perhaps Old Norse would save the world.

Such was my hope when I began writing this book. I expected that Norse mythology would show traces of its origins in an ecological worldview that was fundamentally different from the Western European Christian mainstream's hierarchical dualisms. I sought in these myths a Greener, more harmonious, or simply different way of looking at the relationship between people and "their environment." I took it as an article of faith—always dangerous—that Norse paganism comes from an alternate past that was somehow less anthropocentric, less authoritarian, "closer to Nature" than the disastrous, tragic, self-defeating regimes of exploitation, exhaustion, and extinction which characterize human/nonhuman relationships in what we have come to call the Anthropocene.

My faith in the fundamental Greenness of Norse mythology was largely misplaced. There are certainly differences between the Norse myths' ecopoesis and the foundational ecomyths of the Western tradition that we can identify as challenging conventional paradigms of world-building: Yggdrasill is an excellent representation of the mutual implication of all forms of life in the life of all other life forms; the creation myths reveal that a sense of the transcorporeal, embodied entanglement of all coexistents underlies the structures that are later superimposed onto the cosmos; here, humans are almost an afterthought to creation rather than the teleological purpose of the universe. Nonetheless, the overall impression that arises from an ecocritical analysis of the mythology as a whole is depressingly familiar. The world of the Æsir—the world the Æsir make *for themselves*—betrays any underlying coexistential principles in pagan ecopoesis by depending utterly upon a set of artificial structures, boundaries, and ontological hierarchies that need to be enforced and defended constantly through the expenditure of considerable resources of wealth and power. The gods occupy the subject position that human beings occupy in modernity and its antecedent worldviews, insisting upon an absolute separation of themselves from the objectified Other, whether that Other takes the form of the giants, the physical substance of the cosmos, the female, the animal, or whatever else the gods decide needs to be oppressed and exploited.

In their surviving textual forms, the Norse myths manifest an ingrained anthropocentrism. Although they do not depend explicitly upon a concept of reified Nature, the worldview that they encode effectively mirrors the human/world dualisms that are endemic to Western culture. There is precious little evidence—on the basis of the myths that are still accessible to us—to support the idea that Norse paganism was truly an "Earth-centered" religion. Perhaps these myths do not reflect the lived reality of Norse pagans; perhaps their strict, anthropocentric structuration is the product of Christian "contamination" in either the texts or the historical environments that produced them. We can't rule out that possibility, since even the most ancient textual manifestations of these myths come from a period in which paganism was confronted by, and forced to react to, the challenge offered by Christianity. Both the *Poetic Edda* and *Snorra Edda,* meanwhile, are the products of a self-consciously antiquarian interest in pagan culture among a coterie of educated Christian Icelanders in the thirteenth century. There are grounds, therefore, for saying that these myths might not be a very accurate representation of "Norse paganism," depending on what we mean by that term. But rejecting these myths as inauthentic because of a preconception about the Greenness of pagan religions is methodologically suspect and ultimately self-defeating. Without these texts we would have hardly any knowledge of the Norse gods and their doings. Moreover, we would lack the interpretative key that is essential to understanding those fragments of external evidence concerning the nature of pagan beliefs, practices, and worldviews that do survive in contexts beyond the Icelandic mythopoetic corpus.

Trying to separate pagan wheat from Christian chaff only has the effect of rendering the Norse myths even more obscure than they already are. It is a move driven by a nostalgia for a golden age of pure, uncontaminated paganism—for a world that may never have existed in the way that people like to imagine it. Often, this nostalgia has been entwined with dangerous and unjustified notions of racial or national purity. Christianity, with its geographical origins in the Middle East and its roots in Jewish culture, has often been stigmatized as a parvenu incomer to northern Europe—an invasive species that sought to smother and efface the religion of Scandinavia's native white populations. Old Norse literature and mythology were inordinately influential on the iconography and historical imaginary of the Third Reich, unfortunately, and scholars today still struggle with the fact that much foundational work in this field was carried out by men who were at best fellow travelers with Hitler's regime, and at worst committed Nazis.[2] The political appropriation of medieval Scandinavian culture continues, with far-right groups frequently adopting Norse symbols and appealing to the idea of the Nordic countries as some sort of homeland for whites, and the Viking Age as marking some sort of zenith of white culture.[3] This type of nostalgia must be rejected and challenged by all medievalists.

Jennifer Ladino, however, argues that eco-nostalgia is a concept worth holding on to: "Nostalgia can highlight the material and political dimensions of dislocations. Who knows but that it might also inspire empathy and, potentially, alert more people to a future we should take steps to avoid? . . . Like all narratives about the past, nostalgia is imperfect, incomplete, and sometimes simplistic. But then again, sometimes it is a legitimate, provocative reaction that prompts evaluation or enhances existing perspectives. Too long considered antithetical to politically progressive movements, nostalgia could be enlisted to visualize new kinds of natures and cultures."[4] While agreeing with Ladino's main point about the *potential* value of nostalgia for thinking ecocritically about displacement and disaster, I don't believe that nostalgia for the world of Norse paganism is an appropriate response to any ecologically centered reading of the Norse myths. It also runs the risk of aligning ecological nostalgia with the unsavory, dangerous, and unjustified ethnocentric fantasies that have bedeviled Norse studies throughout the twentieth century and beyond. Indeed, white separatist movements have their own Green wings, which assert that their people's proprietorial claims upon their homelands, the intrinsic connection they perceive between "blood" and "soil," make careful stewardship and conservation of "their" land and its resources a matter of considerable concern within their wider projects of social purification.[5]

Rather than being nostalgic for a lost golden age of a paganism of our own imagining, we can learn much from the Norse myths about the limitations of nostalgia and the failings of all projects of purification. Nostalgia is fundamental to both the myths of the Æsir and the mythologized accounts of land-taking and settlement of the sagas. I would go so far as to suggest that the most important mythic paradigm operative in Old Norse literature generally is the narrative of naturecultural decline and collapse that underlies both the history of the pagan cosmos from creation to Ragnarǫk and the history of the Norse settlements in Vínland (and also, to different extents, in Greenland and Iceland). Nostalgia for a golden age of plenty, for a paradise in which humanity's daily needs are met by a beatific and bountiful nonhuman environment, is absolutely central to these stories. It must have performed important cultural work for Norse people—whether pagan or Christian or both or neither—just as nostalgia for the preindustrial countryside or for untouched wilderness still animates many of our creative and critical responses to today's ecological predicament. But the Æsir's nostalgia for the golden age, the period when they could play chess in their meadow, the leisure society at the dawn of the world, does nothing to prevent Ragnarǫk. When the new world rises up in place of the old, the reborn Æsir continue to look backward, to dwell on their own achievements—the "progress" that resulted in the total annihilation of their society. They are paralyzed by nostalgia, which makes them lethargic, complacent, and conservative. It leads to a stultifying inertia that prevents them from acting effectively to prevent Ragnarǫk or preparing themselves for a different, less catastrophic, way of living in the post-Ragnarǫk cosmos.

It is also important to remember that the Æsir are nostalgic for a particular mode of naturecultural existence that is characterized by and depends upon the absence, or erasure, of the Other from their territory. The gods' golden age is a separatist fantasy. They believe that their prosperity depends upon maintaining spatial and ontological boundaries between themselves and the giants, between male and female, between Inside and Outside. It is easy to see that a distinction between Nature and Society is imbricated with these other dualisms. But the myth of Ragnarǫk is the story of how these boundaries are impossible to maintain. The gods expend massive amounts of energy and actual and symbolic capital to keep the Other out of their gated community— but they cannot keep the Other out, because they also need and desire the Other, and because the Other doesn't really exist except as part of the paranoid, exclusionary imaginary that underlies the Æsir's attempts at world-building.

A progressive reading of the Ragnarǫk-myth therefore draws attention to the sterility and futility of the gods' nostalgia and of the impossibility of their attempts to purify the world of the Other. If we want to learn something from these narratives that might inform our own responses to ecological crisis, then the Æsir's actions can only teach a negative lesson. They show us that dualistic modes of thought are indeed implicated in the collapse of unsustainable anthropocentric worldings. The gods' failure to prevent Ragnarǫk, to delay it or survive it, arises from their determination to double down on their dualisms. If the borders between Ásgarðr and the lands of the giants, between male and female, between Nature and Society, between Us and Them, are crumbling, the Æsir's first response will always be to build a bigger wall. And these walls, both actual and conceptual, always fall down.

Ragnarǫk, the "doom of the divine powers," shows us that however powerful the gods are, they are never powerful enough to escape the apocalypse that is both their fate and a judgment upon them. I have suggested that global warming is our Ragnarǫk, our own self-imposed destiny. Just as it is always already too late for the Æsir to prevent Ragnarǫk, it is already much too late for us to prevent global warming. It is too big, too complicated, too far advanced for us to stop. Our task is to cope with it as best we can—to find a way of living that mitigates the effects of global warming and reduces the suffering it causes as much as possible, while remembering that it is not only humans who are suffering the consequences of human failures. The Æsir never manage to reconcile themselves to the apocalypse: they struggle against it, seeking to prevent that which has already happened. They never change their way of life. They hold onto the dream of mastery of Nature and domin-ion over the Other that brought them to this pass in the first place.

If we retreat into nostalgia for our old world—a world in which Nature seemed to us an uncomplicated home for humanity, a bountiful mother, a source of solace and nourishment, and an endless fountain of prosperity—we will do nothing to prepare ourselves for an era in which the boundaries between the human world and the nonhuman nonworld will become less and less sustainable or enforceable. As anthropogenic climate change becomes even more severe, the effects of the changed climate upon the world will become even more severe in turn. It will be increasingly difficult to maintain the boundary between Nature and Society as these "unnatural" climatic con-ditions have an ever more destabilizing impact on the conditions under which life on Earth must struggle to survive.

Roy Scranton expresses the challenge that faces us in elegant and com-pelling terms: "The crisis of global climate change, the crisis of capitalism, and the crisis of the humanities in the university today are all aspects of the same crisis, which is the suicidal burnout of our carbon-fueled global cap-italist civilization. The odds of that civilization surviving are negligible. . . . We cannot escape our fate. Our future will depend on our ability to con-front it not with panic, outrage, or denial, but with patience, reflection, and love."[6] Scranton could also be describing the crisis of Ragnarǫk here, for the fate of the Norse gods is a reflection of part of the same crisis, the crisis of the Anthropocene. The Æsir do not rely on carbon-based fuel sources, but their regimes of exploitation of natural resources and subordination of Other populations in the pursuit of their own wealth and security are recognizably protocapitalist, protocolonialist, and depend upon the same brutally enforced dualisms that permeate modern worldviews. The Æsir's civilization does not survive, and the few survivors of Ragnarǫk have no good idea about what sort of society they should create to replace it. Scranton proposes that we have a clear choice in our current predicament: we can "continue acting as if tomorrow will be just like yesterday, growing less and less prepared for each new disaster as it comes, and more and more desperately invested in a life we can't sustain"—this is the Æsir's strategy, and it ends up killing them. Their nostalgia kills them. The alternative is to let go of the past, to abandon our fatal attachment to the structures that have been killing us, and to focus on dealing with the very real problems of the present.[7] There is some fear in letting go of modernity's false promise, the illusion of progress with which we have bewitched ourselves, but we have to abandon fear, too. Fear of the future will be one thing that prevents us from having a future.

Whether or not the extant Norse myths—including the settlement myths of Iceland, Greenland, and Vínland—belie the ecological values of an earlier form of Scandinavian paganism, these narratives do not provide us with a Green mythology. They are too dark to be Green. Their ecological outlook is dark because they come from dark places and dark times: they reflect the social anxieties of people experiencing the practical and emotional challenges of conversion to a new religion, but they also reflect the ecological anxieties of communities living marginal existences in unfamiliar and often hostile ecosystems. They are exercises in imaginative world-building that carry with them the recognition and fear that the worlds they construct are unstable, liable to collapse, and under threat from the physical environment and from the Other, whether that Other is conceived as human or nonhuman. They are heavily nostalgic: they project their conceptions of and faith in an idealized world of naturecultural harmony onto a past that can never be recovered.

The myth of a "golden age of Nature" still tacitly or explicitly animates much ecocritical discourse. We still sometimes think of Nature as something we'd like to go *back* to, something that we have lost that might yet be reclaimed. Ecocriticism's romanticist underpinnings show through in these attitudes, since romanticism is founded in a sort of radical nostalgia, a yearning for a prior world in which Man was as yet unalienated from Nature. But we can never go back to this "state of Nature"—since no such thing ever existed—and to think that we might does not help us face the crisis that threatens to bring about the downfall of modern society and cause untold suffering in the process. Medievalist ecocritics should therefore be very careful not to condone or perpetuate lazy nostalgia for the Middle Ages as a possible golden age of harmonious interrelationships between humans and the nonhuman world—to do so is to implicate ourselves in a refusal to address the ecological problems that ecocriticism is supposed to address. I don't mean that we have nothing to learn from taking ecocritical approaches to the medieval period—far from it. We learn a great deal *about* the Middle Ages from an ecocritical approach, and there is still much that we might learn *from* such an endeavor. But nostalgia for a Green Middle Ages is hardly any more justifiable than nostalgia for a white Middle Ages. Both these nostalgias work by appropriating the medieval world for modern political ends, by fossilizing a dynamic and complex network of networks into stasis and homogeneity, and by projecting our present-day desires onto a world that is forever lost to us. Golden ages only exist as such once they are already over.

Without succumbing to the facile teleology that treats modernity as the one true fulfillment of the promise of human society, our ecocritical approaches to the Middle Ages can be forward- and outward-looking rather than intro-verted and nostalgic. Studying the Middle Ages is important because they are not over yet. How can they be over when they never existed as such in the first place? Latour tells us that "we have never been modern"—but we were never premodern, either. The Nature/Society dualism that Latour sees as being at the heart of the "modern constitution" is present in ancient Judaism and Western Christianity; it is all-pervasive in pagan Norse mythology; it is the bedrock of capitalism; it is immanent in all anthropocentric worldviews—and historically, all human worldviews have been anthropocentric, though not identically or equally anthropocentric. Or perhaps it is better to say that some anthropocentrisms have been more damaging than others.

The inevitable outcome of the Æsir's anthropocentric structuration of the cosmos is Ragnarǫk. The inevitable outcome of Western society's "progress" into modernity is global warming. Both phenomena represent the price of admission to the Anthropocene. The Ragnarǫk myths reveal with remark-able clarity that the cost of cleaving the human from the nonhuman, Nature from Society, Us from the Other, is ultimately the destruction of both sides of the binary. These binaries are illusions, what in Old Norse would be called *sjónhverfingar* (sight-turnings), and they require massive amounts of cultural energy to stage. It is precisely because they are not real that they are so expen-sive to maintain, so unsustainable. At Ragnarǫk they collapse into one another, coalescing into a new realm of possibility in which all entities might exist on an equal, nonhierarchical footing. The real tragedy of the Norse myths is that the reborn Æsir are determined to reject this opportunity, choosing instead to repeat the mistakes of their ancestors, enacting over and over again the futile and fatal charade of mastery over a "natural world" that they have to create as an act of will. They are too much invested in their specialness. They are unable to transcend their modernity; nor will we transcend our own benighted situ-ation by retreating into the past. The past is where we've already come from. It is what resulted in this particular present.

The goal of ecocriticism is to help us transcend this modernistic imaginary, to conceive of something new and better that might grow in the ruins of a modernity that is melting along with the ice caps, drowning as the sea rises, facing extinction as it destroys its own habitat. Norse mythology, which I have argued is the product of precisely such a modernistic worldview, does not seem to offer a very hopeful alternative model of how future modes of human existence might be less anthropocentric, less dualistic, more sustainable, and less horrifying than that which faces us today. But it does at least provide us with a symbol for our project of destabilizing the conventional human/

nonhuman dualisms of modernity, in the form of Yggdrasill, the "evergreen ash" of my title. Yggdrasill does not exist *for* gods, humans, or any other category of beings, and their activities cannot exhaust or diminish its life force. Yggdrasill is deeply enmeshed with all other entities; it does not enter into hierarchical relationships with any of them. It provides food for some, shelter for others, but it does not exist to play these roles. Yggdrasill implacably resists all teleologies and myths of human mastery. It is simply there; it simply *is*. Yggdrasill suffices. And Yggdrasill endures. The end of the world is not the end of Yggdrasill. Yggdrasill is the Earth—neither tree nor planet needs saving, because both will outlive by an almost unimaginable distance any world we can conceive of. The Anthropocene, however long it lasts, will be but a blink in the eye when viewed from a planetary or cosmic standpoint. Yggdrasill is life, and life will certainly persist through and beyond global warming; but life will change, as it always does. The challenge that faces us is the same challenge that the Norse gods refuse to acknowledge as their knowledge of Ragnarǫk presses down on them: Yggdrasill is eternal, or might as well be from a human perspective, but our world is ending right now. How much are we prepared to suffer, and how much suffering are we prepared to impose on others, in order to put off the end of this world for another handful of years? How much worse will we allow things to become in order to be able to pretend this crisis is not really happening? The narrator of *Vǫluspá* repeatedly taunts Óðinn, the arch Ragnarǫk denier, with the phrase *vituð er enn—eða hvat?* Do you know yet? What more do you need to know? When will you have made up your mind? These are the same questions we must answer about global warming, the Anthropocene, and the death of modernity. Norse mythology does not answer these questions for us, but it demonstrates with chilling efficiency the necessity and urgency of addressing them: Yggdrasill survives, but the gods do not—and we are not even gods.

Notes

Prologue

1. *Book of Common Prayer* [1549], edited by Cummings, 82.

2. Cremation is still forbidden in the Orthodox churches. It has been permissible among Roman Catholics only since 1963; the Roman church still recommends burial, however. In Anglican circles cremation was finally legitimized in 1969. Wherever possible, a person's cremated remains should be buried in consecrated ground; see *Oxford Dictionary of the Christian Church*, s.v. "cremation."

3. *Manuale ad usum percelebris ecclesie Sarisburiensis*, edited by Collins, 158–59 ("Inhumatio defuncti").

4. In a less common variant of the phoenix myth, the bird dies without burning, decomposes, and comes back to life in the form of a worm, which quickly develops back into the adult creature. By the first century AD this classical tradition had been effaced almost entirely by the immolation motif. In some versions, including the highly influential Greek *Physiologus* and its derivatives, the worm creeps between the versions, now representing a three-day-long intermediate stage between the phoenix's death and its full rebirth. This addition strengthened the correspondence between the phoenix's life cycle and the time that lapsed between Christ's death and resurrection. See J. S. Hall, "The Phoenix"; and Van den Broek, *Myth of the Phoenix*, 146–47. As Van den Broek also notes (9), the phoenix had many symbolic valences, representing at various times "renewal in general as well as the sun, Time, the Empire, metempsychosis, consecration, resurrection, life in the heavenly Paradise, Christ, Mary, virginity, the exceptional man, and certain aspects of Christian life."

5. *Edda*, translated by Faulkes, 9; *Gylfaginning*, edited by Faulkes, 8–9: "Hitt er mest er hann gerði manninn ok gaf honum ǫnd þá er lifa skal ok aldri týnask, þótt líkaminn fúni at moldu eða brenni at ǫsku."

6. In the *Edda*, Snorri produces a sort of simulacrum of what Norse paganism might have been like when viewed from the perspective of a Christian Icelander of the thirteenth century. In another of the works attributed to Snorri—the prologue to the collection of kings' sagas known as *Heimskringla*—the author makes the association between cremation and paganism quite clear. *Heimskringla* states that the first age of Scandinavian history is called the "Age of Burning," since at that time "all dead people had to be burned and memorial stones raised for them" (*Heimskringla I*, translated by Finlay and Faulkes, 3). Snorri's observations about funerary practices in mainland Scandinavia are broadly supported by the archaeological record; see Price, "Dying and the Dead."

7. On the physical and cultural impact of the Laki eruption in Egypt, see Mikhail, "Ottoman Iceland." Mikhail notes that "the volcano's environmental history explains some of the political, economic, and social history of Egypt at the end of the eighteenth century, a history that indeed remains incomplete without an understanding of Laki" (264).

8. An excellent overview of the eruption and its effects in Western Europe is provided by Demarée and Ogilvie, "*Bon baisers d'Islande.*" For a review of the scientific evidence relating to the eruption's effect on the physical environment, see also Þorvaldur Þórðarson and Self, "Atmospheric and Environmental Effects."

9. G. White, *Natural History of Selborne*, 232–33.

10. The total death toll attributable to Laki's eruption is controversial. John Grattan and his collaborators, who take the most inclusive approach to the potential worldwide effects of this event, state that "the climactic disasters that occurred in 1783 . . . encompassed the deaths of millions" (Grattan, Michnowicz, and Rabartin, "Long Shadow," 171). The "official" death toll for the 1783 eruption, however, which only accounts for mortality among the Icelandic population immediately affected, is below 10,000.

11. See Scott, "Apocalypse Narrative, Chaotic System."

12. Grattan, Michnowicz, and Rabartin, "Long Shadow," 157.

13. Þorvaldur Þórðarson and Larsen, "Volcanism in Iceland," 142; Oppenheimer et al., "Eldgjá Eruption." As well as an unparalleled amount of lava, the Eldgjá eruptions emitted more sulfur dioxide into the atmosphere even than Laki in 1783.

14. *Le voyage de saint Brendan,* translated by Mackley, lines 1107–20, in Mackley, *Legend of St Brendan,* 291–92. For the original text, see *Le voyage de saint Brendan,* edited by Short and Merrilees, lines 1103–16.

15. For a thorough appraisal of the topography of *Le voyage de saint Brendan*'s inferno, see Burrell, "Hell as Geological Construct." Although Burrell is frustrated in her attempt to identify the hell that Brendan encounters with a particular historical eruption—she is unable to find evidence of an undersea eruption that would have produced the Surtsey-style offshore volcano necessary to explain the particular form of the island in the narrative—she nonetheless accepts that Iceland lies somewhere in the hinterland of *Le voyage*'s description.

16. *The King's Mirror,* translated by Larson, 131; *Konungs skuggsiá,* edited by Holm-Olsen, 20: "Enn nu má eingi dyliast vid sá er siá má firi augum sier. firi þui at slijkir hlutir eru oss sagdir frá pijslum heluijtis sem nu má siá j þeiri ey er ijsland heitir. Þuiat þar er gnott ellds ofur gangs og ofur efli frosts og iokla. Vellandi votn og strijdleikur ijskalldra vatna."

17. La Martinière, *Voyage des pais septentrionaux,* 171.

18. Sigurður Þórarinsson, *Hekla,* 5.

19. On Hekla's changing public image over the centuries, see Kellerer-Pirklbauer and Eulenstein, "From 'Door to Hell.'"

20. *Islandske annaler indtil 1578,* edited by Storm, 401: "men foru til fiallzins þar sem vpp varpit var ok heyrdiz þeim sem biargi storu væri kastat innam vm fiallit. Þeim synduzst fuglar fliuga i elldinum badi smair ok storir med ymsum laatum. hugdu menn vera saalir."

21. Falk, "Vanishing Volcanoes."

22. *Biskupa sögur,* edited by Jón Sigurðsson and Guðbrandur Vígfússon, 2:5: "Þau eru fjöll önnur þess lands, er ór sér verpa ægiligum eldi með grimmasta grjótkasti, svo at þat brak ok bresti heyrir um allt landit, svo vítt sem menn kalla fjórtán tylftir umbergis at sigla réttleiði fyrir hvert nes. Kann þessi ógn at fylgja svo mikit myrkr forviðris, at um hásumar um miðdegi sér eigi handa grein. Þat fylgir þessum fádæmum, at í sjálfu hafinu viku sjávar suðr undan landinu hefir upp komit af eldsganginum stórt fjall, en annat sökk niðr í staðinn, þat er upp kom í fyrstu með sömu grein. Keldur vellandi ok brennusteinn fær þar ínóg."

23. See *Íslendingabók; Kristni saga,* translated by Grønlie, 49.

24. Þorvaldur Þórðarson and Larsen, "Volcanism in Iceland," 137.

25. The same connection was made in ancient Greek: Homer uses "ash" (μελίη) as a metonym for "spear." See Yates, "Titanic Origin of Humans," 184.

26. See Dumont, "Ash Tree in Indo-European Culture."

27. Hesiod, *Works and Days,* 134–47 from *Theogony,* translated by Athanassakis.

28. The primary source for the Askr and Embla myth is *Voluspá* 17, which forms the basis for Snorri's elaboration of the story in *Gylfaginning.* See chap. 4 for a discussion of these passages.

29. "Ask veit ek standa, / heitir Yggdrasill, / hár baðmr, ausinn / hvíta auri; / þaðan koma doggvar / þærs í dala falla, / stendr æ yfir grœnn / Urðarbrunni." Larrington translates the last line of this stanza as "green, it stands always over the well of fate." *Voluspá* exists in two distinct versions, as I discuss in chap. 2. The siglum [K] indicates that the text given is from *Konungsbók* (the Codex Regius). Readings from *Hauksbók* are indicated by [H].

30. Yggdrasill's species has been the subject of considerable controversy, mostly on account of scholars' reading *yfir grœnn* as "evergreen." The so-called *Icelandic Rune Poem* calls yew—which is the name of one of the characters in the Norse runic alphabet, indicating its long-standing significance in Scandinavian culture—*vetgrønstr viðr* (winter-greenest tree), so the coniferous nature of the yew must have been well known. But the *Rune Poem'*s reference to yew is not a reference to Yggdrasill, pace Fred Hageneder (*Yew,* 147). Hageneder is the strongest recent proponent of the Yggdrasill-as-yew thesis, but his argument has an air of special pleading about it—his book is dedicated to the yew and its cultural significance throughout history, and he is understandably inclined to seek the yew wherever he may. As one of Europe's longest-lived species, with significant naturecultural connotations in many areas, a yew would not be a bad prototype for a Germanic world tree by any means. But the fact remains that the sources call it an ash; they never call it a yew; and it is doubtful whether *æ yfir grœnn* is really supposed to connote a coniferous species. For a summary of these arguments, see Simek, *Dictionary of Northern Mythology,* 376.

31. *Voluspá* and *Grímnismál* both call Yggdrasill an *askr* repeatedly, which is by far the most prominent species name associated with it in the myths. However, in Old Norse–Icelandic poetry it is possible for any tree name to stand in for the concept of "tree" and for a nonspecific tree word to stand in for the name of a particular sort of tree. In *Voluspá* 20, for example, Yggdrasill is called a *þollr,* which properly refers to a pine, but probably is just a synonym for tree in this instance.

32. Dobrowolska et al., *Review of European Ash,* 133, include Iceland in the "natural distribution" of *Fraxinus excelsior.* I have been able to find no confirmation of this,

however: Iceland's only native woodland species is the mountain birch, while the rowan and tea-leaved willow are also considered indigenous to the country but occur generally in isolation. Specimens of *Fraxinus excelsior* have been raised in Iceland on an experimental basis, but despite the warming climate Iceland remains inhospitable to the ash: it requires a sheltered location, better than normal soil fertility, and often a south-facing slope. See Þröstur Eysteinsson, "Noble Hardwoods in Icelandic Forestry."

33. Motz, "Cosmic Ash," 127–28.

34. On the nomenclature of this pathogen, see Baral, Queloz, and Hosoya, "*Hymenoscyphus fraxineus.*" For an account of its characteristics, origins, and transmission from Asia into Europe, see Gross et al., "*Hymenoscyphus pseudoalbidus.*"

35. See the UK Forestry Commission's 2014 report, "Chalara Dieback of Ash (*Hymenoscyphus fraxineus*)," https://www.forestry.gov.uk/ashdieback. For a survey of the disease's ecological impact in the UK, see Mitchell et al. "Ash Dieback in the UK."

36. See Tomlinson, "Discovery of Ash Dieback in the UK."

37. David Derbyshire, "Thought the Threat to Our Noble Ash Trees Was Over? They Could ALL Be Lost in 10 Years." [London] *Daily Mail,* 14 May 2013. Accessed online at http://www.dailymail.co.uk/news/article-2324089/Ash-dieback-Thought-threat-noble-ash-trees-They-ALL-lost-10-years.html.

38. Nick McDermott. "Eat Less Meat or Face Food Shortage: Nannying MPs' Warning 'Unhelpful,' Say Farmers." [London] *Daily Mail,* 3 June 2013. Accessed online at http://www.dailymail.co.uk/news/article-2335424/Eat-meat-face-food-shortage-Nannying-MPs-astonishing-warning-unhelpful-say-farmers.html.

39. Derbyshire, "Thought the Threat to Our Noble Ash Trees Was Over?"

40. UK Forestry Commission, "Chalara Ash Dieback—Key Scientific Facts," https://www.forestry.gov.uk/forestry/infd-8zss7u; see also Solheim et al., "Yggdrasils helsetilstand"; Timmermann et al., "Ash Dieback."

41. *Emerald Ash Borer Information Network,* http://www.emeraldashborer.info/. As in the case of European ash die-back, the transport of wood products across ecological boundaries seems to have been the vector by which this pest reached America; see Poland and McCullough, "Emerald Ash Borer."

42. On the formation of outsiders' impressions of the Icelandic landscape, see Brady, "Sublime, Ugliness and 'Terrible Beauty.'"

43. See Falk, "Vanishing Volcanoes," 6. Lisbeth Torfing, "Volcanoes as Cultural Artefacts," argues that the almost constant volcanic activity of Iceland changed medieval Icelanders' risk perception to the extent that an eruption was seen as no more intrinsically catastrophic than any other comparably destructive geological or meteorological phenomena.

44. See Sverrir Jakobsson, "Centre and Periphery."

45. See Borgþór Magnússon et al., "Plant Colonization, Succession and Ecosystem Development."

46. *Vǫluspá* [K] 51, lines 1–4: "Surtr ferr sunnan / með sviga lævi, / skínn af sverði / sól valtíva." In Larrington's translation, this stanza is number 50: "Surtr travels from the south with branches-ruin. The slaughter-gods' sun glances from his sword."

47. Halink, "Icelandic Mythscape," 209. As Kees Samplonius points out ("Background and Scope of *Vǫluspá,*" 119–20), there is no need to assume an Icelandic origin for the

figure of Surtr in order for the mythological potential of the fire-giant to be actualized in different ways in a volcanic environment. The available evidence, though slim, seems to indicate that Surtr was known in pagan Norway, and his name does not derive from an Icelandic landscape feature: it is cognate with the adjective *svartr* (black).

48. Freyr's fatal encounter with Surtr is not mentioned in *Vǫluspá*, but Snorri is in no doubt about it: "Freyr will fight Surtr and there will be a harsh conflict before Freyr falls" (*Edda,* translated by Faulkes, 54; *Gylfaginning,* edited by Faulkes, 50: "Freyr bersk móti Surt ok verðr harðr samgangr áðr Freyr fellr").

49. "Sól tér sortna, / sígr fold í mar, / hverfa af himni / heiðar stjǫrnar; / geisar eimi / við aldrnara, / leikr hár hiti við himin sjálfan."

50. Oppenheimer et al., "Eldgjá Eruption."

51. The suggestion that the 1014 Katla eruption triggered the description of a volcanic catastrophe was made by Sigurður Þórarinsson, "Tephra Studies and Tephrachronology," 1–2.

1. Ecocriticism and Old Norse

1. Glotfelty, "Introduction," xviii.

2. Oppermann, "Theorizing Ecocriticism," 105.

3. Wood, "Introduction: Eco-historicism," 1.

4. Latour, *Enquiry into Modes of Existence,* 99.

5. Latour, "Attempt at a 'Compositionist Manifesto,'" 476.

6. Plumwood, *Feminism and the Mastery of Nature,* 42–43.

7. Phelpstead, "Ecocriticism and *Eyrbyggja saga*," 2.

8. Nardizzi, "Medieval Ecocriticism," 121. It is notable that the Middle Ages initially went unconsidered by ecocritics, whose praxis during the first wave of the "movement" was concerned with modern literatures and above all with modes of "nature writing" that simply have no parallels in premodern corpuses. Jonathan Bate's pioneering eco-critical study of Romantic poetry, *Song of the Earth,* for example, finds antecedents to nineteenth-century Romantic ecopoesis in ancient Greece and Shakespeare, but mentions nothing of the medieval period. Perhaps the first important intervention by a medievalist into the mainstream of ecocriticism was Sarah Stanbury's article "Ecochaucer." Other important milestones in this subfield have included Alfred Siewers's *Strange Beauty* and Gillian Rudd's *Greenery.* For an overview of developments in medieval ecocriticism, see Nardizzi, "Medieval Ecocriticism"; and Douglass, "Ecocriticism and Medieval Literature."

9. Phelpstead, "Ecocriticism and *Eyrbyggja saga*," 2 n. 4, identifies the work of Ian Wyatt and Eleanor Barraclough as precursors to ecocritical approaches to Old Norse–Icelandic literature, as well as Gillian R. Overing and Marijane Osborn's 1994 book *Landscape of Desire:* Wyatt, "Narrative Functions of Landscape"; Wyatt, "Landscape and Authorial Control"; Wyatt, "Landscape of the Icelandic Sagas"; Barraclough, "Inside Outlawry"; and Barraclough, "Land-Naming in the Migration Myth." See also Jeffrey Jerome Cohen's remarks about *Grettis saga:* "Introduction: All Things," 1–8.

10. Harman, "Well-Wrought Broken Hammer," 200.

11. Wood, "Introduction: Eco-historicism," 4.

12. Nordvig, "Of Fire and Water," 28–29.

13. Taggart, "All the Mountains Shake."

14. Phelpstead, "Ecocriticism and *Eyrbyggja saga*," 4.

15. Moore, "Crisis of Feudalism," 304.

16. On the occasion of the fiftieth anniversary of the publication of White's famous article, a collection of reflections on and critiques of his thesis was published as *Religion and Ecological Crisis,* edited by Todd LeVasseur and Anna Peterson. Particularly important responses to White's treatment of historical paganisms in that volume are Callicott, "Historical Roots of Environmental Philosophy"; Stoll, "Sinners in the Hands of an Ecologic Crisis"; and Krech, "Animism and Reincarnation."

17. L. White, "Historical Roots of Our Ecologic Crisis," 1205.

18. Primavesi, *Sacred Gaia*, 30. For an overview of Primavesi's work with myth and ecology, see Coupe, "Genesis and the Nature of Myth."

19. White, "Historical Roots of Our Ecologic Crisis," 1205.

20. Yi-Fu Tuan, "Discrepancies between Environmental Attitudes and Behaviour," argues convincingly that the fact that the ancient Greeks and Romans were animist pagans did nothing to prevent wholesale and damaging anthropogenic environmental change in the Mediterranean region. See also Callicott, "Historical Roots of Environmental Philosophy," 41–42.

21. Krech, "Animism and Reincarnation," 78–79.

22. Higginbotham and Higginbotham, *Paganism.*

23. Harvey, "Roots of Pagan Ecology," 38; M. Hall, *Plants as Persons,* 132.

24. The case can be made that medieval Irish literature also preserves an important body of pre-Christian mythology which may illustrate a distinctively different ecological worldview—such is one of the contentions made by Alfred Siewers in his book *Strange Beauty.* However, Ireland converted to Christianity so much earlier than any of the Scandinavian polities that the record of historical Irish paganism is perhaps even more susceptible to bias and reinterpretation than the admittedly problematic Old Norse mythological corpus is. As Siewers shows, the distinctive eco-semiotics of medieval Irish culture should probably be explained as arising from a fusion of pre-Christian elements with a distinctively Irish variety of Christian piety.

25. Callaghan, "Myth as a Site of Ecocritical Inquiry," 80.

26. Ibid., 96.

27. Morton, *Ecology without Nature,* 19.

28. Latour, *Politics of Nature,* 25–26.

29. Žižek, *In Defense of Lost Causes,* 445.

30. Mickey, *Coexistentialism,* 53.

31. Harman, *Guerrilla Metaphysics,* 251.

32. Merchant, *Death of Nature,* 2–6.

33. Morton, *Ecological Thought,* 5.

34. See Chenu, *Nature, Man, and Society.*

35. The seminal account of this controversial theory is Colin Morris, *The Discovery of the Individual, 1050–1200;* see also Bynum, "Did the Twelfth Century Discover the Individual?" and, for a summary of subsequent research, Melve, "Revolt of the Medievalists."

36. H. White, *Nature, Sex, and Goodness,* 2.

37. Ritchey, "Rethinking the Twelfth-Century Discovery," 229. For more conventional readings of Natura's place in twelfth-century philosophy and art, see White, *Nature, Sex, and Goodness;* Economou, *Goddess Natura;* P. Dronke, *Intellectuals and Poets,* 53–55.

38. *Alexanders saga,* edited by Finnur Jónsson, 126.

39. See Abram, "*Gylfaginning* and Early Medieval Conversion Theory"; Perron, "Face of the 'Pagan.'"

40. Harvey, "Animals, Animists, and Academics," 11.

41. Ibid. See also David-Bird, "'Animism' Revisited"; also, more generally, Harvey, *Animism.*

42. Morton, *Ecological Thought,* 8.

43. Ibid., 110.

44. *Norges gamle love,* edited by Keyser and Munch, 308. See Brink, "Mythologizing Landscape," 89–90.

45. See Meylan, "La (re)conversion des «esprits de la terre»."

46. See Hafstein, "Elves' Point of View"; Ármann Jakobsson, "Beware of the Elf!"

47. Buell, *Environmental Imagination,* 10.

48. Oppermann, "Theorizing Ecocriticism," 103.

49. Phelpstead, "Ecocriticism and *Eyrbyggja saga,*" 16.

50. Phelpstead has recently expanded on his concerns about the limitations that mainstream Western ecocriticisms place on our conceptions of possible interactions between people and the universes—physical, mental, spiritual, earthly, and ethereal—that they inhabit and interact with. As he puts it, "The physical environment extends beyond earth's atmosphere and encompasses our larger cosmological context" ("Beyond Ecocriticism," 5–6).

51. I am by no means the first to issue the call to move beyond "nature writing" in ecocritical literary studies. See, most notably, the 2001 anthology of essays edited by Karla Armbruster and Kathleen Wallace, *Beyond Nature Writing.*

52. Schatz, "Importance of Apocalypse," 21.

53. Eliade, *Sacred and the Profane,* 88.

54. Morton, *Hyperobjects,* 7.

55. Johnston and Mueller, "Kant in King Arthur's Court."

56. Parham, "Editorial," 4. Parham's editorial opens a special issue of the journal *Green Letters* devoted to premodernist ecocriticism.

57. Miller, "Anachronistic Reading," 76.

58. Ibid., 82.

2. *Remembering and Dismembering a Transcorporeal Cosmos*

1. Lincoln, *Theorizing Myth,* xii.

2. Lovelock, *Ages of Gaia,* 208.

3. See Fidjestøl, *Dating of Eddic Poetry;* Gunnell, "Eddic Poetry."

4. On *Vǫluspá*'s Christian elements, see Samplonius, "Background and Scope of *Vǫluspá*"; Steinsland, "*Vǫluspá* and the Sibylline Oracles"; Pétur Pétursson, "Manifest

and Latent Biblical Themes"; McKinnell, "*Vǫluspá* and the Feast of Easter"; and, approaching the same question from the opposite direction, McKinnell, "Heathenism in *Vǫluspá*."

5. On these two poetic cosmologies, see Larrington, "*Vafþrúðnismál* and *Grímnismál*."

6. For an overview of this text and the questions surrounding its authorship, integrity, and intended purpose, see Wanner, *Snorri Sturluson and the Edda*.

7. On the Prologue to *Snorra Edda* and its relationship to the mythographic material contained in the rest of the work, see Faulkes, "Descent from the Gods" and "Pagan Sympathy"; Ursula Dronke and Peter Dronke, "The Prologue of the Prose *Edda*"; and See, "Snorri Sturluson and Norse Cultural Ideology."

8. *Edda,* translated by Faulkes, 1; *Gylfaginning,* edited by Faulkes, 3: "Almáttigr guð skapaði himin ok jǫrð ok alla þá hluti er þeim fylgja, ok síðarst menn tvá er ættir eru frá komnar, Adam ok Evu, ok fjǫlgaðisk þeira kynslóð ok dreifðisk um heim allan. En er fram liðu stundir, þá ójafnaðisk mannfólkit: váru sumir góðir ok rétt trúaðir, en myklu fleiri snerusk eptir girndum heimsins ok órœktu guðs boðorð, ok fyrir því drekti guð heiminum í sjávargangi ok ǫllum kvikvendum heimsins nema þeim er í ǫrkinni váru með Nóa."

9. These three figures, with their strange names and ambiguous hierarchy, have suggested Christian influence to some commentators. As Rory McTurk puts it: "Gylfi's three interlocutors, Hár, Jafnhár, and Þriði, whose names turn out, as we have seen, to belong also to the god Óðinn, are meant to suggest the Holy Trinity" ("Fooling Gylfi," 21).

10. See McTurk, "Fooling Gylfi" and "*Snorra Edda* as Menippean Satire." Abram, "*Gylfaginning* and Early Medieval Conversion Theory," offers some parallels to Snorri's approach in earlier Christian theorizing about best how to reveal pagans' illogical folly to them.

11. *Edda,* translated by Faulkes, 8–9; *Gylfaginning,* edited by Faulkes, 8–9: "Gangleri hóf svá mál sitt: 'Hverr er œztr eða elztr allra goða?' Hár segir: 'Sá heitir Alfǫðr at váru máli, en í Ásgarði inum forna átti hann tólf nǫfn [. . .] Þá spyrr Gangleri: 'Hvar er sá guð, eða hvat má hann, eða hvat hefir hann unnit framaverka?' Hár segir: 'Lifir hann of allar aldir ok stjórnar ǫllu ríki sínu ok ræðr ǫllum hlutum stórum ok smám.' Þá mælir Jafnhár: 'Hann smíðaði himin ok jǫrð ok loptin ok alla eign þeira.' Þá mælti Þriði: 'Hitt er mest er hann gerði manninn ok gaf honum ǫnd þá er lifa skal ok aldri týnask, þótt líkaminn fúni at moldu eða brenni at ǫsku. Ok skulu allir menn lifa þeir er rétt eru siðaðir ok vera með honum sjálfum þar sem heitir Gimlé eða Vingólf, en vándir menn fara til Heljar ok þaðan í Niflhel, þat er niðr í inn níunda heim.'"

12. Óðinn is a master of disguise in the Norse myths, and All-father (*Alfǫðr*) is listed among an array of his aliases in *Grímnismál* 48. It is not, however, one of his more common cognomens. It occurs in the legendary poem *Helgakviða Hundingsbani I* and in a single stanza by the eleventh-century Orkney poet, Arnórr jarlaskáld. See Simek, *Dictionary of Northern Mythology,* 9.

13. *Edda,* translated by Faulkes, 9; *Gylfaginning,* edited by Faulkes, 9: "Gangleri mælti: 'Hvat var upphaf? Eða hversu hófsk? Eða hvat var áðr?' Hár svarar: 'Svá sem segir í Vǫluspá: Ár var alda / þat er ekki var. / Vara sandr né sær né svalar unnir. / Jrð fannsk æva / né upphiminn, / gap var ginnunga, en gras hvergi.'" I have reformatted

Faulkes's translation of the stanza from *Vǫluspá* to emphasize the poem's difference from the prose that surrounds it.

14. Cole, "Towards a Typology of Absence," 141.

15. "Ór Ymis holdi / var jǫrð um skǫpuð / en ór beinum bjǫrg, / himinn ór hausi / ins hrímkalda jǫtuns / en ór sveita sjór."

16. "Ór Ymis holdi / var jǫrð um skǫpuð / en ór sveita sær / bjǫrg ór beinum, / baðmr ór hári / en ór hausi himinn. // En ór hans brám / gerðu blíð regin / Miðgarð manna sonum; / en ór hans heila / váru þau in harðmóðgu / ský ǫll um skǫpuð."

17. *Edda*, translated by Faulkes, 10; *Gylfaginning*, edited by Faulkes, 10: "Þá mælti Þriði: 'Svá sem kalt stóð af Niflheimi ok allir hlutir grimmir, svá var þat er vissi námunda Muspelli heitt ok ljóst, en Ginnungagap var svá hlætt sem lopt vindlaust. Ok þá er moettisk hrímin ok blær hitans svá at bráðnaði ok draup, ok af þeim kvikudropum kviknaði með krapti þess er til sendi hitann, ok varð manns líkandi, ok var sá nefndr Ymir.'"

18. *Edda*, translated by Faulkes, 10; *Gylfaginning*, edited by Faulkes, 10–11: "Ok svá er sagt at þá er hann svaf, fekk hann sveita. Þá óx undir vinstri hǫnd honum maðr ok kona, ok annarr fótr hans gat son við ǫðrum. En þaðan af kómu ættir. Þat eru hrímþursar."

19. Auðhumla may be Snorri's invention, since she appears nowhere else in the Norse myths as they survive. Scholars have noted, however, the widespread importance of cows as maternal figures in cultures across time and space, of which trope Snorri's Auðhumla may be a reflection. See Davidson, "Milk and the Northern Goddess"; Simek, *Dictionary of Northern Mythology*, 22. The name Auðhumla means something like "hornless cow of prosperity."

20. *Edda*, translated by Faulkes, 11; *Gylfaginning*, edited by Faulkes, 11: "Ok þat er mín trúa at sá Óðinn ok hans brœðr munu vera stýrandi himins ok jarðar; þat ætlum vér at hann muni svá heita. Svá heitir sá maðr er vér vitum mæstan ok ágætzan, ok vel megu þér hann láta svá heita."

21. Alaimo, "Trans-Corporeal Feminisms," 238.

22. Hird, "Naturally Queer," 85–86.

23. *Edda*, translated by Faulkes, 11–12; *Gylfaginning*, edited by Faulkes, 11: "Þá svarar Hár: 'Synir Bors drápu Ymi jǫtun. En er hann fell, þá hljóp svá mikit blóð ór sárum hans at með því drektu þeir allri ætt hrímþursa, nema einn komsk undan með sínu hýski [. . .] Þeir tóku Ymi ok fluttu í mitt Ginnungagap, ok gerðu af honum jǫrðina, af blóði hans sæinn ok vǫtnin. Jǫrðin var gǫr af holdinu en bjǫrgin af beinunum, grjót ok urðir gerðu þeir af tǫnnum ok jǫxlum ok af þeim beinum er brotin váru.'"

24. Cohen, *Of Giants*, 10–11.

25. The "sons of Burr" mentioned here are presumably identical with the "sons of Borr" whom Snorri mentions in the same context in *Gylfaginning*. Since Burr/Borr is a very obscure figure in the mythology, despite his paternity of Óðinn, it is impossible to say which spelling of the name is more likely to be its original form.

26. "Áðr Burs synir / bjǫðum um ypðu, / þeir er Miðgarð / maran skópu; / sól skein sunnan / á salar steina, / þá var grund gróin / grœnum lauki." Larrington translates *grœnum lauki* as "with the green leek," which to my mind is excessively specific about the botany of the newly created world.

27. *Edda*, translated by Faulkes, 12; *Gylfaginning*, edited by Faulkes, 12: "Þá mælir Gangleri: 'Þetta eru mikil tíðindi er nú heyri ek. Furðu mikil smíð er þat ok hagliga

gert. Hvernig var jǫrðin háttuð?' Þá svarar Hár: 'Hon er kringlótt útan, ok þar útan um liggr hinn djúpi sjár, ok með þeiri sjávar strǫndu gáfu þeir lǫnd til bygðar jǫtna ættum. En fyrir innan á jǫrðunni gerðu þeir borg umhverfis heim fyrir ófriði jǫtna, en til þeirar borgar hǫfðu þeir brár Ymis jǫtuns, ok kǫlluðu þá borg Miðgarð. Þeir tóku ok heila hans ok kǫstuðu í lopt ok gerðu af skýin.' "

28. Lévi-Strauss, *Elementary Structures of Kinship,* xxix.

29. *Útgarðr* does not occur in the *Poetic Edda,* and is used as a name for a place but once in *Gylfaginning.* Its occurrence in *Gylfaginning* is part of Snorri's strange and unique narration of Þórr's journey to a "castle" (*borg*) named Útgarðr, where he enters into a series of contests with a mysterious and treacherous giant named Útgarða-Loki.

30. Hastrup, *Culture and History,* 146–48.

31. As a noun, *útgarðr* appears twice in the sagas of Icelanders as part of the phrase *fœra e-n við útgarða* (to lead someone into *útgarðr*). The editor of *Víga-Glúms saga* explains this phrase as meaning "to drive someone away from their home" (*að hrekja hann brott af heimili sínu*): "Víga-Glúms saga," edited by Jónas Kristjánsson, 30. The other occurrence is found in *Gísla saga:* "Gísla saga Súrssonar," edited by Björn K. Þórólfsson and Guðni Jónsson, 19.

32. *Alþingi* is the name of medieval Iceland's national assembly, incorporating the functions of a parliament and supreme court, which took place each summer at Þingvellir, a remarkable cleft in the landscape formed by the gradual pulling apart of the North American and European tectonic plates.

33. Hastrup, *Culture and History,* 144.

34. Ibid., 137–45.

35. See Van Houts, "Vocabulary of Exile"; Riisøy, "Outlawry"; Barraclough, "Inside Outlawry."

36. Hastrup, *Culture and History,* 144–45.

37. See Ármann Jakobsson, "Where Do the Giants Live?"

38. The term *innangarðr* is sometimes used in neo-pagan cosmology to refer to a spatial or social enclosure, on the inside of which are the members of the coreligionists' own community, while outsiders are said to dwell in *útgarðr.* (See Snook, "Reconsidering Heathenry.") *Innangarðr* is found very rarely in Old Norse sources, however. The only citation of a cognate term offered by Cleasby-Vigfusson comes from a fourteenth-century collection of ecclesiastical documents known as *Pétrsmáldagi,* in which the form *innangarða* occurs adverbially.

39. Kress, "Taming the Shrew," 83.

40. As I write in May 2017, the gods' creation of Miðgarðr resonates depressingly with the campaign promises made by US President Donald Trump to build a wall along the length of the Mexican border and to initiate a program of full-scale deportations of Mexican people out of the United States. One of the rationales given for this grotesque piece of nationalistic rabble-rousing was the alleged criminality of immigrants from Mexico, though Trump said that he might let the "good" Mexicans back in afterward. Richard Cole explores these ideas in "Make Ásgarðr Great Again!"

41. As Jonas Wellendorf points out, the very fact that we believe in the *possibility* of a systematic pre-Christian Norse cosmology is probably down to Snorri's success in conceiving of such a thing in *Gylfaginning:* "The fact of the matter is that the cosmology

and the entire system of belief was hardly a system at all, but an indefinite amalgam of mutually contradictory but complementary notions" ("Homogeneity and Heterogeneity," 52).

42. Hastrup, *Culture and History,* 150–51. One of the greatest structuralist critics of Old Norse mythology, Aron Gurevich, regarded the "vertical axis" of the cosmology as being Snorri's direct imposition of a schema from his Christian worldview onto a pagan cosmos that was configured entirely around a horizontal spatial structure (Gurevich, "Space and Time," 42–53). See also Schjødt, "Horizontale und Vertikale Achsen" and "Kosmologimodeller og mytekredse"; Wellendorf, "Homogeneity and Heterogeneity," 51.

3. The Nature of World in a World without Nature

1. Clark, *Ecocriticism on the Edge,* 30.
2. "Ek man jǫtna / ár um borna, / þá er forðum mik / fœdda hǫfðu; / níu man ek heima, / níu íviðjur, / mjǫtvið mæran / fyr mold neðan."
3. In stanza 43 of *Vafþrúðnismál,* 6–8, Vafþrúðnir tells Óðinn that he has traveled in "every world; nine worlds I have traveled through to Niflhel" (þvíat hvern hefi ek heim um komit; / níu kom ek heima / fyr Niflhel neðan). Snorri agrees that Niflhel is "down in the ninth world" (*Gylfaginning,* edited by Faulkes, 9).
4. Snorri's *Gylfaginning* is the only source to mention all nine of these worlds. In the *Poetic Edda,* Álfaheimr and Vanaheimir are mentioned in passing one time each (*Grímnismál* 5 and *Vafþrúðnismál* 39); Svartálfheimr, Niflheimr, and Muspellsheimr do not occur in the Eddic poems, though Niflheimr might be equated with the Niflhel of *Vafþrúðnismál* 43.
5. Howarth, "Some Principles of Ecocriticism," 69.
6. Jakob Benediktsson, "Veraldar saga," 691.
7. *Edda,* translated by Faulkes, 1; *Gylfaginning,* edited by Faulkes, 3. "Eptir Nóa flóð lifðu átta menn þeir er heiminn bygðu ok kómu frá þeim ættir, ok varð enn sem fyrr at þá er fjǫlmentisk ok bygðisk verǫldin þá var þat allr fjǫlði mannfólksins er elskaði ágirni fjár ok metnaðar en afrœktusk guðs hlýðni, ok svá mikit gerðisk af því at þeir vildu eigi nefna guð."
8. The *OED* gives "Human existence; a period of this" as its first definition of "world" and cites examples of this usage as far back as the ninth century.
9. *Edda,* translated by Faulkes, 1; *Gylfaginning,* edited by Faulkes, 4: "Verǫldin var greind í þrjár hálfur. Frá suðri í vestr ok inn at Miðjarðarsjá, sá hlutr var kallaðr Affrica. Hinn syðri hlutr þeirar deildar er heitr ok brunninn af sólu. Annarr hlutr frá vestri ok til norðrs ok inn til hafsins, er sá kallaðr Evropa eða Enea."
10. "Valði henni Herfǫðr / hringa ok men, / fekk spjll spaklig / ok spá ganda, / sá hon vítt ok um vítt / of verǫld hverja." I have altered Larrington's text (number 30 in her reconstruction of the poem) to reflect the reading of the Íslenzk fornrit edition, which emends the Codex Regius's *fe* (for *fé,* "money" or "treasure") to *fekk,* "received," in the third line. If the manuscript reading stands, the verse should be translated as "Father of Hosts chose for her rings and necklaces / wise speech / and spirits of divination," which would make the *vǫlva's* divinatory powers part of Óðinn's gift to her. It makes

better sense for Óðinn to receive her counsels in exchange for the necklaces and rings he gives her.

11. "Brœðr munu berjask / ok at bǫnom verðask, / munu systrungar / sifjum spilla; / hart er í heimi, / hórdómr mikill, / skeggǫld, skálmǫld, / skildir ro klofnir, / vindǫld, vargǫld / áðr verǫld steypisk; / mun engi maðr / ǫðrum þyrma."

12. The idea of "the mesh" appears frequently across Morton's ecocritical writings. His use of the term is most conveniently explained in *Ecological Thought,* 28–31.

13. Morton, "Coexistence and Coexistents," 169.

14. "Jǫrð heitir með mǫnnum / en með ásum fold, / kalla vega Vanir, / ígrœn jǫtnar, / álfar gróandi, / kalla aur uppregin."

15. The precise signification of *ígrœnn,* which appears to be an elision of the preposition *í* (in/into) with the adjective, is uncertain. *Í* may simply be an intensifier; like Larrington, the editors of the Íslenzk fornrit edition treat it as such (439, note to stanza 10 of *Alvíssmál:* "mjög grœn").

16. On the ways in which *Alvíssmál* structures and presents its information, see Lindow, "Poetry, Dwarfs and Gods."

17. On the etymology of this term, see Bjorvand, "Eytmologien til *aur* og *golv."*

18. Lovelock, *Revenge of Gaia,* 32.

19. Lovelock's Gaia theory has proved popular, but it is by no means universally accepted as the most plausible model to explain the development and maintenance of life on Earth. There have certainly been many cases where scientific data do not seem to fit with the most fundamental tenets of the model. For criticism of the concept, see (among very many others) Williams, "Gaia, Nature Worship"; Kirchner, "Gaia Hypothesis"; Schneider, "Goddess of Earth"; Tyrell, *On Gaia.* Bruno Latour ("Why Gaia Is Not a God of Totality") has made a robust defense of Gaia theory in response to Tyrell's highly critical book, emphasizing that Lovelock's Gaia must not be viewed as a separate entity that has a providential, controlling function over life on earth. As Latour points out, Gaia's foremost importance is as a (constantly evolving) metaphor, not a scientific theory along the lines of evolution.

20. Lovelock, *Age of Gaia,* 153.

21. Morton, *Hyperobjects,* 156.

22. *Edda,* translated by Faulkes, 31; *Gylfaginning,* edited by Faulkes, 30: "Jǫrð, móðir Þórs, ok Rindr, móðir Vála, eru talðar með Ásynjum."

23. *Edda,* translated by Faulkes, 13; *Gylfaginning,* edited by Faulkes, 13: "Jǫrðin var dóttir hans ok kona hans."

24. The four main manuscripts disagree on the relationships within this branch of the giants' genealogy, sometimes making Jǫrð the mother of Dagr (Day) and wife of Dellingr and sometimes placing Nótt in that position. It seems likely that this tangle of names reflects the general obscurity of this manifestation of Jǫrð, who is much better attested as a personification of Earth than as a giantess. See Haukur Þorgeirsson, "Hinn fagri foldar son."

25. King, "Healing the Wounds," 115–16.

26. See, e.g., Roach, "Loving Your Mother"; Berman, "Rape of Mother Nature?"; Murphy, *Literature, Nature, and Other,* 59–72.

27. Plumwood, *Feminism and the Mastery of Nature,* 81.

28. Ibid., 84.

29. Frank, "Lay of the Land," 175.

30. See Abram, *Myths of the Pagan North*, 134–38.

31. Although Earl Hákon's identity as the subject and recipient of these verses is widely accepted, their attribution to Hallfreðr has been disputed: see Fidjestøl, *Det nørrone fyrstediktet*, 102–3. In the new edition of Old Norse–Icelandic skaldic poetry, however, Hallfreðr continues to be named as the author of this *Hákonardrápa* ("Poem about Hákon").

32. Hallfreðr vandræðaskáld Óttarsson, "Hákonardrápa," translated and edited by Heslop, 5–8: "Sannyrðum spenr sverða / snarr þiggjandi viggjar / barrhaddaða byr-jar / biðkvn und sik Þriðja. // Því hykk fleygjanda frægjan /—ferr Jǫrð und menþverri / ítran—eina at láta / Auðs systur mjǫk trauðan. // Rð lukusk, at sá síðan / snjallráðr konungs spjalli / átti eingadóttur / Ónars viði gróna. // Breiðleita gat brúði / Báleygs at sér teygja / stefnir stǫðvar Hrafna / stála ríkismlum."

33. Ónarr may be another byname for Óðinn, which would add an incestuous element to this already unpleasant metaphor. See Clunies Ross, *Prolonged Echoes*, 1:58.

34. Ström, "Hallfreðr Óttarsson," 263.

35. The fullest treatment of the sacred marriage motif in Norse religious culture is found in Steinsland, *Det hellige bryllup* and "Myte og ideologi."

36. Frank, "Lay of the Land," 182–84.

37. Snorri Sturluson, "Háttatal," edited by Gade, 3: "Úlfs bága verr ægis / ítrbals hati málu; / sett eru bǫrð fyr bratta / brún Míms vinar rúnu. / Orms váða kann eiðu allvaldr gǫfugr halda; menstríðir, njót móður / mellu dólgs til elli."

38. Frank, "Lay of the Land," 185, suggests that Snorri may intend a sardonic effect with his treatment of Jǫrð as both mother figure and sexual conquest in this stanza, perhaps tacitly drawing attention to the youth and inexperience of King Hákon Hákonarson of Norway, to whom his poem was dedicated.

39. See Berman, "Rape of Mother Earth?"

40. Stearney, "Feminism, Ecofeminism," 145.

41. This section of *Vǫluspá* is discussed in more detail in chap. 7, below.

42. "Sól tér sortna / sígr fold í mar, / hverfa af himni / heiðar stjǫrnur; / geisar eimi / við aldrnara, / leikr hár hiti / við himin sjálfan."

43. "Sér hon upp koma / ǫðru sinni / jǫrð ór ægi / iðjagrœna; / falla forsar, / flýgr ǫrn yfir, / sá er á fjalli / fiska veiðir."

44. Berman, "Rape of Mother Earth?" 264.

45. Morton, *Dark Ecology*, 10–11.

4. Tree-People and People-Trees

I must acknowledge the influence of Michael Bintley on this chapter and its title. Bintley uses "Tree People in Old Norse Poetry" as a subheading in chap. 4 of *Trees in the Religions of Early Medieval England*, and being unable to improve on this phrase, I have borrowed it here. The present chapter is much indebted to Bintley's work.

1. *Edda*, translated by Faulkes, 17; *Gylfaginning*, edited by Faulkes, 17: "hǫfuð-staðrinn eða helgistaðrinn goðanna . . . er at aski Yggdrasils. Þar skulu guðin eiga dóma sína hvern dag."

2. *Edda,* translated by Faulkes, 17; *Gylfaginning,* edited by Faulkes, 17: "Askrinn er allra tréa mestr ok beztr. Limar hans dreifask yfir heim allan ok standa yfir himni. Þrjár rœtr trésins halda því upp ok standa afar breitt. Ein er með Ásum, en ǫnnur með hrímþursum, þar sem forðum var Ginnungagap. In þriðja stendr yfir Niflheimi, ok undir þeiri rót er Hvergelmir, en Níðhǫggr gnagar neðan rótna. En undir þeiri rót er til hrímþursa horfir, þar er Mímis brunnr, er spekð ok mannvit er í fólgit . . . þriðja rót asksins stendr á himni, ok undir þeiri rót er brunnr sá er mjǫk er heilagr er heitir Urðar brunnr. Þar eigu guðin dómstað sinn."

3. For an overview of the importance of trees in historical Norse paganisms, see Andrén, *Tracing Old Norse Cosmology,* 27–63; Cusack, *Sacred Tree,* 146–70.

4. Gunanarsson, *Träden och människan,* 26–30; Brink, "Mythologizing Landscape," 99.

5. See Hastrup, "Cosmology and Society."

6. "Þaðan koma meyjar / margs vitandi / þrjár ór þeim sæ, / er und þolli stendr; / Urð hétu eina, / aðra Verðandi /—skáru á skíði—/ Skuld ina þriðju. / Þær lǫg lǫgðu, / þær líf kuru / alda bǫrnum, / ørlǫg seggja." I do not know why Larrington splits this stanza into two, as both the Codex Regius and *Hauksbók* versions have the single twelve-line text.

7. The first two Norns have names derived, respectively, from the past and present participles of the Old Norse *verða* (to become). Old Norse does not have a proper future tense, so the third Norn, Skuld, has a name that derives from the modal auxiliary verb *skulu,* which can express futurity or obligation, like the English verb "shall." On these figures, see Bek-Pedersen, *Norns in Old Norse Mythology.*

8. "Þrjár rœtr / standa á þrjá vega / undan aski Yggdrasils; / Hel býr undir einni, / annarri hrímþursar, / þriðju mennskir men."

9. The name Hel is given both to the chthonic realm of the dead in Norse mythology and to a personification of that realm. Hel is always represented as being below the ground: its etymology derives from a Germanic word for "something concealed," perhaps a "cave" or "grave." In the *Poetic Edda,* the "goddess" Hel—like Jǫrð, she is neither properly a goddess nor a giantess, but something of both or something between—is mentioned only rarely. See Abram, "Hel in Early Norse Poetry."

10. In stanza 21 of Egill Skallagrímsson's long memorial poem *Sonatorrek,* the poet speaks of his dead son as having gone *upp í Goðheim* (up into the world of the gods), which is the only explicit surviving reference to the gods inhabiting a realm above the world of people in a work that can be contextualized in a pagan Norse milieu. In *Gylfaginning* (ed. Faulkes, 13), Snorri states clearly that the Æsir live on the same plane as humankind, with Ásgarðr—which he identifies with Troy—forming the absolute center of the realm we know as Miðgarðr.

11. *Edda,* translated by Faulkes, 9; *Gylfaginning,* edited by Faulkes, 9. Faulkes translates *mold* as "dust" here, but "earth" seems preferable by analogy, e.g., with stanza 2 of *Vǫluspá's mjǫtvið mæran / fyr mold neðan* (mighty measuring-tree below the earth).

12. "Eikþyrnir heitir hjǫrtr / er stendr á hǫllu á Herjafǫðrs / ok bítr af Læraðs limum; / en af hans hornum / drýpr í Hvergelmi, / þaðan eigu vǫtn ǫll vega."

13. See Egeler, "Eikþyrnir and the Rivers of Paradise," 24–25, for a summary of the debate over Læraðr's identity. Egeler goes on to suggest the tree, animals, and rivers

of *Grímnismál* 25–26 have important correlations with Christian iconography, which is an interesting idea, but not germane to my topic here. Hageneder (*Yew,* 147) glosses *læraðr* as "glossy" and uses this alleged glossiness to support his contention that Ygg-drasill is a specimen of yew, which has much shinier foliage that the ash. I can't tell how Hageneder has come upon this interpretation, however, which certainly is not supported by other etymological work on this word; see Simek, *Dictionary of Northern Mythology,* 185.

14. US Geological Survey, "Evapotranspiration—The Water Cycle." https://water.usgs.gov/edu/watercycleevapotranspiration.html.

15. "Ratatoskr heitir íkorni / er renna skal / at aski Yggdrasils; / arnar orð / hann skal ofan bera / ok segja Níðhǫggvi niðr. // Hirtir eru ok fjórir, / þeirs af hœfinar á / gagháls gnaga: / Dáinn ok Dvalinn, / Dúneyrr and Duraþrór."

16. *Gylfaginning,* edited by Faulkes, 19: "Sú dǫgg er þaðan af fellr á jǫrðina, þat kalla men hunangfall, ok þar af fœðask býflugur. Fuglar tveir fœðask í Urðar brunni. Þeir heita svanir, ok af þeim fuglum komit þat fugla kyn er svá heitir."

17. These data are taken from a report published by Natural England in 2014: "Assessing and Addressing the Impacts of Ash Dieback on UK Woodlands and Trees of Conservation Importance," http://publications.naturalengland.org.uk/publication /5273931279761408.

18. Battles, *Tree,* 124.

19. "Askr Yggdrasils / drýgir erfiði / meira enn menn viti: / hjǫrtr bítr ofan, / en á hliðu fúnar, / skerðir Níðhǫggr neðan."

20. Bintley, "Plant Life in the *Poetic Edda,*" 235.

21. M. Hall, *Plants as Persons,* 127.

22. Ibid., 124.

23. Bintley, "Plant Life in the *Poetic Edda,*" 242.

24. Del Tredici, "Gestalt Dendrology," 5 and 8.

25. Ibid., 3.

26. Motz, "Cosmic Ash," 132.

27. Ibid., 140. See also Cusack, *Sacred Tree;* and Tolley, "What Is a World Tree?"

28. The evidence in favor of plants' abilities to communicate among themselves and perhaps even with different types of organisms is reviewed by M. Hall, *Plants as Persons,* 137–56. See also the essays collected in Baluška, Mancuso, and Volkmann, *Communication in Plants.*

29. See Hultgård, "Askr and Embla Myth."

30. *Edda,* translated by Faulkes, 13; *Gylfaginning,* edited by Faulkes, 13: "Þá er þeir Bors synir gengu með sævar strǫndu, fundu þeir tré tvau, ok tóku upp tréin ok skǫpuðu af menn. Gaf hinn fyrsti ǫnd ok líf, annarr vit ok hrœring, þriði ásjónu, mælit ok heyrn ok sjón; gáfu þeim klæði ok nǫfn. Hét karlmaðrinn Askr, en konan Embla, ok ólusk þaðan af mannkindin þeim er bygðin var gefin undir Miðgarði."

31. Bintley, *Trees in the Religions of Early Medieval England,* 138.

32. After more than four decades, the best introduction to skaldic poetry remains, in my opinion, Roberta Frank's *Old Norse Court Poetry;* for a comprehensive history of the form, see Clunies Ross, *History of Old Norse Poetry.*

33. There have been many attempts to define the Old Norse–Icelandic kenning system in linguistic, stylistic, or philosophical terms, and I don't think that a single definition has yet been arrived at that encompasses this figure of speech's remarkable complexity. See Holland, "Kennings, Metaphors"; Fidjestøl, "Kenning System"; Bergsveinn Birgisson, *Inn í skaldens sinn;* Broz, "Kennings as Blends"; Abram, "Kennings and Things."

34. See Meissner, *Die Kenningar der Skalden,* 266–72.

35. *Den norsk-islandske skjaldediktning,* edited by Finnur Jónsson, B1, 53.

36. Andrew McGillivray, however, does see a close enough resemblance in form that this similarity can work as part of a complex that makes a human the "microcosm of the tree," by which McGillivray means Yggdrasill: "The synergetic relationship between humans and the tree, as seen in the creation of humans from the pieces of wood, suggests that a human may be a microcosm of the tree, for both grow from a common material and interact in a life-giving cycle with the same regenerative force. Moreover, the human shape resembles that of a tree in appearance, the arms representative of the branches of the tree and the torso of the trunk" ("Mythic Transformations," 60–61).

37. See Frank, *Old Norse Court Poetry,* 43; Weber, "Of Trees and Men."

38. Gerd Wolfgang Weber takes issue with the idea that these kennings have anything to do with actual trees: "In kennings for 'humans,' words for 'trees' are reduced to their basic qualities of 'standing upright' and 'conveying the notion of male or female gender.'" In Weber's analysis, this type of kenning does not really produce hybrid image-objects: rather, the determinants "of swords," "of battle," "of linen," and so on, become simply a badge that marks off these tree-people as "not real trees" ("Of Trees and Men," 431). I have used these examples elsewhere, as part of an analysis of what I suggest we can call an "object-oriented skaldic poetics" (Abram, "Kennings and Things").

39. *Skáldskaparmál,* edited by Faulkes, 1:64–65; *Edda,* translated by Faulkes, 116–17.

40. *Icelandic-English Dictionary,* s.v. *meiðr.*

41. As Bintley puts it ("Plant Life in the *Poetic Edda,*" 242), "an interim assessment of the proliferation of treeish terms for humans points to a certain pre-Christian antiquity in this trope in Norse culture." Bintley provides the fullest and best overview of the connections between people and trees in skaldic verse in *Trees in the Religions of Early Medieval England,* 129–41.

42. *Egils saga,* edited by Bjarni Einarsson, 144–46. Egill Skallagrímsson lived in the middle of the tenth century, and the composition of *Sonatorrek* took place, on the basis of the saga's internal chronology, around 960.

43. Ibid., 38–40.

44. Ibid., 136 and 98.

45. All translations from *Sonatorrek* are by me, and based on the text of *Egils saga,* edited by Bjarni Einarsson, where the poem is found at 146–54.

46. *Sonatorrek* 4: "Því at ætt mín / á enda stendr, / hræbarnir / sem hlynir marka, / era karskr maðr / sá er kǫgla berr / frænda hrørs / af fletjum niðr."

47. *Sonatorrek* 5: "Þó mun ek mitt / ok móður hrør / fǫður fall / fyrst um telja; / þat ber ek út / ór orðhofi / mærðar timbr / máli laufgat."

48. *Egils saga,* edited by Bjarni Einarsson, 145.

49. Bintley, "Life-Cycles of Men and Trees" and *Trees in the Religions of Early Medieval England,* 131–32; see also Turville-Petre, *Scaldic Poetry,* 39.

50. *Sonatorrek* 21: "Þat man ek enn / er upp um hóf / í goðheim / Gauta spjalli / ættar ask / þann er óx af mér / ok kynvið / kvánar minnar."

5. *Trees, Vines, and the Golden Age of Settlement*

1. Kissane, "Seeing the Forest," 7.

2. See Þröstur Eysteinsson, *Forestry in a Treeless Land.*

3. Oslund, "Imagining Iceland," 315.

4. Þröstur Eysteinsson, *Forestry in a Treeless Land,* 3.

5. *Íslendingabók. Landnámabók,* edited by Jakob Benediktsson, 1:5: "Ingolfr hét maðr nórœnn, es sannliga es sagt at fœri fyrst þaðan til Íslands, þá es Haraldr enn hárfagri vas sextán vetra gamall, en í annat sinn fám vetrum síðarr; hann byggði suðr í Reykjarvík. Þar es Ingolfshǫfði kallaðr fyr austan Minþakseyri, sem hann kom fyrst á land, en þar Ingolfsfell fyr vestan Ǫlfossá, es hann lagði sína eigu á síðan. Í þann tíð vas Ísland viði vaxit á miðli fjalls ok fjǫru."

6. Ashwell and Jackson, "Sagas as Evidence," 165.

7. See, e.g., Hörður Kristinsson, "Post-Settlement History"; Smith, *"Landnám"*; Amorosi et al., "Raiding the Landscape."

8. Hörður Kristinsson, "Post-Settlement History," 31–32.

9. *Egils saga,* edited by Bjarni Einarsson, 38: "Síðan kannaði Skalla-Grímr landit og var þar mýrlendi mikit og skógar víðir, langt í milli fjalls og fjǫru, selveiðar gnógar og fiskifang mikit."

10. *Íslendingabók. Landnámabók,* edited by Jakob Benediktsson, 1:38: "Þeir sigldu um sumarit eptir til Nóregs. Ok er menn spurðu af landinu, þá lét Flóki illa yfir, en Herjólfr sagði kost ok lǫst landinu, en Þórólfr kvað drjúpa smjǫr af hverju strái á landinu, því er þeir hǫfðu fundit; því var hann kallaðr Þórólfr smjǫr."

11. Rudd, *Greenery,* 13.

12. Andrés Arnalds, "Ecosystem Disturbance"; Dugmore and Erskine, "Local and Regional Patterns."

13. Sigurður Gylfi Magnússon, *Wasteland with Words,* 149.

14. Orri Vésteinsson, McGovern, and Keller, "Enduring Impacts." See also Dugmore et al., "Norse *landnám.*"

15. Stewart, *On Longing,* 23. See also Davies, "Sustainable Nostalgia."

16. Morton, *Ecology without Nature,* 23.

17. Rudd, *Greenery,* 53.

18. For a thorough discussion of the name, the sources of our knowledge for it, and the various interpretations that have been proposed for it, see Magnús Stefánsson, "Vínland or Vinland?" Magnús argues forcefully that the name should be given as *Vinland* with a short *i* and interpreted as "land of meadows." Magnús's reasoning is that *vín* (wine) is a manmade product rather than a natural property of the land, and thus naming this place "Wineland" would contradict normal Norse naming practices.

19. The myth of "Vínland the Good" first appears in the German historian Adam of Bremen's eleventh-century *Descriptio insularum Aquilonis* (Description of the Northern islands) in his *Gesta Hammaburgensis ecclesiae pontificum* (History of the bishops of the church of Hamburg), wherein Adam states that grapes grew uncultivated in a

place he knew as *Winland.* For a survey of these sources and their possible interrelationships, see Sverrir Jakobsson, "Vinland and Wishful Thinking," 494–97.

20. "Eiríks saga rauða," edited by Einar Ól. Sveinsson and Matthías Þórðarson, 201: "því at hann kvað menn þat mjǫk mundu fýsa þangat, ef landit héti vel." Translations from *Eiríks saga* are by me, as the most reliable published translation—"Eirik the Red's Saga," translated by Keneva Kunz—follows a variant manuscript that does not form the basis of the standard edition.

21. For an overview of Greenland's treatment in the sagas, see Grove, "Place of Greenland."

22. "The Saga of the Greenlanders," translated by Kunz, 637; "Grœnlendinga saga," edited by Einar Ól. Sveinsson and Matthías Þórðarson, 246: "landit var ófjǫllótt ok skógi vaxit, ok smár hæðir á landinu."

23. "The Saga of the Greenlanders," 638; "Grœnlendinga saga," 249.

24. "The Saga of the Greenlanders," 639; "Grœnlendinga saga," 250: "Af kostum skal þessu landi nafn gefa ok kalla Markland."

25. "The Saga of the Greenlanders," 639; "Grœnlendinga saga," 250: "þóttusk ekki jafnsœtt kennt hafa, sem þat var."

26. "The Saga of the Greenlanders," 639; "Grœnlendinga saga," 250–51: "en þegar sjór fell undir skip þeira, þá tóku þeir bátinn ok reru til skipsins ok fluttu þat upp í ána, síðan í vatnit, ok kǫstuðu þar akkerum ok báru af skipi húðfǫt sín ok gerðu þar búðir; tóku þat ráð síðan, at búask þar um þann vetr, ok gerðu þar hús mikil. Hvárki skorti þar lax í ánni né í vatninu, ok stœrra lax en þeir hefði fyrr sét. Þar var svá góðr landskostr, at því er þeim sýndisk, at þar myndi engi fénaðr fóðr þurfa á vetrum; þar kómu engi frost á vetrum, ok lítt rénuðu þar grǫs. Meira var þar jafndœgri en á Grœnlandi eða Íslandi; sól hafði þar eyktar stað ok dagmála stað um skammdegi."

27. *Tyrkir* is an obviously foreign name in an Old Norse–Icelandic context, and it is identical with the nominative plural form *Tyrkir,* "Turks." If this derivation is correct, we should probably interpret the name as referring to the character's exotic origins in what to Icelanders would seem like the far south of Europe (the difference between a Turk and a German is relatively small from the perspective of the continent's northern periphery). When the saga first introduces Tyrkir, it calls him a *suðrmaðr*—a "man of the south." His identification as German rests on the saga's identification of his language as *þýsk.*

28. "The Saga of the Greenlanders," 640; "Grœnlendinga saga," 252. "Þá mælti Leifr til hans: 'Hví vartu svá seinn, fóstri minn, ok fráskili fǫruneytinu?' Hann talaði þá fyrst lengi á þýzku ok skaut marga vega augunum ok gretti sik, en þeir skilðu eigi, hvat er hann sagði. Hann mælti þá á norrœnu, er stund leið: 'Ek var genginn eigi miklu lengra en þit. Kann ek nǫkkur nýmæli at segja; ek fann vínvið ok vínber.' 'Mun þat satt, fóstri minn?' kvað Leifr. 'At vísu er þat satt,' kvað hann, 'því at ek var þar fœddr, er hvárki skorti vínvið né vínber.'"

29. Magnús Stefánsson, "Vínland or Vinland?" 142; Halldór Hermannsson, "Tyrkir, Leif Erikson's Foster-Father," 392; Brown and Magoun, "Tyrkir, First German in North America."

30. "The Saga of the Greenlanders," 640; "Grœnlendinga saga," , 252–53: "Nú skal hafa tvennar sýslur fram, ok skal sinn dag hvárt, lesa vínber eða hǫggva vínvið ok fella mǫrkina, svá at þat verði farmr til skips míns."

31. "Eiríks saga rauða," edited by Einar Ól. Sveinsson and Matthías Þórðarson, 211: "Váru þar hveitiakrar sjálfsánir ok vínviðr vaxinn. Þar váru þau tré, er mǫsurr heita, ok hǫfðu þeir af þessu ǫllu nǫkkur merki."

32. As noted by Hoidal, "Norsemen and the North American Forests," 202, the proposed sites of the Norse landings in Newfoundland are well within the present-day range of the sugar maple; specimens of the silver maple and red maple are also found this far north, though less frequently near the coast. The etymology of *mǫsurr* refers to the spottiness of the wood, which may refer to the characteristic bird's-eye figuring one sometimes finds in maple.

33. "The Saga of the Greenlanders," 651; "Grœnlendinga saga," 268. On the nature and significance of Karlsefni's strange wooden *húsasnotra,* see Sayers, "Karlsefni's *husasnotra.*" Sayers identifies the object as a "wind vane" (346), while other critics have been inclined to interpret it as some form of decorative prow ornament for his ship.

34. "Eiríks saga rauða," edited by Einar Ól. Sveinsson and Matthías Þórðarson, 223: "En er þeir hǫfðu siglt fyrir Furðustrandir, þá létu þeir ina skozku men á land ok báðu þau hlaupa suðr á landit at leita landskosta ok koma aptr, áðr þrjú dœgr væri liðin . . . En er þau kómu aptr, hafði annat í hendi vínberjakǫngul, en annat hveitiax sjálfsáit."

35. Ibid., 223–24.

36. Ibid., 226–27: "Þeir fundu þar á landi sjálfsána hveitakra, þar sem lægðir váru, en vínvið allt þar sem holta vissi. Hverr lœkr var þar fullr af fiskum. Þeir gerðu grafar, þar sem mœttisk landit ok flóðit gekk ofast, ok þá er út fell sjórinn, váru helgir fiskar í grǫfunum. Þar var mikill fjǫlði dýra á skóginum, með ǫllu móti. Þeir váru þar hálfan mánuð ok skemmtuðu sér ok urðu við ekki varir. Fé sitt hǫfðu þeir með sér."

37. "The Saga of the Greenlanders," 648; "Grœnlendinga saga," 264: "sú ferð þykkir bæði góð til fjár ok virðingar."

38. See Lethbridge and Hartman, "Inscribing Environmental Memory"; Barraclough, "Land-Naming."

39. On the sagas' descriptions of Vínland as literary fabrications, see Barnes, "Vínland the Good"; Williamsen, "Boundaries of Difference"; Larrington, "'Undruðusk þá, sem fyrir var'"; Baumgartner, "Freydís in Vinland."

40. On the concept of *Bestand* and its relevance to ecocritical thinking, see Garrard, *Ecocriticism,* 31.

41. Borlik, *Ecocriticism,* 75–76.

42. "The Saga of the Greenlanders," 646; "Grœnlendinga saga," 261: "Þann máldaga gerðu þeir Karlsefni ok hásetar hans, at jǫfnum hǫndum skyldi þeir hafa allt þat, er þeir fengi til gœða. Þeir hǫfðu með sér alls konar fénað, því at þeir ætluðu at byggja landit, ef þeir mætti þat."

43. It is difficult to know how best to refer to the inhabitants of Vínland as they appear in these sagas. The term *skræling* is quite possibly pejorative. Kolodny (*In Search of First Contact,* 58) calls it a "nasty and contemptuous term, meaning 'little wretches' or 'wretches who screech.'" Treating the *skrælingar* as if they were historical personages, Kolodny chooses to call them "American Indians." In her translations of the sagas, Kunz regularly uses the noun "native," which is not entirely free of imperialist connotations of alterity and inferiority. Frakes ("Vikings, Vínland," 167 n. 33) discusses the problems surrounding this nomenclature; he opts for "Americans" as a gloss for *skrælingar,* which,

in his opinion, is anachronistic but less offensive than some of the alternatives. In my discussion of these figures, I prefer to retain the Old Norse term.

44. "Eiríks saga rauða," edited by Einar Ól. Sveinsson and Matthías Þórðarson, 227: "Þeir váru svartir menn ok illiligr ok hǫfðu illt hár á hǫfði; þeir váru mjǫk eygðir ok breiðir í kinnum."

45. See Cole, "Racial Thinking"; Jochens, "Race and Ethnicity"; Lindow, "Supernatural Others." A useful comparison between medieval and modern conceptions of "race" is made by Bartlett, "Medieval and Modern Concepts."

46. For a thorough survey of the classical and medieval sources for the idea of the uniped, see Pàroli, "How Many Are the Unipeds' Feet?"

47. As Krech has shown, the idea of the "ecological Indian" is a western fantasy of North American colonialism that vastly oversimplifies the relationship between these people and their environments (Ecological Indian, 15). And as Ladino demonstrates, contemporary discourse continues lazily to "uphold a human-nature binary that affiliates Indians with the latter [and that creates] an opposition between Native Americans and the rest of America," shifting the burden of ecological consciousness from white people onto those who have already been deprived of the possibility of dwelling in their own oikos (Reclaiming Nostalgia, 122).

48. "The Saga of the Greenlanders," 642; "Grœnlendinga saga," 255: "Hér er fagrt, ok hér vilda ek bœ minn reisa."

49. "The Saga of the Greenlanders," 646–47; "Grœnlendinga saga," 261: "Eptir þann vetr inn fyrsta kom sumar; þá urðu þeir varir við Skrælinga, ok fór þar ór skógi fram mikill flokkr manna. Þar var nær nautfé þeira, en graðungr tók at belja ok gjalla ákafliga hátt; en þat hræddusk Skrælingar ok lǫgðu undan með byrðar sínar, en þat var grávara ok safali ok alls konar skinnavara."

50. "The Saga of the Greenlanders," 647; "Grœnlendinga saga," 262: "Ok nú leitar hann ráðs með þeim hætti, at hann bað konur bera út búnyt at þeim; ok þegar er þeir sá búnyt, þá vildu þeir kaupa þat, en ekki annat. Nú var sú kaupfǫr Skrælinga, at þeir báru sinn varning í brott í mǫgum sínum, en Karlsefni ok fǫrunautar hans hǫfðu eptir bagga þeira ok skinnavǫru; fóru þeir við svá búit í burt."

51. Kolodny, In Search of First Contact, 65.

52. Frakes, "Vikings, Vínland," 181

53. See Baumgartner, "Freydís in Vinland"; Wolf, "Amazons in Vínland"; Kolodny, In Search of First Contact, 88.

54. Frakes, "Vikings, Vínland," 194.

55. "Eiríks saga rauða," edited by Einar Ól. Sveinsson and Matthías Þórðarson, 228–29: "Þat sá þeir Karlsefni, at Skrælingar fœrðu upp á stǫng knǫtt stundar mikinn, því nær til at jafna sem sauðarvǫmb, ok helzt blán at lit, ok fleygðu af stǫnginni upp á landit yfir lið þeira Karlsefnis, ok lét illiliga við, þar sem niðr kom."

56. "The Saga of the Greenlanders," 647; "Grœnlendinga saga," 263: "Nú hafði einn þeira Skrælinga tekit upp øxi eina ok leit á um stund ok reiddi at félaga sínum ok hjó til hans."

57. "Eiríks saga rauða," edited by Einar Ól. Sveinsson and Matthías Þórðarson, 230: "Þeir Skrælingar fundu ok mann dauðan, ok lá øx í hjá. Einn þeira tók upp øxina ok høggr með tré ok þá hverr at ǫðrum, ok þótti þeim vera gersimi ok bíta vel. Síðan tók

einn ok hjó í stein, svá at brotnaði øxin, ok þá þótti þeim engu nýt, er eigi stózk grjótit, ok kǫstuðu niðr."

58. Frakes, "Vikings, Vínland," 182.

59. "Eiríks saga rauða," edited by Einar Ól. Sveinsson and Matthías Þórðarson, 229: "Þeir Karlsefni þóttusk nú sjá, þótt þar væri landskostir góðir, at þar myndi jafnan ótti ok ófriðr á liggja af þeim, er fyrir bjuggu."

60. Although the sagas are silent on the matter, Ari Þorgilsson does claim in *Íslendingabók* that early settlers of Greenland discovered traces of prior human presence there: "They found signs of human habitation there both in the east and west of the country, fragments of skin-boats and stone implements, from which it may be deduced that the same kind of people had passed through there as had settled Vínland and the Greenlanders call Skrælingar" (*Íslendingabók; Kristni saga,* translated by Grønlie, 7.) There is no secure archaeological evidence of Norse-Inuit contact in Greenland before about 1200, however.

61. As Kolodny has shown in *Lay of the Land,* later North American colonialist discourse deployed the metaphor of "land as woman" promiscuously. Even if this metaphor is only implicit in the Norse accounts of Vínland, it is another example of how the Viking expansion around the North Atlantic anticipates in many ways later European attitudes toward the claiming of new territories in terra incognita.

62. The Norse presence in Greenland certainly lasted long enough to be classed as a stable settlement, but worsening climatic conditions, disease, and changing economic and political circumstances in Scandinavia threatened the viability of the colony over the course of the fifteenth century. By 1500 the Norse presence in Greenland was effectively over. For an overview of these developments, see Dugmore, Keller, and McGovern, "Norse Greenland Settlement."

6. The Æsir and the Anthropocene

1. Schatz, "Importance of Apocalypse," 21.

2. Buell, *Environmental Imagination,* 285.

3. *Homilies of Wulfstan,* edited by Bethurum, 254: "ðeos woruld is on ofste & hit nealæcð þam ende. & þy hit is on worulde aa swa leng swa wyrse."

4. See Abram, *Myths of the Pagan North,* 166–68.

5. Paul Crutzen and Eugene Stoermer seem to deserve most credit for popularizing the coinage with their 2000 article "The Anthropocene." Crutzen gives a succinct definition of the term in a 2006 paper also entitled "The 'Anthropocene.'" See also Steffen, Crutzen, and McNeill, "The Anthropocene."

6. Steffen et al., "Trajectory of the Anthropocene"; see also McNeill and Engelke, *Great Acceleration.*

7. Some critics of the term "Anthropocene" object to the universality of the term and argue that it is particular groups of humans, rather than human beings as a species, to whom anthropogenic trauma in earth systems should be attributed, whether these groups are Westerners, moderns, capitalists, or whatever. Depending on one's preference, the same concept could be referred to under the rubrics "Technocene," "Econocene," "Occidentocene," or "Capitalocene," although in my view "Anthropocene"

can do useful work as an umbrella term that encompasses all these different works of attribution (and blaming). See Malm and Hornborg, "Geology of Mankind?"; Rudiak-Gould, "Social Life of Blame"; Haraway, "Anthropocene"; Schneiderman, "Naming the Anthropocene."

8. See, e.g., Ruddiman, "Atmospheric Greenhouse Era." A compromise between the early and late onset theories of Anthropocene origins has been proposed with the introduction of the term "Palaeoanthropocene," which refers to "the diffuse, transitional period between early Holocene environmental modification by humans and the clear, global changes brought about by the Industrial Revolution" (Catlyn, "Archaeology for the Anthropocene," 13.)

9. Fuller et al., "Contribution of Rice Agriculture." The issue of the journal *Holocene* in which this article appears was a special number devoted to the early-Anthropocene debate, with contributions from scholars on both sides.

10. Ruddiman, "Anthropocene."

11. Morton, *Hyperobjects, 7.*

12. Ibid., 7.

13. As Aidan Davison puts it: "All ways of life inhabit worlds that exceed them. Extinction, then, involves not just a discrete loss, but a multispecies unravelling of possibility and purpose: the end of a storied world. Different ways of life ravel the real into narrative threads that cannot be unpicked from the tapestry of any given world. The mass extinction event that may define the Anthropocene, then, is a colossal unravelling of collective realities that include but exceeds the loss of much human possibility and purpose." ("Beyond the Mirrored Horizon," 304.)

14. Morton, *Hyperobjects*, 16.

15. Gräslund and Price, "Twilight of the Gods?"; Nordvig, "Of Fire and Water," 120–85.

16. Davison, "Beyond the Mirrored Horizon," 301.

17. Latour, *We Have Never Been Modern*, 30–32.

18. Ibid., 10–11.

19. See Jón Hnefill Aðalsteinsson, "Gods and Giants"; Schulz, *Riesen.*

20. "Hittusk æsir / á Iðavelli, / þeir er hǫrg ok hof / hátimbruðu; / afla lǫgðu, / auð smíðuðu, / tangir skópu / ok tól gørðu."

21. Simek, *Dictionary of Northern Mythology, 170.*

22. *Vǫluspá* [K] 8, lines 1–4: "Teflðu í túni, / teitir váru, / var þeim vettergis / vant ór gulli . . ."

23. *Edda*, translated by Faulkes, 16; *Gylfaginning*, edited by Faulkes, 15: "Þar næst gerðu þeir þat at þeir lǫgðu afla ok þar til gerðu þeir hamar ok tǫng ok steðja ok þaðan af ǫll tól ǫnnur. Ok því næst smíðuðu þeir málm ok stein ok tré, ok svá gnógliga þann málm er gull heitir at ǫll búsgǫgn ok ǫll reiðigǫgn hǫfdu þeir af gulli, ok er sú ǫld kǫlluð gullaldr."

24. See Zutter, "Cultural Landscape of Iceland," 63–64.

25. *Vǫluspá* [K] 8, 5–8: ". . . unz þrjár kvómu / þursa meyjar / ámáttakr mjǫk / ór jǫtunheimum."

26. *Edda*, translated by Faulkes, 16; *Gylfaginning*, edited by Faulkes, 15.

27. Lönnroth, "The Founding of Miðgarðr," 18–19.

28. U. Dronke, *Poetic Edda II*, 120. See also Hamel, "Game of the Gods."

29. Latour, *We Have Never Been Modern*, 98–99.

30. Ibid., 99–100.

31. For an overview and analysis of this type of narrative, see McKinnell, *Meeting the Other.*

32. Jochens, "*Vǫluspá*," 351.

33. "Þá gengu regin ǫll / á røkstóla, / ginnheilǫg goð, / ok um þat gættusk, / hverr skyldi dverga / dróttin skepja, / ór Brimis blóði / ok ór Bláins leggjum."

34. U. Dronke, *Poetic Edda II*, 38.

35. *Edda*, translated by Faulkes, 16; *Gylfaginning*, edited by Faulkes, 15: "Þar næst settusk guðin upp í sæti sín ok réttu dóma sína ok mintusk hvaðan dvergar hófðu kviknat í moldunni ok niðri í jǫrðunni svá sem maðkar í holdi. Dvergarnir hǫfðu skipazk fyrst ok tekit kviknun í holdi Ymis ok váru þá maðkar, en af atkvæði guðanna urðu þeir vitandi mannvits ok hǫfðu manns líki ok búa þó í jorðu ok í steinum."

36. Latour, *We Have Never Been Modern*, 41.

37. Lindow, *Norse Mythology*, 100.

38. Bragg, *Oedipus Borealis*, 154–55; Motz, *Wise One of the Mountain*, 116–17.

39. See, e.g., Cantor, "Image of the Negro"; Ellingson, *Myth of the Noble Savage;* Haller, *Outcasts from Evolution.*

40. "Þat man hon fólkvíg / fyrst í heimi, / er Gullveigu / geirum studdu / ok í hǫll Hárs / hana brenndu; / þrysvar brenndu / þrysvar borna, / opt, ósjaldan, / þó hon enn lifir."

41. Lindow, *Norse Mythology*, 53.

42. Müllenhoff, *Deutsche Altertumskunde*, 5:96.

43. Borovsky, "'En hon er blandin mjök,'" 6.

44. My reading omits discussion of stanza 22, which is usually treated as a companion piece to stanza 21, with Gullveig referred to by the name Heiði (which means "shiny" or something like it). In stanza 22, this figure is called a *vǫlu vel spá* (a seeress who prophesies well) and *angan illrar þjóðar/brúðar* (delight of an evil people/woman [the two main manuscripts of *Vǫluspá* have different readings at this point]). Although the identification of Gullveig with Heiði in these two verses is perfectly plausible, I believe it is also possible that stanza 23 refers to the *vǫlva* who is narrating the poem and that this stanza properly belongs to *Vǫluspá*'s frame narrative rather than the story of the Æsir-Vanir war.

45. "Þá gengu regin ǫll / á røkstóla, / ginnheilǫg goð, / ok um þat gættusk, / hvárt skyldu æsir / afráð gjalda / eða skyldu goðin ǫll / gildi eiga." I depart from Larrington in translating *eiga gildi* as "receive payment" rather than her "share sacrificial feasts." Although "feast" is an attested gloss for *gildi*, I feel that Larrington is overly specific about the nature of the thing—an honor or a payment—that the gods will receive. Larrington is following Ursula Dronke's interpretation of the poem at this point: "The Æsir are faced with surrendering their monopoly of godhead and its revenues and joining in with the all-too-popular Vanir . . . if they do agree to share with the Vanir, then they must be all gods together. . . . The Æsir's only alternative to this unprofitable and demeaning share-policy is to attack again: which they do" (*Poetic Edda II*, 134).

46. *Vǫluspá* [K] 24, 5–8; 25 in Larrington: ". . . brotinn var borðveggr / borgar ása, / knáttu vanir / vígspá / vǫllu sporna."

47. "Þá gengu regin ǫll / á rǫkstóla, / ginnheilǫg goð, / ok um þat gættusk, / hverr hefði lopt allt / lævi blandit / eða ætt jǫtuns / Óðs mey gefna." I translate *hverr* as "who," instead of Larrington's "which people," which I view as tendentiously suggesting that it is a group, rather than an individual, which is responsible for these actions.

48. *Edda,* translated by Faulkes, 35; *Gylfaginning,* edited by Faulkes, 34: "Þat var snimma í ǫndverða bygð goðanna, þá er goðin hǫfðu sett Miðgarð ok gert Valhǫll, þá kom þar smiðr nokkvorr ok bauð at gera þeim borg á þrim misserum svá góða at trú ok ørugg væri fyrir bergrisum ok hrímþursum þótt þeir komi inn um Miðgarð. En hann mælir sér þat til kaups at hann skyldi eignask Freyju, ok hafa vildi hann sól ok mána. Þá gengu Æsirnir á tal ok réðu ráðum sínum, ok var þat kaup gert við smiðinn at hann skyldi eignask þat er hann mælir til ef hann fengi gert borgina á einum vetri, en hinn fyrsta sumars dag ef nokkvorr hlutr væri ógjǫrr at borginni þá skyldi hann af kaupinu."

49. *Edda,* translated by Faulkes, 26; *Gylfaginning,* edited by Faulkes, 26–27: "Sá er enn talðr með Ásum er sumir kalla rógbera Ásanna ok frumkveða flærðanna ok vǫmm allra goða ok manna. Sá er nefndr Loki eða Loptr, sonr Fárbauta jǫtuns. Móðir hans er Laufey eða Nál . . . Loki er fríðr ok fagr sýnum, illr í skaplyndi, mjǫk fjǫlbreytinn at háttum. Hann hafði þá speki um fram aðra menn er sloegð heitir, ok vælar til allra hluta. Hann kom Ásum jafnan í fullt vandræði ok opt leysti hann þá með vælræðum."

50. *Edda,* translated by Faulkes, 26–27; *Gylfaginning,* edited by Faulkes, 27: "Enn átti Loki fleiri bǫrn. Angrboða hét gýgr í Jǫtunheimum. Við henni gat Loki þrjú bǫrn. Eitt var Fenrisúlfr, annat Jǫrmungandr (þat er Miðgarðsormr), þriðja er Hel. En er goðin vissu til at þessi þrjú systkin fœddusk upp í Jǫtunheimum ok goðin rǫkðu til spadóma at af systkinum þessum mundi þeim mikit mein ok óhapp standa ok þótti ǫllum mikils ills af væni, fyrst af móðerni ok enn verra af faðerni."

51. Morton, *Hyperobjects,* 122.

52. Blanchot, *Writing of the Disaster,* 1.

53. Morton, *Hyperobjects,* 120.

54. Ibid., 2.

55. The best guides to the myth of Baldr's death and its aftermath in a social context are Lindow, *Murder and Vengeance;* and Lieberman, "Some Controversial Aspects."

56. *Edda,* translated by Faulkes, 48; *Gylfaginning,* edited by Faulkes, 45: "Frigg tók svardaga til þess at eira skyldu Baldri eldr ok vatn, járn ok alls konar málmr, steinar, jǫrðin, viðirnir, sóttirnar, dýrin, fuglarnir, eitr, ormar."

57. *Edda,* translated by Faulkes, 48; *Gylfaginning,* edited by Faulkes, 45: "En er þetta var gert ok vitat, þá var þat skemtun Baldrs ok Ásanna at hann skyldi standa upp á þingum en allir aðrir skyldu sumir skjóta á hann, sumir hǫggva til, sumir berja grjóti. En hvat sem at var gert, sakaði hann ekki, ok þótti þetta ǫllum mikill frami."

58. *Edda,* translated by Faulkes, 23; *Gylfaginning,* edited by Faulkes, 23: "Annarr son Óðins er Baldr, ok er frá honum gott at segja. Hann er beztr ok hann lofa allir. Hann er svá fagr álitum ok bjartr svá at lýsir af honum, ok eitt gras er svá hvítt at jafnat er til Baldrs brár. Þat er allra grasa hvítast, ok þar eptir mátþu marka hans fegrð bæði á hár ok á líki [. . .] Hann býr þar sem heitir Breiðablik. Þat er á himni. Í þeim stað má ekki vera óhreint."

59. See Busygin, "White-Christ," 2. Whereas earlier scholarship had tended to see Christ's "whiteness" in Old Norse sources as a borrowing from pagan iconography,

Busygin convincingly shows that epithets like "White-Christ" were in circulation among Christians in the British Isles before the conversion of Scandinavia and that the probable direction of influence between the two figures should be reversed.

60. *Edda,* translated by Faulkes, 23; *Gylfaginning,* edited by Faulkes, 23: "sú náttúra fylgir honum at engi má haldask dómr hans."

61. Loki's structural identity with other trickster figures from world mythology was first proposed by de Vries, *Problem of Loki;* see also Rooth, *Loki in Scandinavian Mythology;* Frakes, "Loki's Mythological Function."

7. Reading Rangarǫk at the End of the World

1. "Austr sat in aldna / í Járnviði / ok fœddi þar / Fenris kindir; / verðr af þeim llum / einna nøkkurr / tungls tjúgari / í trolls hami." Larrington translates the verb *fœða* (cognate with English "feed") as "to give birth to." This is an attested meaning of *fœða* but not its primary meaning. Since the identity of *in aldna* in this stanza is utterly obscure, there is no need to assume that she is the parent of the wolves in her care.

2. "Fyllisk fjǫrvi / feigra manna, / rýðr ragna sjǫt / rauðum dreyra; / svǫrt verða sólskin / of sumur eptir, / veðr ǫll válynd. / Vituð ér enn—eða hvat?" Larrington translates the refrain at the end of this verse as "do you want to know more: and what?" It has been impossible for critics to arrive at a consensus over how this important but ambiguous phrase should be rendered in English.

3. *Edda,* translated by Faulkes, 53; *Gylfaginning,* translated by Faulkes, 49: "Þá mælir Gangleri: 'Hver tíðindi eru at segja frá um ragnarøkr? Þess hefi ek eigi fyrr heyrt getit.' Hár segir: 'Mikil tíðindi eru þaðan at segja ok mǫrg. Þau í fyrstu at vetr sá kemr er kallaðr er fimbulvetr. Þá drífr snær ór ǫllum áttum. Frost eru þá mikil ok vindar hvassir. Ekki nýtr sólar. Þeir vetr fara þrír saman ok ekki sumar milli. En áðr ganga svá aðrir þrír vetr at þá er um alla verǫld orrostur miklar.'"

4. See Hultgård, "Fimbulvintern."

5. "Brœðr munu berjask / ok at bǫnum verðask, / munu systrungar / sifjum spilla; / hart er í heimi, / hórdómr mikill, / skeggǫld, skálmǫld, / skildir ro klofnir, / vindǫld, varǫld, / áðr verǫld steypisk; / mun eigi maðr / ǫðrum þyrma."

6. Hsiang, Burke, and Miguel, "Quantifying the Influence of Climate," 12353667–10.

7. Salehyan, "Climate Change and Conflict"; Salehyan, "From Climate Change to Conflict?"

8. Gräslund and Price, "Twilight of the Gods?"; see also Gräslund, "Fimbulvintern."

9. Gräslund and Price, "Twilight of the Gods?" 438–40; see also Haraldur Bernharðsson, "Old Icelandic *ragnarök.*" In the *Hauksbók* version of the poem, the verse that contains the first reference to *ragna rǫk* occurs earlier than in the Codex Regius—in the thirty-sixth stanza, though this stanza is also repeated in *Hauksbók* as the forty-sixth verse in the sequence, just as it recurs in the Codex Regius as stanza 47.

10. *Vǫluspá* [K] 45 says *mælir Óðinn / við Míms hǫfuð* (Óðinn speaks with Mímir's head), which implies that Mímir's head is no longer attached to his body. However, no story survives that explains how Mímir came to be decapitated. Mímir is an obscure figure, known only for his wisdom and his connection to Óðinn. See Simek, *Dictionary of Northern Mythology,* 216.

11. "Skelfr Yggdrasils / askr standandi, / ymr it aldna tré / en jǫtunn losnar." My translation here follows a different stanza division to Larrington's. In Larrington's translation, this stanza is elided with stanza 45, following *Snorra Edda*'s example and making stanzas 44 and 45 both twelve lines long. *Vǫluspá*'s stanzas are most commonly eight lines in length, although it would be unwise to assume that its structure is inflexible in this regard and that longer or shorter stanzas are somehow "faulty."

12. Rigby, *Dancing with Disaster,* 19 (italics mine).

13. "Sól tér sortna / sígr fold í mar, / hverfa af himni / heiðar stjǫrnur; / geisar eimi / við aldrnara, / leikr hár hiti / við himin sjálfan."

14. *Vǫluspá* [K] 56, 6–8: "fram sé ek lengra / um ragna røk / rǫm sigtíva."

15. "Sér hon upp koma / ǫðru sinni / jǫrð ór ægi / iðjagrœna; / falla forsar, / flýgr ǫrn yfir, / sá er á fjalli / fiska veiðir."

16. "Finnask æsir / á Iðavelli / ok um Moldþinur / máttkan dœma, / ok minnask þar / á megindóma / ok á Fimbultýs / fornar rúnar." Lines 5–6 of stanza 58 are missing from the Codex Regius text and are supplied from *Hauksbók*. Although a six-line stanza would be by no means impossible in *Vǫluspá*'s meter, an eight-line stanza is more regular, and the *Hauksbók* text makes slightly better sense. I therefore follow the Íslenzk fornrit edition in presenting a hybrid text in this instance.

17. "Þar munu eptir / undrsamligar / gullnar tǫflur / í grasi finnask, / þærs í árdaga / áttar hǫfðu. // Munu ósánir / akrar vaxa, / bǫls mun alls batna, / Baldr mun koma; / búa þeir Hǫðr ok Baldr / Hropts sigtóptir / vel, valtívar. / Vituð ér enn—eða hvat?" I have substituted "slain gods" for Larrington's "slaughter gods" in translating *valtívar* in line 7. The meaning of this word is ambiguous, but seems to me to make better sense if we treat it as "slain gods," assuming that it is in apposition with the names Baldr and Hǫðr earlier in the stanza: both these gods are killed earlier in the narrative, and neither is conventionally connected with battle or violent death, as "slaughter gods" implies.

18. "Sal sér hon standa / sólu fegra, / gulli þakðan, / á Gimlé; / þar skulu dyggvar / dróttir byggja / ok um aldrdaga / ynðis njóta."

19. "Lif ok Lífþrasir, / en þau leynask munu / í holti Hoddmímis; / morgindǫggvar / þau sér at mat hafa, / þaðan af aldr alask."

20. *Edda,* translated by Faulkes, 57.

21. Latour, "Attempt at a 'Compositionist Manifesto,' " 486.

22. "Þar kømr inn dimmi / dreki fljúgandi, / naðr fránn, neðan / frá Niðafjǫllum; / berr sér í fjǫðrum /—flýgr vǫll yfir—/ Níðhǫggr nái. / Nú mun hon søkkvask."

23. "Þá kemr inn ríki / at regindómi, / ǫflugr ofan, / sá er ǫllu ræðr."

24. Latour, "Attempt at a 'Compositionist Manifesto,' " 486.

25. Trexler, *Anthropocene Fictions,* 5.

26. Eliade, *Sacred and the Profane,* 88.

27. Hartman et al., "Medieval Iceland, Greenland," 2.

28. Clark, *Ecocriticism on the Edge,* 80.

29. McMurry, "Slow Apocalypse," § 34.

30. See Vésteinn Ólason, "*Vǫluspá* and Time."

31. In the Codex Regius version of *Vǫluspá,* this refrain is found mostly in the central third of the poem: in stanzas 27 and 28 (verses belonging to the frame narrative, both of which address Óðinn directly); 33 and 34 (immediately following Baldr's death); 38

and 40 (respectively the stanzas that introduce Níðhǫggr and the fearful weather of Fimbulvetr); and stanza 50, which concludes with the *vituð* refrain and marks the final assembly of the Æsir before the climactic battle of Ragnarǫk. Finally, the same refrain reappears in the postapocalyptic coda to the poem, after the returning gods have been named (stanza 61).

32. Morton, *Hyperobjects*, 7.

33. Alberts, "Responsibility towards Life," 7.

34. Latour, *We Have Never Been Modern*, 139.

35. Rudiak-Gould, "Social Life of Blame," 49–53.

36. Sunstein, "On the Divergent American Reactions," 543.

37. Malm and Hornborg, "Geology of Mankind?" 64.

38. Rudiak-Gould, "Social Life of Blame," 52.

39. Scranton, *Learning to Die*, 85.

40. See Jochens, "*Vǫluspá*," 352–53. In *Snorra Edda*'s version of the Ragnarǫk mythos, female figures are slightly more prominent and play more active roles, especially in the person of Frigg, who attempts to protect Baldr by having everything in the world promise not to harm him and, when this first move fails, has Heimdallr ride to Hel to request Baldr's release back to the land of the living. Hel—who is personified in *Snorra Edda* in a way that she is not in *Vǫluspá*, where the name may refer only to a chthonic realm of the dead—agrees only on the condition that everything in the universe should weep for Baldr. In a mirroring of the earlier narrative, all of creation save for one individual complies with this request: Loki, unrecognizable in drag as an old woman, refuses.

41. Colebrook and Weinstein, "Introduction," 176. The term "Androcene" has also been used by Sharp, "Endangered Life," 278; Schneiderman, "Naming the Anthropocene," 182, mentions the term without discussing it.

42. Plumwood, *Feminism and the Mastery of Nature*, 49; Latour, *We Have Never Been Modern*, 61.

43. Plumwood, *Feminism and the Mastery of Nature*, 9.

44. Kompridis, "Romanticism," 259. I owe my knowledge of this reference to Gibson-Graham, "Feminist Project of Belonging."

45. Haraway, "Anthropocene," 161.

46. Gibson-Graham, "Feminist Project of Belonging," 5.

47. Davison, "Beyond the Mirrored Horizon," 303.

48. Latour, "Agency at the Time of the Anthropocene," 15.

Conclusion

1. Nardizzi, "Medieval Ecocriticism," 121.

2. See See, *Ideologie und Philologie*; See and Zernack, *Germanistik und Politik*; Mees, "*Germanische Sturmflut*."

3. See Teitelbaum, *Lions of the North*, 29–60, for a survey of new nationalist impulses in late twentieth-century Scandinavia. Gardell, *Gods of the Blood*, traces the connections between contemporary pagan revivalism and white supremacist movements. See also Schnurbein, "Tales of Reconstruction."

4. Ladino, *Reclaiming Nostalgia*, 230–31.

5. See Mix, "Greening of White Separatism"; Olsen, *Nature and Nationalism*. The "Green credentials" of the Nazi regime in 1930s Germany have often been asserted, and just as often brought into question; on this issue, see the essays collected in *How Green Were the Nazis?* edited by Brüggemeier, Cioc, and Zeller.

6. Scranton, *Learning to Die*, 26–27.

7. Ibid., 27.

Bibliography

By convention, Icelanders are referred to by—and alphabetized according to—their given names rather than their patro- or matronymics. In this bibliography, I have adhered to this practice. Authors whose names begin with the characters Þ or Ö are found at the end of the bibliography, which also reflects Icelandic norms.

Abram, Christopher. "*Gylfaginning* and Early Medieval Conversion Theory." *Saga-Book* 33 (2009): 5–24.
———. "Hel in Early Norse Poetry." *Viking and Medieval Scandinavia* 2 (2006): 1–29.
———. "Kennings and Things: Towards an Object-Oriented Skaldic Poetics." Forthcoming in *Early English Poetics and the History of Style*, edited by Irina Dumitrescu and Eric Weiskott. Kalamazoo: Medieval Institute Publications.
———. *Myths of the Pagan North: The Gods of the Norsemen*. London: Continuum, 2011.
Acker, Paul, and Carolyne Larrington, eds. *The Poetic Edda: Essays on Old Norse Mythology*. New York: Routledge, 2002.
Alaimo, Stacy. "Trans-Corporeal Feminisms and the Ethical Space of Nature." In *Material Feminisms*, edited by Stacy Alaimo and Susan Hekman, 237–64. Bloomington: Indiana University Press, 2008.
Alberts, Paul. "Responsibility towards Life in the Early Anthropocene." *Angelaki* 16 (2011): 5–17.
Amorosi, Thomas, et al. "Raiding the Landscape: Human Impact in the Scandinavian North Atlantic." *Human Ecology* 25 (1997): 491–518.
Anderson, Sarah M., and Karen Swenson, eds. *Cold Counsel: Women in Old Norse Literature and Mythology*. New York: Routledge, 2002.
Andrén, Anders. *Tracing Old Norse Cosmology: The World Tree, Middle Earth, and the Sun from Archaeological Perspectives*. Lund: Nordic Academic Press, 2014.
Andrén, Anders, Kristina Jennbert, and Catharina Raudvere, eds. *Old Norse Religion in Long-Term Perspectives: Origins, Changes, and Interactions*. Lund: Nordic Academic Press, 2006.
Andrés Arnalds. "Ecosystem Disturbance in Iceland." *Arctic and Alpine Research* 19 (1987): 508–13.
Ármann Jakobsson. "Beware of the Elf! A Note on the Evolving Meaning of Álfar." *Folklore* 126 (2015): 215–23.

―――. "Where Do the Giants Live?" *Arkiv för nordisk filologi* 121 (2006): 101–12.

Armbruster, Karla M., and Kathleen R. Wallace, eds. *Beyond Nature Writing: Expanding the Boundaries of Ecocriticism.* Charlottesville: University Press of Virginia, 2001.

Ashwell, Ian, and Edgar Jackson. "The Sagas as Evidence of Early Deforestation in Iceland." *Canadian Geographer* 14 (1970): 158–66.

Baluška, František, Stefano Mancuso, and Dieter Volkmann, eds. *Communication in Plants: Neuronal Aspects of Plant Life.* Berlin: Springer, 2006.

Baral, Hans-Otto, Valentin Queloz, and Tsuyoshi Hosoya. "*Hymenoscyphus fraxineus,* the Correct Scientific Name for the Fungus Causing Ash Dieback in Europe." *IMA Fungus* 5 (2014): 79–80.

Barnes, Geraldine. "Vínland the Good: Paradise Lost?" *Parergon* 12 (1995): 75–96.

Barraclough, Eleanor Rosamond. "Inside Outlawry in *Grettis saga Ásmundarsonar* and *Gísla saga Súrssonar:* Landscape in the Outlaw Sagas." *Scandinavian Studies* 82 (2010): 365–88.

―――. "Land-Naming in the Migration Myth of Medieval Iceland: Constructing the Past in the Present and the Present in the Past." *Saga-Book* 36 (2012): 79–101.

Bartlett, Robert. "Medieval and Modern Concepts of Race and Ethnicity." *Journal of Medieval and Early Modern Studies* 31 (2001): 39–26.

Bate, Jonathan. *The Song of the Earth.* 2nd edition. London: Picador, 2001.

Battles, Matthew. *Tree.* London: Bloomsbury, 2017.

Baumgartner, W. "Freydís in Vinland oder die Vertreibung aus dem Paradies." *Skandinavistik* 23 (1993): 16–35.

Bek-Pedersen, Karen. *The Norns in Old Norse Mythology.* Edinburgh: Dunedin, 2011.

Bergsveinn Birgisson. *Inn í skaldens sinn: Kognitive, estetiske og historiske skatter i den norrøne skaldediktingen.* Bergen: University of Bergen, 2007.

Berman, Tzeporah. "The Rape of Mother Nature? Women in the Language of Environmental Discourse." In *The Ecolinguistics Reader: Language, Ecology and Environment,* edited by Alwin Fill and Peter Mühlhäusler, 258–69. London: Continuum, 2001.

Bethurum, Dorothy, ed. *The Homilies of Wulfstan.* Oxford: Clarendon, 1957.

Bintley, Michael D. J. "Life-Cycles of Men and Trees in *Sonatorrek.*" *Opticon1826* 6 (2009). http://www.ucl.ac.uk/opticon1826/archive/Issue6/AH_Bintley.pdf.

―――. "Plant Life in the *Poetic Edda.*" In *Sensory Perception in the Medieval West,* edited by Simon C. Thomson and Michael D. J. Bintley, 227–44. Turnhout: Brepols, 2016.

―――. *Trees in the Religions of Early Medieval England.* Woodbridge: Boydell, 2015.

Bjarni Einarsson, ed. *Egils saga.* London: Viking Society for Northern Research, 2003.

Björn K. Þórólfsson, and Guðni Jónsson, eds. "Gísla saga Súrssonar." In *Vestfirðinga sǫgur,* edited by Björn K. Þórólfsson and Guðni Jónsson, 3–118. Reykjavik: Íslenzka fornritafélag, 1943.

Bjorvand, Harald. "Eytmologien til *aur* og *golv.*" *Maal og Minne* 2006, 97–106.

Blanchot, Maurice. *The Writing of the Disaster.* Translated by Ann Smock. Lincoln: University of Nebraska Press, 1995.

Borgþór Magnússon, et al. "Plant Colonization, Succession and Ecosystem Development on Surtsey with Reference to Neighbouring Islands." *Biogeosciences* 11 (2014): 5521–37.

Borlik, Todd. *Ecocriticism and Early Modern English Literature: Green Pastures.* New York: Routledge, 2011.

Borovsky, Zoe. "'En hon er blandin mjök': Women and Insults in Old Norse Literature." In *Cold Counsel,* edited by Anderson and Swenson, 1–14.

Brady, Emily. "The Sublime, Ugliness and 'Terrible Beauty' in Icelandic Landscapes." In *Conversations with Landscape,* edited by Karl Benediktsson and Katrín Anna Lund, 125–36. Farnham: Ashgate, 2010.

Bragg, Lois. *Oedipus Borealis: The Aberrant Body in Old Icelandic Myth and Saga.* Madison, NJ: Fairleigh Dickinson University Press, 2004.

Brink, Stefan. "Mythologizing Landscape: Place and Space of Cult and Myth." In *Kontinuitäten und Brüche in der Religionsgeschichte,* edited by M. Stausberg, 76–116. Berlin: De Gruyter, 2001.

Brown, Madelaine R., and Francis P. Magoun Jr. "Tyrkir, First German in North America." *Modern Language Notes* 61 (1946): 547–51.

Broz, Vlatko. "Kennings as Blends and Prisms." *Linguistics (Jeziklovlje)* 12 (2011): 165–86.

Brüggemeier, Franz Josef, Mark Cioc, and Thomas Zeller, eds. *How Green Were the Nazis? Nature, Environment and Nation in the Third Reich.* Athens: Ohio University Press, 2005.

Buell, Lawrence. *The Environmental Imagination: Thoreau, Nature Writing, and the Formation of American Culture.* Cambridge, MA: Belknap, 1995.

Burrell, Margaret. "Hell as a Geological Construct." *Florilegium* 24 (2007): 37–54.

Busygin, A. V. "White-Christ." *Viking and Medieval Scandinavia* 7 (2011): 1–6.

Bynum, Caroline Walker. "Did the Twelfth Century Discover the Individual?" *Journal of Ecclesiastical History* 31 (1980): 1–17.

Callaghan, Patsy. "Myth as a Site of Ecocritical Inquiry: Disrupting Anthropocentrism." *Interdisciplinary Studies in Literature and Environment* 22 (2015): 80–97.

Callicott, J. Baird. "The Historical Roots of Environmental Philosophy." In *Religion and Ecological Crisis,* edited by LeVasseur and Peterson, 33–46.

Cantor, Milton. "The Image of the Negro in Colonial Literature." *New England Quarterly* 36 (1963): 452–77.

Catlyn, Kathryn. "Archaeology for the Anthropocene: Scale, Soil, and the Settlement of Iceland." *Anthropocene* 15 (2016): 13–21.

Chenu, Marie-Dominique. *Nature, Man, and Society in the Twelfth Century: Essays on New Theological Perspectives in the Latin West.* Translated by Jerome Taylor and Lester K. Little. Chicago: University of Chicago Press, 1968.

Clark, Timothy. *Ecocriticism on the Edge: The Anthropocene as a Threshold Concept.* London: Bloomsbury, 2015.

Clunies Ross, Margaret. *A History of Old Norse Poetry and Poetics.* Cambridge: Brewer, 2005.

———. *Prolonged Echoes: Old Norse Myths in Medieval Northern Society.* 2 volumes. Odense: Odense University Press, 1994–98.

Cohen, Jeffrey Jerome. "Introduction: All Things." In *Animal, Vegetable, Mineral: Ethics and Objects,* edited by Cohen, 1–8. Washington, DC: Oliphaunt, 2012.

———. *Of Giants: Sex, Monsters, and the Middle Ages.* Minneapolis: University of Minnesota Press, 1999.

Cole, Richard. "Make Ásgarðr Great Again!" *Notre Dame Medieval Studies Research Blog,* January 20, 2017. https://sites.nd.edu/manuscript-studies/2017/01/20/make-asgardr-great-again/.

———. "Racial Thinking in Old Norse Literature: The Case of the Blámaðr." *Saga-Book* 39 (2015): 21–40.

———. "Towards a Typology of Absence in Old Norse Literature." *Exemplaria* 28 (2016): 137–60.

Colebrook, Claire, and Jami Weinstein. "Introduction: Anthropocene Feminisms: Rethinking the Unthinkable." *philoSOPHIA* 5 (2015): 167–78.

Collins, A. Jeffries, ed. *Manuale ad usum percelebris ecclesie Sarisburiensis.* London: Henry Bradshaw Society, 1960.

Coupe, Laurence. "Genesis and the Nature of Myth." *Green Letters* 11 (2009): 9–22.

Crutzen, Paul J. "The 'Anthropocene.'" In *Earth System Science in the Anthropocene,* edited by Eckart Ehlers and Thomas Krafft, 13–18. Berlin: Springer, 2006.

Crutzen, Paul J., and Eugene F. Stoermer. "The Anthropocene." *Global Change Newsletter* 41 (2000): 17–18.

Cummings, Brian, ed. *The Book of Common Prayer: The Texts of 1549, 1559, and 1662.* Oxford: Oxford University Press, 2013.

Cusack, Carole M. *The Sacred Tree: Ancient and Medieval Manifestations.* Newcastle-upon-Tyne: Cambridge Scholars, 2011.

David-Bird, Nurit. "'Animism' Revisited: Personhood, Environment, and Relational Epistemology." In *Readings in Indigenous Religions,* edited by Graham Harvey, 73–105. London: Continuum, 2002.

Davidson, Hilda Ellis. "Milk and the Northern Goddess." In *The Concept of the Goddess,* edited by Sandra Billington and Miranda Green, 91–106. New York: Routledge, 2002.

Davies, Jeremy. "Sustainable Nostalgia." *Memory Studies* 3 (2010): 262–68.

Davison, Aidan. "Beyond the Mirrored Horizon: Modern Ontology and Amodern Possibilities in the Anthropocene." *Geographical Research* 53 (2015): 298–305.

Del Tredici, Peter. "Gestalt Dendrology: Looking at the Whole Tree." *Arnoldia* 61 (2002): 3–8.

Demarée, G. R., and A. E. J. Ogilvie. "*Bons baisers d'Islande:* Climatic, Environmental, and Human Dimensions of the *Lakagígar* Eruption (1783–1784) in Iceland." In *History and Climate: Memories of the Future?,* edited by P. D. Jones et al., 219–46. New York: Kluwer, 2001.

Dobrowolska, Dorota, et al. "A Review of European Ash (*Fraxinus excelsior* L.): Implications for Silviculture." *Forestry* 84 (2011): 133–48.

Douglass, Rebecca. "Ecocriticism and Medieval Literature." *Studies in Medievalism* 10 (1998): 136–63.

Dronke, Peter. *Intellectuals and Poets in Medieval Europe.* Rome: Edizioni di Storia e Letteratura, 1992.

Dronke, Ursula, ed. *The Poetic Edda II: Mythological Poems.* Oxford: Oxford University Press, 1997.

Dronke, Ursula, and Peter Dronke. "The Prologue of the Prose *Edda:* Explorations of a Latin Background." In *Sjötíu ritgerðir helgaðar Jakobi Benediktssyni 20. júli 1977,* edited by Einar G. Pétursson and Jónas Kristjánsson, 1:153–76. Reykjavik: Stofnun Árnamagnússonar í íslenskum fræðum, 1977.

Dugmore, Andrew J., and Camilla C. Erskine. "Local and Regional Patterns of Soil Erosion in Southern Iceland." In *Environmental Change in Iceland,* edited by Johann Stötter and Friedrich Wilhelm, 63–78. Munich: Institut für Geographie der Universität München, 1994.

Dugmore, Andrew J., Christian Keller, and Thomas H. McGovern. "Norse Greenland Settlement: Reflections on Climate Change, Trade, and the Contrasting Fates of Human Settlements in the North Atlantic Islands." *Arctic Anthropology* 44 (2007): 12–36.

Dugmore, Andrew J., et al. "The Norse *landnám* on the North Atlantic Islands: An Environmental Impact Assessment." *Polar Record* 41 (2005): 21–37.

Dumont, Darl J. "The Ash Tree in Indo-European Culture." *Mankind Quarterly* 32 (1992): 323–36.

Economou, George. *The Goddess Natura in Medieval Literature.* 2nd edition. Notre Dame: University of Notre Dame Press, 2002.

Egeler, Matthias. "Eikþyrnir and the Rivers of Paradise: Cosmological Perspectives on Dating *Grímnismál* 26–28." *Arkiv för nordisk filologi* 128 (2013): 17–39.

Einar Ól. Sveinsson, and Matthías Þórðarson, eds. "Eiríks saga rauða." In *Eyrbyggja saga; Brands þáttr ǫrva; Eiríks saga rauða; Grœnlendinga saga; Grœnlendinga þáttr,* edited by Einar Ól. Sveinsson and Matthías Þórðarson, 195–237. Reykjavik: Íslenzka fornritafélag, 1935.

———, eds. "Grœnlendinga saga." In *Eyrbyggja saga . . .* , edited by Einar Ól. Sveinsson and Matthías Þórðarson, 241–67.

Eliade, Mircea. *The Sacred and the Profane.* Translated by W. R. Trask. New York: Harcourt Brace Jovanovich, 1959.

Ellingson, Ter. *The Myth of the Noble Savage.* Berkeley and Los Angeles: University of California Press, 2001.

Falk, Oren. "The Vanishing Volcanoes: Fragments of Fourteenth-Century Icelandic Folklore." *Folklore* 118 (2007): 1–22.

Faulkes, Anthony. "Descent from the Gods." *Mediaeval Scandinavia* 11 (1979–80): 92–125.

———. "Pagan Sympathy: Attitudes to Heathendom in the Prologue to *Snorra Edda.*" In *Edda: A Book of Essays,* edited by R. J. Glendinning and Haraldur Bessason, 283–314. Winnipeg: University of Manitoba Press, 1983.

Fidjestøl, Bjarne. *The Dating of Eddic Poetry: A Historical Survey and Methodological Investigation.* Copenhagen: Arnamagnaean Institute, 1999.

———. *Det nørrone fyrstediktet.* Øvre Ervik: Alvheim and Eide, 1982.

———. "The Kenning System. An Attempt at a Linguistic Analysis." In Fidjestøl, *Selected Papers,* edited by Odd Einar Haugen and Else Mundal, translated by Peter Foote, 16–67. Odense: Odense University Press, 1997.

Finnur Jónsson, ed. *Alexanders saga: Islandsk oversættelse ved Brandr Jónsson.* Copenhagen: Gyldendal, 1925.

———, ed. *Den norsk-islandske skjaldediktning.* 4 volumes. Copenhagen: Gyldendal, 1912–15.

Fleck, Jere. "Óðinn's Self-Sacrifice—a New Interpretation II: The Ritual Landscape." *Scandinavian Studies* 43 (1971): 385–413.

Frakes, Jerold C. "Loki's Mythological Function in the Tripartite System." *JEGP* 86 (1987): 473–86.

———. "Vikings, Vínland and the Discourse of Eurocentrism." *JEGP* 100 (2001): 157–99.

Frank, Roberta. "The Lay of the Land in Skaldic Praise Poetry." In *Myth in Early Northwest Europe,* edited by Stephen Glosecki, 175–95. Tempe: Arizona Center for Medieval and Renaissance Studies, 2007.

———. *Old Norse Court Poetry: The Dróttkvætt Stanza.* Ithaca: Cornell University Press, 1978.

Fuller, Dorian, et al. "The Contribution of Rice Agriculture and Livestock Pastoralism to Prehistoric Methane Levels: An Archeological Assessment." *Holocene* 21 (2011): 743–59.

Gade, Kari Ellen, and Edith Marold, eds. *Poetry from Treatises on Poetics.* 2 volumes. Turnhout: Brepols, 2017.

Gardell, Mattias. *Gods of the Blood: The Pagan Revival and White Separatism.* Durham, NC: Duke University Press, 2003.

Garrard, Greg. *Ecocriticism.* Abingdon: Routledge, 2004.

Gibson-Graham, J. K. "A Feminist Project of Belonging for the Anthropocene." *Gender, Place, and Culture* 18 (2011): 1–21.

Glotfelty, Cheryll. Introduction to *The Ecocriticism Reader,* edited by Glotfelty and Fromm, xv–xxxvii.

Glotfelty, Cheryll, and Harold Fromm, eds. *The Ecocriticism Reader: Landmarks in Literary Ecology.* Athens: University of Georgia Press, 1996.

Gräslund, Bo. "Fimbulvintern, Ragnarök och klimatkrisen år 536–537 e.Kr." *Saga och Sed* 2007, 93–123.

Gräslund, Bo, and Neil Price. "Twilight of the Gods? The 'Dust Veil Event' of AD 536 in Critical Perspective." *Antiquity* 86 (2012): 428–43.

Grattan, John, Sabina Michnowicz, and Roland Rabartin. "The Long Shadow: Understanding the Influence of the Laki Fissure Eruption on Human Mortality in Europe." In *Living under the Shadow: Cultural Impacts of Volcanic Eruptions,* edited by John Grattan and Robin Torrence, 153–74. New York: Routledge, 2016.

Grønlie, Siân, trans. *Íslendingabók; Kristni saga.* London: Viking Society for Northern Research, 2006.

Gross, Andrin, et al. "*Hymenoscyphus pseudoalbidus,* the Causal Agent of European Ash Dieback." *Molecular Plant Pathology* 15 (2014): 5–21.

Grove, Jonathan. "The Place of Greenland in Medieval Icelandic Saga Narrative." *Journal of the North Atlantic* 2 (2009): 30–51.

Gunnarsson, Allan. *Träden och människan.* Kristianstad: Rabén and Sjögren, 1988.

Gunnell, Terry. "Eddic Poetry." In *A Companion to Old Norse–Icelandic Literature and Culture,* edited by Rory McTurk, 82–100. Malden, MA: Blackwell, 2005.

Gunnell, Terry, and Annette Lassen, eds. *The Nordic Apocalypse: Approaches to Vǫluspá and Nordic Days of Judgement.* Turnhout: Brepols, 2013.

Gurevich, A. Y. "Space and Time in the *Weltmodell* of the Old Scandinavian Peoples." *Mediaeval Scandinavia* 2 (1969): 42–53.

Hafstein, Valdimar. "The Elves' Point of View: Cultural Identity in Contemporary Icelandic Elf-Traditions." *Fabula* 41 (2000): 87–104.

Hageneder, Fred. *Yew.* London: Reaktion, 2013.

Halink, Simon. "The Icelandic Mythscape: Sagas, Landscapes and National Identity." *National Identities* 16 (2014): 209–33.

Hall, John Spencer. "The Phoenix." *Religion and Literature* 16 (1984): 61–66.

Hall, Matthew. *Plants as Persons: A Philosophical Botany.* Albany: State University of New York Press, 2011.

Halldór Hermannsson. "Leif Erikson's Foster-Father." *Modern Language Notes* 69 (1954): 388–93.

Haller, John S., Jr. *Outcasts from Evolution: Scientific Attitudes on Racial Inferiority, 1859–1900.* Urbana: University of Illinois Press, 1971.

Hallfreðr vandræðaskáld Óttarsson. "Hákonardrápa." Translated and edited by Kate Heslop. In *Poetry from Treatises on Poetics,* edited by Gade and Marold, 1:212–27.

Hamel, A. G. van. "The Game of the Gods." *Arkiv för nordisk filologi* 50 (1934): 218–42.

Haraldur Bernharðsson. "Old Icelandic *ragnarök* and *ragnarökkr.*" In *Verba docenti: Studies in Historical and Indo-European Linguistics presented to Jay H. Jasanoff by Students, Colleagues, and Friends,* edited by A. J. Nussbaum, 25–38. Ann Arbor, MI: Beech Stave, 2007.

Haraway, Donna. "Anthropocene, Capitalocene, Plantationocene, Chthulucene: Making Kin." *Environmental Humanities* 6 (2015): 159–65.

Harman, Graham. *Guerrilla Metaphysics.* Chicago: Open Court, 2005.

———. "The Well-Wrought Broken Hammer: Object-Oriented Literary Criticism." *New Literary History* 43 (2012): 183–203.

Hartman, Stephen, et al. "Medieval Iceland, Greenland, and the New Human Condition: A Case Study." *Global and Planetary Change* 156 (2017): 123–39.

Harvey, Graham. "Animals, Animists, and Academics." *Zygon* 41 (2006): 9–19.

———. *Animism: Respecting the Living World.* London: Hurst, 2005.

———. "The Roots of Pagan Ecology." *Religion Today* 9 (1994): 38–41.

Hastrup, Kirsten. *Culture and History in Medieval Iceland.* Oxford: Clarendon, 1985.

———. "Cosmology and Society in Medieval Iceland: A Social Anthropological Perspective on World-View." In Hastrup, *Island of Anthropology: Studies in Past and Present Iceland,* 25–43. Odense: Odense University Press, 1990.

Haukur Þorgeirsson. "Hinn fagri foldar son." *Gripla* 19 (2008): 159–68.

Hesiod. *Works and Days. Shield.* Translated by A. Athanassakis. Baltimore: Johns Hopkins University Press, 2004.

Higginbotham, Joan, and River Higginbotham. *Paganism: An Introduction to Earth-Centered Religions.* Woodbury, MN: Llewellyn, 2002.

Hiltner, Ken. "Renaissance Literature and Our Contemporary Attitude toward Global Warming." *Interdisciplinary Studies in Literature and Environment* 16 (2009): 429–41.

Hird, Myra J. "Naturally Queer." *Feminist Theory* 5 (2004): 85–89.

Hoidal, Oddvar K. "Norsemen and the North American Forests." *Journal of Forest History* 24 (1980): 200–203.

Holland, Gary. "Kennings, Metaphors, and Semantic Formulae in Norse *Dróttkvætt.*" *Arkiv för nordisk filologi* 120 (2005): 123–47.

Holm-Olsen, Ludvig, ed. *Konungs skuggsiá.* Oslo: Kjeldeskriftfondet, 1945.

Hörður Kristinsson. "Post-Settlement History of Icelandic Forests." *Búvísindi* 9 (1995): 31–35.

Houts, Elisabeth van. "The Vocabulary of Exile and Outlawry in the North Sea Area around the First Millennium." In *Exile in the Middle Ages: Selected Proceedings from the International Medieval Congress, University of Leeds, 8–11 July 2002,* edited by Laura Napran and Elisabeth van Houts, 13–28. Turnhout: Brepols, 2004.

Howarth, William, "Some Principles of Ecocriticism." In *The Ecocriticism Reader,* edited by Glotfelty and Fromm, 69–91.

Hsiang, Solomon M., Marshall Burke, and Edward Miguel. "Quantifying the Influence of Climate on Human Conflict." *Science* 341 (2013): 1235367-1-14.

Hultgård, Anders. "The Askr and Embla Myth in a Comparative Perspective." In *Old Norse Religion in Long-Term Perspectives,* edited by Andrén et al., 58–62.

———. "Fimbulvintern—ett mytmotiv och dess tolkning." *Saga och Sed* 2004, 51–69.

An Icelandic-English Dictionary. Edited by Richard Cleasby and Gudbrand Vigfusson. 2nd edition. Oxford: Oxford University Press, 1957.

Jakob Benediktsson, ed. *Íslendingabók, Landnámabók.* 2 volumes. Reykjavik: Íslenzka fornritafélag, 1968.

———, ed. "*Veraldar saga.*" In *Medieval Scandinavia: An Encyclopedia,* edited by Pulsiano and Wolf, 691.

Jochens, Jenny. "Race and Ethnicity in the Old Norse World." *Viator* 30 (1999): 79–104.

———. "*Vǫluspá:* Matrix of Norse Womanhood." *JEGP* 88 (1989): 344–62.

Johnston, Michael, and Alex Mueller. "Kant in King Arthur's Court: Charges of Anachronism in Book Reviews." *In the Medieval Middle,* August 24, 2016. http://www.inthemedievalmiddle.com/2016/08/kant-in-king-arthurs-court-charges-of.html.

Jón Hnefill Aðalsteinsson. "Gods and Giants in Old Norse Mythology." *Temenos* 26 (1990): 7–21.

Jón Sigurðsson, and Guðbrandur Vigfússon, eds. *Biskupa sögur.* 2 volumes. Copenhagen: Möller, 1856–78.

Jónas Kristjánsson, ed. "*Víga-Glúms saga.*" In *Eyfirðinga sögur,* edited by Jónas Kristjánsson, 3–98. Reykjavik: Íslenzka fornritafélag, 1956.

Jónas Kristjánsson, and Vésteinn Ólason, eds. *Eddukvæði.* 2 volumes. Reykjavik: Íslenzka fornritafélag, 2014.

Kellerer-Pirklbauer, A., and J. Eulenstein. "From 'Door to Hell' to an Advertising Medium: The Volcano Hekla in Iceland—1100 Years of Man-Volcano Interaction." *Mitteilungen der österreichischen geographischsen Gesellschaft* 145 (2003): 239–62.

Keyser, R., and P. A. Munch, eds. *Norges gamle love indtil 1387, I: Norges love ældre end Kong Magnus Haakonssöns regjerings-tiltrædelse i 1263.* Christiania: Gröndahl, 1846.

King, Ynestra. "Healing the Wounds: Feminism, Ecology, and Nature/Culture Dualism." In *Gender/body/knowledge: Feminist Reconstructions of Being and Knowing,* edited by Alison M. Jaggar and Susan Bordo, 115–44. New Brunswick, NJ: Rutgers University Press, 1989.

Kirchner, James W. "The Gaia Hypothesis: Conjectures and Refutations." *Climatic Change* 58 (2003): 21–45.

Kissane, Michael. "Seeing the Forest for the Trees: Land Reclamation in Iceland." *Scandinavian Review* 86 (1998): 4–7.

Kolodny, Annette. *In Search of First Contact: The Vikings of Vinland, the Peoples of the Dawnland, and the Anglo-American Anxiety of Discovery.* Durham: Duke University Press, 2012.

———. *The Lay of the Land: Metaphor as Experience and History in American Life and Letters.* Chapel Hill: University of North Carolina Press, 1975.

Kompridis, Nikolas. "Romanticism." In *The Oxford Handbook of Philosophy and Literature,* edited by Richard Eldridge, 247–70. Oxford: Oxford University Press, 2009.

Krech, Shepard, III. "Animism and Reincarnation: Lynn White in Indian Country." In *Religion and Ecological Crisis,* edited by LeVasseur and Peterson, 75–88.

———. *The Ecological Indian: Myth and History.* New York: Norton, 1999.

Kress, Helga. "Taming the Shrew: The Rise of Patriarchy and the Subordination of the Feminine in Old Norse Literature." In *Cold Counsel,* edited by Anderson and Swenson, 81–92.

Kunz, Keneva, trans. "Eirik the Red's Saga." In *The Sagas of Icelanders,* edited by Örnólfur Þorsson, 653–74.

———. trans. "The Saga of the Greenlanders." In *The Sagas of Icelanders,* edited by Örnólfur Þorsson, 636–52.

La Martinière, Pierre Martin de. *Voyage des pays septentrionaux.* Paris: Louis Vandosme, 1671.

Ladino, Jennifer K. *Reclaiming Nostalgia: Longing for Nature in American Literature.* Charlottesville: University of Virginia Press, 2012.

Larrington, Carolyne, trans. *The Poetic Edda.* 2nd edition. Oxford: Oxford University Press, 2014.

———. "'Undruðusk þá, sem fyrir var': Wonder, Vínland and Mediaeval Travel Narratives." *Mediaeval Scandinavia* 14 (2004): 91–114.

———. "*Vafþrúðnismál* and *Grímnismál:* Cosmic History, Cosmic Geography." In *The Poetic Edda,* edited by Acker and Larrington, 59–78.

Larson, Laurence Marcellus, trans. *The King's Mirror—Speculum regale—Konungs skuggsjá.* New York: American-Scandinavian Foundation, 1917.

Latour, Bruno. "Agency at the Time of the Anthropocene." *New Literary History* 45 (2014): 1–18.

———. "An Attempt at a 'Compositionist Manifesto.'" *New Literary History* 41 (2010): 471–90.

———. *An Enquiry into Modes of Existence: An Anthropology of the Moderns.* Translated by Catherine Porter. Cambridge, MA: Harvard University Press, 2013.

———. *Politics of Nature: How to Bring the Sciences into Democracy.* Translated by Catherine Porter. Cambridge, MA: Harvard University Press, 2004.

———. *We Have Never Been Modern.* Translated by Catherine Porter. Cambridge, MA: Harvard University Press, 1993.

————. "Why Gaia Is Not a God of Totality." *Theory, Culture, and Society* 34 (2017): 61–81.

Lethbridge, Emily, and Steven Hartman. "Inscribing Environmental Memory in the Icelandic Sagas and the *Icelandic Saga Map*." *PMLA* 131 (2016): 381–91.

LeVasseur, Todd, and Anna Peterson, eds. *Religion and Ecological Crisis: The "Lynn White Thesis" at Fifty.* New York: Routledge, 2017.

Lévi-Strauss, Claude. *The Elementary Structures of Kinship.* Translated by H. H. Bell and J. R. von Sturmer. 2nd edition. London: Eyre and Spottiswode, 1969.

Lieberman, Anatoly. "Some Controversial Aspects of the Myth of Baldr." *Alvíssmál* 11 (2004): 17–54.

Lincoln, Bruce. *Theorizing Myth: Narrative, Ideology and Scholarship.* Chicago: University of Chicago Press, 1999.

Lindow, John. *Murder and Vengeance among the Gods: Baldr in Scandinavian Mythology.* Helsinki: Suomalainen Tiedeakatemia, 1997.

————. *Norse Mythology: A Guide to the Gods, Heroes, Rituals, and Beliefs.* New York: Oxford University Press, 2001.

————. "Poetry, Dwarfs and Gods: Understanding *Alvíssmál.*" In *Learning and Understanding in the Old Norse World: Essays in Honour of Margaret Clunies Ross.* Edited by Judy Quinn, Kate Heslop, and Tarrin Wills, 287–305. Turnhout: Brepols, 2007.

————. "Supernatural Others and Ethnic Others: A Millennium of World View." *Scandinavian Studies* 67 (1995): 8–31.

Lovelock, James. *The Ages of Gaia: The Biography of Our Living Earth.* Oxford: Oxford University Press, 1989.

————. *The Revenge of Gaia: Why the Earth Is Fighting Back—and How We Can Still Save Humanity.* London: Penguin, 2007.

Lönnroth, Lars. "The Founding of Miðgarðr: *Vǫluspá* 1–8." In *The Poetic Edda,* edited by Acker and Larrington, 1–26.

Mackley, J. S. *The Legend of St Brendan: A Comparative Study of the Latin and Anglo-Norman Versions.* Leiden: Brill, 2008.

Magnús Stefánsson. "Vínland or Vinland?" *Scandinavian Journal of History* 23 (1998): 139–52.

Malm, Andreas, and Alf Hornborg. "The Geology of Mankind? A Critique of the Anthropocene Narrative." *Anthropocene Review* 1 (2014): 62–69.

McGillivray, Andrew. "Mythic Transformations: Tree Symbolism in the Norse Plantation." MA thesis, University of Manitoba, 2011. http://mspace.lib.umanitoba.ca /handle/1993/4433.

McKibben, Bill. *The End of Nature.* Revised edition. New York: Random House, 2006.

McKinnell, John. "Heathenism in *Vǫluspá*: A Preliminary Survey." In *The Nordic Apocalypse,* edited by Gunnell and Lassen, 93–112.

————. *Meeting the Other in Norse Myth and Legend.* Cambridge: Brewer, 2005.

————. "*Vǫluspá* and the Feast of Easter." *Alvíssmál* 12 (2008): 3–28.

McMurry, Andrew. "The Slow Apocalypse: A Gradualistic Theory of the World's Demise." *Postmodern Culture* 6 (1996). http://pmc.iath.virginia.edu/text-only/issue .596/pop-cult.596.

McNeill, John Robert, and Peter Engelke. *The Great Acceleration: An Environmental History of the Anthropocene since 1945.* Cambridge, MA: Harvard University Press, 2014.

McTurk, Rory. "Fooling Gylfi: Who Tricks Who?" *Alvíssmál* 3 (1994): 3–18.

———. "*Snorra Edda* as Menippean Satire." In *Myths, Legends, and Heroes: Essays on Old Norse and Old English Literature in Honour of John McKinnell,* edited by Daniel Anlezark, 109–32. Toronto: University of Toronto Press, 2011.

Medieval Scandinavia: An Encyclopedia. Edited by Phillip Pulsiano and Kirsten Wolf. New York: Garland, 1993.

Mees, Bernard. "*Germanische Sturmflut:* From the Old Norse Twilight to the Fascist New Dawn." *Studia Neophilologica* 78 (2006): 184–98.

Meissner, Rudolf. *Die Kenningar der Skalden: Ein Beitrag zur skaldischen Poetik.* Bonn: Schroeder, 1921.

Melve, Leidulf. "'The Revolt of the Medievalists': Directions in Recent Research on the Twelfth-Century Renaissance." *Journal of Medieval History* 32 (2006): 231–52.

Merchant, Carolyn. *The Death of Nature: Women, Ecology and the Scientific Revolution.* Revised edition. New York: Harper, 1989.

Meylan, Nicolas. "La (re)conversion des «esprits de la terre» dans l'Islande médiévale." *Revue de l'histoire des religions* 230 (2013): 330–54.

Mickey, Sam. *Coexistentialism and the Unbearable Intimacy of Ecological Emergency.* Lanham, MD: Lexington, 2016.

Mikhail, Alan. "Ottoman Iceland: A Climate History." *Environmental History* 20 (2015): 262–84.

Miller, J. Hillis. "Anachronistic Reading." *Derrida Today* 3 (2010): 75–91.

Mitchell, R. J., et al. "Ash Dieback in the UK: A Review of the Ecological and Conservation Implications and Potential Management Options." *Biological Conservation* 175 (2014): 95–109.

Mix, Tamara L. "The Greening of White Separatism: Use of Environmental Themes to Elaborate and Legitimize Extremist Discourse." *Nature + Culture* 4 (2009): 138–66.

Moore, Jason W. "The Crisis of Feudalism: An Environmental History." *Organization and Environment* 15 (2002): 301–22.

Morris, Colin. *The Discovery of the Individual, 1050–1200.* Toronto: University of Toronto Press, 1972.

Morton, Timothy. "Coexistence and Coexistents: Ecology without a World." In *Ecocritical Theory: New European Approaches,* edited by Axel Goodbody and Kate Rigby, 168–80. Charlottesville: University of Virginia Press, 2011.

———. *Dark Ecology: For a Logic of Future Coexistence.* New York: Columbia University Press, 2016.

———. *The Ecological Thought.* Cambridge, MA: Harvard University Press, 2010.

———. *Ecology without Nature: Rethinking Environmental Aesthetics.* Cambridge, MA: Harvard University Press, 2007.

———. *Hyperobjects: Philosophy and Ecology after the End of the World.* Minneapolis: University of Minnesota Press, 2013.

Motz, Lotte. "The Cosmic Ash and Other Trees of Germanic Myth." *Arv* 1991, 127–41.

————. *The Wise One of the Mountain: Form, Function, and Significance of the Subter-ranean Smith.* Göppingen: Kümmerle, 1983.

Müllenhoff, Karl. *Deutsche Altertumskunde.* 5 volumes. Berlin: Weidmann, 1891.

Murphy, Patrick D. *Literature, Nature, and Other: Ecofeminist Critiques.* Albany: State University of New York Press, 1995.

Nardizzi, Vin. "Medieval Ecocriticism." *Postmedieval* 4 (2013): 112–23.

Nordvig, A. Mathias Valentin. "Of Fire and Water: The Old Norse Mythical Worldview in an Eco-Mythological Perspective." PhD dissertation, Aarhus University, 2013.

Olsen, Jonathan. *Nature and Nationalism: Right-Wing Ecology and the Politics of Iden-tity in Contemporary Germany.* New York: St. Martin's, 1999.

Oppenheimer, Clive, et al. "The Eldgjá Eruption: Timing, Long-Range Impacts and Influence on the Christianisation of Iceland." *Climatic Change* 147 (2018): 369–81.

Oppermann, Serpil. "Theorizing Ecocriticism: Toward a Postmodern Ecocritical Prac-tice." *Interdisciplinary Studies in Literature and Environment* 13 (2006): 103–28.

Orri Vésteinsson, Thomas H. McGovern, and Christian Keller. "Enduring Impacts: Social and Environmental Aspects of Viking Age Settlement in Iceland and Green-land." *Archaeologia Islandica* 2 (2002): 98–136.

Overing, Gillian R., and Marijane Osborn. *Landscape of Desire: Partial Stories of the Medieval Scandinavian World.* Minneapolis: University of Minnesota Press, 1994.

Oslund, Karen. *Iceland Imagined: Nature, Culture, and Storytelling in the North Atlan-tic.* Seattle: University of Washington Press, 2011.

————. "Imagining Iceland: Narratives of Nature and History in the North Atlantic." *British Journal for the History of Science* 35 (2002): 313–34.

The Oxford Dictionary of the Christian Church. Edited by F. L. Cross. 3rd edition revised. Edited by E. A. Livingstone. Oxford: Oxford University Press, 2005.

Parham, John. "Editorial." *Green Letters* 11 (2009): 4–8.

Pàroli, Theresa. "How Many Are the Unipeds' Feet? Their Tracks in Texts and Sources." In *Analecta Septentrionalia,* edited by Wilhelm Heizmann, Klauz Böldl, and Hein-rich Beck, 281–327. Berlin: De Gruyter, 2009.

Perron, Anthony. "The Face of the 'Pagan': Portraits of Religious Deviance on the Medieval Periphery." *Journal of the Historical Society* 9 (2009): 467–92.

Pétur Pétursson. "Manifest and Latent Biblical Themes in *Vǫluspá.*" In *The Nordic Apocalypse,* edited by Gunnell and Lassen, 185–204.

Phelpstead, Carl. "Beyond Ecocriticism: A Cosmocritical Reading of Ælfwine's Prayerbook." Forthcoming in *Review of English Studies.* https://doi.org/10.1093/res /hgy037.

————. "Ecocriticism and *Eyrbyggja saga.*" *Leeds Studies in English* 45 (2014): 1–18.

Plumwood, Val. *Feminism and the Mastery of Nature.* New York: Routledge, 1993.

Poland, Therese M., and Deborah G. McCullough. "Emerald Ash Borer: Invasion of the Urban Forest and the Threat to North America's Ash Resource." *Journal of For-estry* 104 (2006): 118–24.

Price, Neil. "Dying and the Dead: Viking Age Mortuary Behaviour." In *The Viking World,* edited by Stefan Brink and Neil Price, 257–73. Abingdon: Routledge, 2008.

Primavesi, Anne. *Sacred Gaia: Holistic Theology and Earth System Science.* London: Routledge, 2000.

Rigby, Kate. *Dancing with Disaster: Environmental Histories, Narratives, and Ethics for Perilous Times.* Charlottesville: University of Virginia Press, 2015.

Riisøy, Anne Irene. "Outlawry: From Western Norway to England." In *New Approaches to Early Law in Scandinavia,* edited by Stefan Brink and Lisa Collinson, 101–29. Turnhout: Brepols, 2014.

Ritchey, Sara. "Rethinking the Twelfth-Century Discovery of Nature." *Journal of Medieval and Early Modern Studies* 39 (2009): 226–55.

Roach, Catherine. "Loving Your Mother: On the Woman-Nature Relation." *Hypatia* 6 (1991): 46–59.

Rooth, Anna Birgitta. *Loki in Scandinavian Mythology.* Lund: Gleerup, 1961.

Rudd, Gillian. *Greenery: Ecocritical Readings of Late Medieval English Literature.* Manchester: University of Manchester Press, 2007.

Ruddiman, William F. "The Anthropocene." *Annual Review of Earth Planet Sciences* 41 (2013): 45–68.

———. "The Atmospheric Greenhouse Era Began Thousands of Years Ago." *Climate Change* 61 (2003): 261–93.

Rudiak-Gould, Peter. "The Social Life of Blame in the Anthropocene." *Environment and Society* 6 (2015): 48–65.

The Sagas of Icelanders: A Selection. Edited by Örnólfur Þorsson. New York: Viking, 2000.

Salehyan, Idean. "Climate Change and Conflict: Making Sense of Disparate Findings." *Political Geography* 43 (2014): 1–5.

———. "From Climate Change to Conflict? No Consensus Yet." *Journal of Peace Research* 45 (2008): 315–26.

Samplonius, Kees. "The Background and Scope of *Vǫluspá.*" In *The Nordic Apocalypse,* edited by Gunnell and Lassen, 113–45.

Sayers, William. "Karlsefni's *húsasnotra:* The Divestment of Vinland." *Scandinavian Studies* 75 (2003): 341–50.

Schatz, J. L. "The Importance of Apocalypse: The Value of End-of-the-World Politics While Advancing Ecocriticism." *Journal of Ecocriticism* 4 (2012): 20–33.

Schjødt, Jens Peter. "Horizontale und vertikale Achsen in der vorchristlichen skandinavischen Kosmologie." In *Old Norse and Finnish Religions and Cultic Place-Names,* edited by Tore Ahlbäck, 35–57. Stockholm: Almqvist and Wiksell, 1990.

———. "Kosmologimodeller og mytekredse." In *Ordning mot kaos,* edited by Anders Andrén, Kristina Jennbert, and Catharina Raudvere, 123–33. Lund: Nordic Academic Press, 2004.

Schneider, Stephen H. "A Goddess of Earth or the Imagination of a Man?" *Science* 291 (2001): 1906–7.

Schneiderman, Jill S. "Naming the Anthropocene." *philoSOPHIA* 5 (2015): 179–201.

Schnurbein, Stefanie von. "Tales of Reconstruction: Intertwining Germanic Neopaganism and Old Norse Scholarship." *Critical Research on Religion* 3 (2015): 148–67.

Schulz, Katja. *Riesen: Von Wissenshütern und Wildnisbewohnern in Edda und Saga.* Heidelberg: Winter, 2004.

Scott, Heidi. "Apocalypse Narrative, Chaotic System: Gilbert White's *Natural History of Selborne* and Modern Ecology." *Romanticism and Victorianism on the Net* 56 (2009). http://id.erudit.org/iderudit/1001095ar.

Scranton, Roy. *Learning to Die in the Anthropocene: Reflections on the End of a Civilization*. San Francisco: City Lights, 2015.

See, Klaus von. *Ideologie und Philologie: Aufsätze zur Kultur- und Wissenschaftsgeschichte*. Heidelberg: Winter, 2006.

———. "Snorri Sturluson and Norse Cultural Ideology." *Saga-Book* 25 (2001): 366–93.

See, Klaus von, and Julia Zernack. *Germanistik und Politik in der Zeit des Nationalsozialismus: Zwei Fallstudien: Hermann Schneider und Gustav Neckel*. Heidelberg: Winter, 2004.

Sharp, Hasana. "Endangered Life: Feminist Posthumanism in the Anthropocene?" In *Feminist Philosophies of Life*, edited by Hasana Sharp and Chloë Taylor, 272–82. Montreal: McGill-Queen's University Press, 2016.

Short, Ian, and Brian Merrilees, eds. *Le voyage de saint Brendan*. Paris: Champion, 2006.

Siewers, Alfred K. *Strange Beauty: Ecocritical Approaches to Early Medieval Landscape*. New York: Palgrave, 2009.

Sigurður Gylfi Magnússon. *Wasteland with Words: A Social History of Iceland*. London: Reaktion, 2010.

Sigurður Þórarinsson. *Hekla—a Notorious Volcano*. Translated by Johann Hannesson and Pétur Karlsson. Reykjavik: Almenna bókafélagið, 1970.

———. "Tephra and Tephrachronology: A Historical Review with Special Reference to Iceland." In *Tephra Studies: Proceedings of the NATO Advanced Study Institute "Tephra Studies as a Tool in Quaternary Research," held in Laugarvatn and Reykjavík, Iceland, June 18–29, 1980*, edited by S. Self and R. S. J. Sparks, 1–12. Dordrecht: Reidel, 1981.

Simek, Rudolf. *Dictionary of Northern Mythology*. Translated by Angela Hall. Cambridge: Brewer, 1993.

Smith, Kevin. "*Landnám:* The Settlement of Iceland in Archaeological and Historical Perspective." *World Archaeology* 26 (1995): 319–47.

Snook, Jennifer. "Reconsidering Heathenry: The Construction of an Ethnic Folkway as Religio-Ethnic Identity." *Nova Religio: The Journal of Alternative and Emergent Religions* 13 (2013): 52–76.

Snorri Sturluson. *Edda*. Translated by Anthony Faulkes. London: Dent, 1987.

———. *Edda. Prologue and Gylfaginning*. Edited by Anthony Faulkes. 2nd edition. London: Viking Society for Northern Research, 2005.

———. "Háttatal." Translated and edited by Kari Ellen Gade. In *Poetry from Treatises on Poetics*, edited by Gade and Marold, 2:1094–1212.

———. *Heimskringla*. Translated by Alison Finlay and Anthony Faulkes. 3 volumes. London: Viking Society for Northern Research, 2011–14.

Solheim, H., et al. "Yggdrasils helsetilstand—Askeskuddsjuke er på frammarsj." *Skogeiren* 96 (2011): 34–36.

Soper, Kate. *What Is Nature? Culture, Politics and the Non-Human*. Oxford: Blackwell, 1995.

Stanbury, Sarah. "Ecochaucer: Green Ethics and Medieval Nature." *Chaucer Review* 39 (2004): 1–16.

Stearney, Lynn M. "Feminism, Ecofeminism, and the Maternal Archetype: Motherhood as a Feminine Universal." *Communication Quarterly* 42 (1994): 145–59.

Steffen, Will, Paul J. Crutzen, and John R. McNeill. "The Anthropocene: Are Humans Now Overwhelming the Great Forces of Nature?" *Ambio* 36 (2007): 614–21.

Steffen, Will, et al. "The Trajectory of the Anthropocene: The Great Acceleration." *Anthropocene Review* 2 (2015): 81–98.

Steinsland, Gro. *Det hellige bryllup og norrøn kongeideologi: En analyse av hierogamimyten i Skírnismál, Ynglingatal, Háleygjatal og Hyndluljóð.* Oslo: Solum, 1991.

———. "Myte og ideologi: Bryllupsmyten i eddadiktning og hos Snorri—om det mytologiske grunnlaget for norrøn kongeideologi." In *Snorrastefna,* edited by Úlfar Bragason, 226–40. Reykjavik: Stofnun Sigurðar Nordals, 1992.

———. "Treet i *Vǫluspá.*" *Arkiv för nordisk filologi* 94 (1979): 120–50.

———. "*Vǫluspá* and the Sibylline Oracles with a Focus on the 'Myth of the Future.'" In *The Nordic Apocalypse,* edited by Gunnell and Lassen, 147–60.

Stewart, Susan. *On Longing: Narratives of the Miniature, the Gigantic, the Souvenir, the Collection.* Durham: Duke University Press, 1993.

Stoll, Mark R. "Sinners in the Hands of an Ecologic Crisis: Lynn White's Environmental Jeremiad." In *Religion and Ecological Crisis,* edited by LeVasseur and Peterson, 47–60.

Storm, Gustav, ed. *Islandske annaler indtil 1578.* Christiania: Grøndahl, 1888.

Ström, Folke. "Hallfreðr Óttarsson." In *Medieval Scandinavia: An Encyclopedia,* edited by Pulsiano and Wolf, 263–64.

Sunstein, Cass R. "On the Divergent American Reactions to Terrorism and Climate Change." *Columbia Law Review* 107 (2007): 503–57.

Sverrir Jakobsson. "Centre and Periphery in Icelandic Medieval Discourse." In *'Á austrvega': Saga and East Scandinavia, Preprint Papers of the Fourteenth International Saga Conference, Uppsala, 9–15 August 2009,* edited by Agnete Ney, Henrik Williams, and Fredrik Charpentier Ljungqvist, 2:918–24. Gävle: Gävle University Press, 2009.

———. "Vínland and Wishful Thinking: Medieval and Modern Fantasies." *Canadian Journal of History* 47 (2012): 493–514.

Taggart, Declan. "All the Mountains Shake: Seismic and Volcanic Imagery in the Old Norse Literature of Þórr." *Scripta Islandica* 68 (2017): 99–122.

Teitelbaum, Benjamin R. *Lions of the North: Sounds of the New Nordic Radical Nationalism.* New York: Oxford University Press, 2017.

Timmermann, V., et al. "Ash Dieback: Pathogen Spread and Diurnal Patterns of Ascospore Dispersal, with Special Emphasis on Norway." *EPPO Bulletin* 41 (2011): 14–20.

Tolley, Clive. "What Is a World Tree, and Should We Expect to Find One Growing in Anglo-Saxon England?" In *Trees and Timber in the Anglo-Saxon World,* edited by Michael D. J. Bintley and Michael G. Shapland, 177–85. Oxford: Oxford University Press, 2013.

Tomlinson, Isobel. "The Discovery of Ash Dieback in the UK: The Making of a Focusing Event." *Environmental Politics* 25 (2016): 709–28.

Torfing, Lisbeth H. "Volcanoes as Cultural Artefacts in Iceland: Risk Perception, Metaphors and Categorisation in a Society with No 'Before.'" In *Past Vulnerability: Volcanic Eruptions and Human Vulnerability in Traditional Societies Past and Present,* edited by Felix Riede, 89–108. Aarhus: Aarhus University Press, 2015.

Trexler, Adam. *Anthropocene Fictions: The Novel in a Time of Climate Change.* Charlottesville: University of Virginia Press, 2015.

Tuan, Yi-Fu. "Discrepancies between Environmental Attitude and Behaviour: Examples from Europe and China." *Canadian Geographer* 12 (1968): 176–91.

Turville-Petre, E. O. G. *Scaldic Poetry.* Oxford: Clarendon, 1976.

Tyrrell, Toby. *On Gaia: A Critical Investigation of the Relationship between Life and Earth.* Princeton: Princeton University Press, 2013.

Van den Broek, R. *The Myth of the Phoenix: According to Classical and Early Christian Traditions.* Leiden: Brill, 1972.

Vésteinn Ólason. "*Vǫluspá* and Time." In *The Nordic Apocalypse,* edited by Gunnell and Lassen, 25–44.

Vikstrand, Per. "Ásgarðr, Miðgarðr, and Útgarðr: A Linguistic Approach to a Classic Problem." In *Old Norse Religion in Long-Term Perspectives,* edited by Andrén et al., 354–57.

Vries, Jan de. *The Problem of Loki.* Helsinki: Suomalainen Tiedeakatemia, 1933.

Wanner, Kevin J. *Snorri Sturluson and the Edda: The Conversion of Cultural Capital in Medieval Scandinavia.* Toronto: University of Toronto Press, 2008.

Weber, Gerd Wolfgang. "Of Trees and Men: Some Thoughts on Kennings and Metaphors—and on Ludvig Holberg's Arboresque Anthropology." In *Twenty-Eight Papers Presented to Hans Bekker-Nielsen on the Occasion of His Sixtieth Birthday, 28 April 1993,* edited by Hans Frede Nielsen and Erik Hansen, 419–46. Odense: Odense University Press, 1993.

Wellendorf, Jonas. "Homogeneity and Heterogeneity in Old Norse Cosmology." In *Old Norse Religion in Long-Term Perspective,* edited by Andrén et al., 50–53.

White, Gilbert. *The Natural History of Selborne.* Edited by Anne Secord. Oxford: Oxford University Press, 2013.

White, Hugh. *Nature, Sex, and Goodness in a Medieval Literary Tradition.* New York: Oxford University Press, 2000.

White, Lynn, Jr. "The Historical Roots of Our Ecologic Crisis." *Science* 155 (1967): 1203–7.

Williams, George C. "Gaia, Nature Worship and Biocentric Fallacies." *Quarterly Review of Biology* 67 (1992): 479–86.

Williamsen, E. A. "Boundaries of Difference in the Vínland Sagas." *Scandinavian Studies* 77 (2005): 451–78.

Winkler, Karen J. "Scholars Embark on Study of Literature about the Environment." *Chronicle of Higher Education,* 9 August 1996, A8–A9, A15

Wolf, Kirsten. "Amazons in Vínland." *JEGP* 95 (1996): 469–85.

Wood, Gillen D'Arcy. "Introduction: Eco-historicism." *Journal of Early Modern Cultural Studies* 8 (2008): 1–7.

Wyatt, Ian. "Landscape and Authorial Control in the Battle of Vigrafjǫrðr in *Eyrbyggja saga.*" *Leeds Studies in English* 35 (2004): 43–56.

———. "The Landscape of the Icelandic Sagas: Text, Place and National Identity." *Landscapes* 5 (2004): 55–73.

———. "Narrative Functions of Landscape in the Old Icelandic Family Sagas." In *Land, Sea, Home,* edited by John Hines, Alan Lane, and Mark Redknap, 272–82. Leeds: Maney, 2004.

Yates, Velvet. "The Titanic Origin of Humans: The Melian Nymphs and Zagreus." *Greek, Roman, and Byzantine Studies* 44 (2004): 183–98.

Žižek, Slavoj. *In Defense of Lost Causes*. London: Verso, 2008.

Zutter, Cynthia. "The Cultural Landscape of Iceland: A Millennium of Human Transformation and Environmental Change." PhD dissertation, University of Alberta, 1997.

Þorvaldur Þórðarson, and Stephen Self. "Atmospheric and Environmental Effects of the 1783–1784 Laki Eruption: A Review and Reassessment." *Journal of Geophysical Research: Atmospheres* 108 (2003): 4011.

Þorvaldur Þórðarson, and G. Larsen. "Volcanism in Iceland in Historical Time: Volcano Types, Eruption Styles and Eruptive History." *Journal of Geodynamics* 43 (2007): 118–52.

Þröstur Eysteinsson. "Noble Hardwoods in Icelandic Forestry." In *EUFORGEN Noble Hardwoods Network, Report of the Sixth (9–11 June 2002, Alter do Chão, Portugal) and Seventh Meetings (22–24 April 2004, Arezzo, Italy)*, edited by M. Bozzano et al., 17–20. Rome: International Plant Genetic Resources Institute, 2006.

———. *Forestry in a Treeless Land*. Egilsstaðir: Iceland Forest Service, 2009.

Index

By convention, Icelanders are referred to by—and alphabetized according to—their given names rather than their patro- or matronymics. This index follows this practice. Entries beginning with the character Þ are found at the end of the index, which also reflects Icelandic norms.

Anthropocene: Æsir as precursors of, 132, 133; Androcene, as new coinage for, 166, 169; apocalypticism of, 37; blame as founding premise of, 164–65; compared to Norse paganism, 172; compared to pathogen in its effect on Gaia (Earth), 72–73; as epoch of human intervention leading to apocalyptic damage to Earth, 69, 126–30, 150, 202n8; future possibilities for, 127, 162, 171, 202n13; as gendered phenomenon, 165–66; inevitability of, 170; kin-making, founded on principles of mutual belonging, 167–68; linking Ragnarǫk to our experience of, 158–66; new world as possible outcome of, 170; objection to use of term, 201n7; origin of, trying to determine time of, 160–61; pre-Anthropocene era as nonexistent, 127; sense of time and our place in relation to chronology of, 161–62; *verǫld* term equated with, 69, 72, 82; Yggdrasill's existence in comparison to, 179. *See also* modernity

anthropocentric worldview: detrimental to biosphere, 65; Earth and, 81–82; Nature/Society dualism in, 178; Norse paganism and, 172

apocalypse: of ash trees, 11–13; difficulty of contemporary humans to relate to, 37–38; as ecocritical trope, 37, 125; as end of "a world" triggering a transformation, 153; as inevitable effect of entropy, 164; pervasiveness in Scandinavian mythology, 37; postapocalyptic pastoral and, 154–58; temporal deference of, 17; twenty-first century view of, 124; volcanic eruption akin to, 3–4; as world ages, we hasten toward, 122–23, 125. *See also* Ragnarǫk

Ari Þorgilsson (Icelandic historian), 103–4, 201n60

Arnórr Þórðarson jarlaskáld (Icelandic poet), 188n12

Ásgarðr (realm of gods), 10, 58, 62, 64, 88, 194n10

ash, 8–14; clouds of ash, effect of, 16; distinguished from earth or dust, 1; mythologies of, 14–18; rising from ashes, import of, 2; as type of tree, 8–10; uses of, 1–2. *See also* common or European ash trees

Ashwell, Ian, 104

askr ("ash"), 9–10, 102, 183n31

Askr (first man), 9, 94–95, 97, 101, 183n28

Ásynjur (female Æsir), 74

atom bombs, 128, 166. *See also* nuclear weapons and technology

Auðhumla (cow, in creation myth), 52, 54, 189n19

Bacon, Francis, 31

Baldr (god), 145–47, 155, 157, 160, 162, 169, 206n17, 207n40

Bárðarbunga (volcano), 4, 8

Barraclough, Eleanor, 185n9

Bate, Jonathan, *Song of the Earth,* 185n8

Battles, Matthew, 91

Berger, James, 153

Berman, Tzeporah, 81

Bernard Silvestris, 33; *Cosmographia,* 32

Bintley, Michael, 91–92, 94–95, 101, 193, 196n41

biosphere, 72

birch trees, 184n32

Bjarni Herjólfsson, 108–9

Blanchot, Maurice, 144

Book of Common Prayer, 1, 2

Borlik, Todd, 116

Borovsky, Zoe, 139

boundaries, consequences of failure to maintain, 134–35, 139–41, 153, 160, 168–69, 175–76

Bragg, Lois, 138

Brendan, Saint, 5, 182n15

British Conservative Party, 9

Bronze age, 9

Buell, Lawrence, 35, 125

dualistic worldviews: as anti-ecological modes of thought, 70; Christian dualism of in-space and out-space, 62; contemporary systems of thought and, 37; Enlightenment's Cartesian revolution and, 26–27; in Gaia theory, 74; hyperseparation as endpoint of, 166–67, 178; of Judeo-Christian tradition, 27, 41, 83, 178; Miðgarðr's construction and, 58, 134–35; in modern Western culture, 172; Nature/Society dichotomy, 56–57, 75, 130, 136, 138, 142, 145, 147, 160, 166–67, 175–76, 178; in Old Norse pagan cosmology, 62, 83, 172; patriarchal cultures and, 21–22, 31, 42, 54; *Snorra Edda* compared to Western worldview, 56–57; between Us and the rest of the world, 30, 83. *See also* Others and otherness

dust, Adam made of and to return to, 1

dwarfs in Old Norse mythology, 64–65, 87, 135–40

Earth Mother. *See* Gaia; *Jǫrð*

Earth vs. world, 63; *heimr* ("home" concept), 64–66, 82, 126; *jǫrð* ("earth" concept), 70–81, 82; three conceptions and one worldview, 81–83; *verǫld* ("age of men" concept), 66–70, 82, 126–30, 152

Eastern religious traditions, 27

ecocriticism, 19–22; anachronism and, 38–39; apocalypse as ecocritical trope, 37, 125; as approach to Old Norse–Icelandic literary studies, 22–26; contemporary purpose of, 124, 178; definition of, 19; ecology as all-inclusive, 20; eco-nostalgia and, 173–74; historically oriented, purpose of studying, 21–22, 38–39; on human displacement from Nature, 69; medieval studies and, 171, 177, 185n8; nostalgia and, 106–7; *oikos* and, 64–65; Old Norse–Icelandic literary studies' potential contribution to,

26–38, 171; postapocalyptic pastoral and, 154; premodern ecology's setting up life in absence of Nature, 31–32; preoccupation with realist modes of literature, 35; Ragnarǫk events in ecocritical reading, 161; Renaissance studies and, 171

ecofeminism, 75, 80

ecomythology: Fimbulvetr and, 152; of Norse America, 107–14; principles of, 25

Egeler, Matthias, 194–95n13

Egill Skallagrímsson, 100–102, 194n10, 196n42

Egils saga, 100, 101, 104

Egypt, 3, 182n7

Eiríkr Þorvaldsson (Eiríkr the Red), 108

Eiríks saga rauða, 108, 111–14, 116–17, 119–20

Eldgjá (volcano), 4–5, 17

Eliade, Mircea, 37, 159

Elizabeth II (Queen), 103

elves, 35, 64

Embla (first woman), 9, 94–95, 97, 101, 183n28

emerald ash borer, 13, 184n41

end of the world. *See* apocalypse

England: ash dieback (fungus attacking ash trees) in, 10–12; ash trees associated with range of other organisms in, 90; conversion to Christianity in, 29; Iceland volcano's effect on, 3–4; Knútr (Cnut the Great) in, 78

Enlightenment, 19, 22, 26, 31, 166

environmental crisis and changes: degradation of Iceland by first settlers, 105–7; global, 20; how human cultures adapted to, 24. *See also* climate change and global warming

environmental humanities, field of, 20

Europe, 3, 5, 182n8; ash dieback in, 10–12, 184n41. *See also* Christianity

European ash. *See* common or European ash trees

extinction, 202n13

Eyjafjallajökull (volcano), 3, 4, 8
Eyrbyggja saga, 26, 36

Falk, Oren, 6
Faroes, 121
fate, 86–87, 89, 91, 100, 108, 123–24, 128, 138
Faulkes, Anthony, 52, 74, 97–98
feminist scholars, 75, 168
Fenrir (Fenrisúlfr, offspring of Loki), 142–44, 148, 152, 153, 163
feudalism, 26–27
Fimbulvetr (terrible winter), 149–52, 207n31
Finnbogadóttir, Vigdís, 103
Flateyjarbók Annals, 6
Flóki (Norwegian settler), 104–5, 109, 113
fold (ground), 70–71, 80
Frakes, Jerold, 119, 199–200n43
Frank, Roberta, 77, 78, 195n32
Fraxinus excelsior. See common or European ash trees
Freudian interpretation, 139
Freydís (daughter of Eiríkr the Red), 119
Freyja (goddess), 139–42, 165
Freyr (god of fertility, hearth, and home-field), 16, 137, 185n48
Frigg (goddess, wife of Óðinn and mother of Baldr), 145, 146–47, 165, 169, 207n40
Frost, Robert, 97
frost-giants, 50, 52–55, 74, 84, 88, 140

Gaia (deity), 33, 42–43, 75, 79–81
Gaia theory (Lovelock), 42, 72–74, 153, 192n19
Gardell, Mattias, 207n3
garðr, 64–66, 82
gender. *See* women and gender in Old Norse–Icelandic literature
Genesis: *1:1,* 49; *1:28–29,* 27, 41–42; *3:19,* 1; Gaia myth in juxtaposition to, 43; Old Norse creation myth in

parallel to, 48, 49, 50, 53, 61, 82–83, 191n42; *Snorra Edda* compared to, 47
geography, conceptions of, 67
Germanic pagan cultures, 15, 25, 92, 110–11, 183n30
Giant Builder myth, 140–41, 142
giants: entering into Miðgarðr ("middle-yard"), 66; figured as the Other in Norse mythology, 131, 134, 166; women giants, 75, 133–35, 165. *See also* frost-giants; Jǫtunheimar; Útgarðr; Ymir; *specific giant by name*
Gibson-Graham, J. K., 168
Ginnungagap (void that exists before creation of universe), 51–52, 55, 131
Gísla saga, 190n31
global warming. *See* climate change and global warming
Glotfelty, Cheryll, 19
God (Christian), 2, 27, 31, 34, 48
golden age: of Æsir, 123, 132–34, 155–56, 174; appropriation of for modern political ends, 177–78; Icelandic trope of, 105–6, 113, 115, 123; of Middle Ages, nostalgia for unhelpful in modern situation, 177; fantasy in Norse mythology of, 175
grapes. *See* wine and grapes
Gräslund, Bo, 151–52
Grattan, John, 182n10
Great Acceleration, 126–27, 143, 152
Greenland: earlier settlement and inhabitants of, 201n60; naming of, 2, 108, 113, 114; Norse settlement of, 107–9, 121, 201n62. *See also* Vínland
Green spirituality and mythology, 28, 172, 177
greenwashing, 108
Grímnismál (Eddic poem), 45, 50–51, 57, 61, 83, 88–93, 195n13
Grímsvötn (volcano), 6, 7
Grœnlendinga saga, 108–13, 116, 117–18, 120
Guðmundar saga byskups, 6–7
Guðmundr Arason (Icelandic bishop), 7

61; uninhabited at time of Norse discovery of, 121, 122; unique medieval polity in, 24, 26–27, 105, 171; volcanic eruptions, conditions related to, 2–8; as young landmass in geological terms, 23. *See also* migration; Old Norse–Icelandic literature
Icelandic Rune Poem, 183n30
imperialism, 19, 199n43
indigenous cultures, contemporary, 33, 34, 36, 79
Industrial Revolution, 22, 26, 126–28, 159, 166, 202n8
Irish literature of medieval period, 186n24
Íslendingabók (Ari Þorgilsson), 103–4, 201n60
Íslenginga sögur (sagas of Icelanders), 24, 35–37, 108

Jackson, Edgar, 104
Járnviðr (Iron-wood), 148
Johnston, Michael, 38
jǫrð (earth), 63, 70–81, 82
Jǫrð (female personification of Earth), 33, 122; equated with Gaia, 72–74; gender of, 75–76, 80; genealogy of, 75, 192n24; as giantess, 75; mother of Þórr, 74; subordinate status in Old Norse literature, 78–80; wife of Óðinn, 75, 76–77
Jǫrmungandr (Miðgarðr-serpent), 142–44, 163
Jórunn skáldmær (female skáld), 97
Jǫtunheimar (realms of giants), 64, 66, 131, 135
Judeo-Christian tradition: creation myth, 41, 47–49, 51, 61; dualistic worldview of, 27, 41, 83, 178; entry into northern Europe, 173; Old Norse myths outside of, 43, 171; parallel in Old Norse creation myth, 48, 49, 50, 53, 61, 82–83, 191n42

Karlsefni (from *Eiríks saga*), 112–14, 116, 118–21

Katla (volcano), 4, 17, 185n51
kennings in skaldic poetry, 96–99, 100, 196n33, 196n38
King, Ynestra, 75
kinship, founded on principles of mutual belonging, 167–68
Kipling, Rudyard, 11
Knútr (Cnut the Great, Danish and English ruler), 78
Kolodny, Annette, 118, 199n43, 201n61
Kompridis, Nikolas, 167
Konrad III (German emperor), 67
Konungs skuggsjá (*The King's Mirror*), 5–6
Kormákr Ǫgmundarson, 98
Krech, Shepard, 28, 200n47
Kress, Helga, 60
Kristni saga (vernacular history), 7–8
Kunz, Keneva, 199n43

Ladino, Jennifer, 173–74, 200n47
Læraðr (tree, probably Yggdrasill), 89–90, 194–95n13
Laki (volcano), 3–4, 182n7, 182n10
La Martiniere, Pierre Martin de, 6
Landnámabók (*The Book of Settlements*), 104–5, 109, 123
Larrington, Carolyne, 70, 71, 132, 191n10, 205n1, 206n11, 206n17
Latour, Bruno: on distributing agency, 168; on Gaia, 192n19; on hybridization, 136–38; on hyper-incommensurability, 166; on moderns' inability to conceive of their future, 156, 158; on Nature, 20, 31, 55; on partition between Nature and Society, 134, 146, 163, 168, 178; *We Have Never Been Modern*, 130–32
Leifr Eiríksson (Leifr the Lucky), 109, 112, 113, 116
Lévi-Strauss, Claude, 58
Líf and Lífþrasir (humans who repopulate world after Ragnarǫk), 156
Lincoln, Bruce, 42
Lindow, John, 137

Loðurr (god), 94

Lokasenna (Eddic poem), 74

Loki, 141–47; accommodation by Æsir as better method of dealing with, 169; gender-shifting ability of, 135, 142, 146, 163, 166, 207n40; hybridity of, as affront to gods, 163–66; identity with other trickster figures from world mythology, 205n61; killing Baldr (god), 145–47, 160; problematic nature of boundary crossing by, 168–69; Ragnarǫk and, 144–45, 153, 160; start of Ragnarǫk and, 160, 164

Lönnroth, Lars, 133

loss and nostalgia, feelings of, 15, 21, 31, 99–102, 106–7, 128, 173–77, 202

Lovelock, James, 42, 72–74, 80, 153, 192n19; *The Revenge of Gaia,* 73

Lucifer, 6

Lutherans, 6

Magnús Stefánsson, 197n18

Malm, Andreas, 165

Manhattan Project, 128

maple trees, 112, 114, 199n32

Markland (Forest-land), 109

McGillivray, Andrew, 196n36

McMurry, Andrew, 161

McTurk, Rory, 188n9

Meadowland, 108, 110. *See also* Newfoundland; Vínland

medieval studies: anachronism and, 38–39; contribution to ecocritical studies from, 22, 171; ecocriticism and, 171, 177, 185n8; "white" culture of far-right groups, needs to reject, 173

Merchant, Carolyn, 31

Meylan, Nicolas, 34–35

Mickey, Sam, 31

Middle Ages: benefits of study of, 177–78; ecocriticism in light of, 177, 185n8; feudalism of, 26–27; geographic conceptions of, 67; less dualistic worldview than in Western modernity, 26, 35; Nature and, 32;

nostalgia for golden age of, unhelpful in modern situation, 177

Miðgarðr ("middle-yard"): construction of, 56–62, 64, 163, 190n40; failure to keep boundary between giants and gods, 134–35; giants entering into, 66; as home-making world-building, 65; as symbol of hyperseparation, 167; in schematization of universe, 88, 194n10; serpent of (Jǫrmungandr), 142–44; as world in *Vǫluspá,* 64

migration: to Greenland, 108; to Iceland, 13, 23, 100, 103–7

Mikhail, Alan, 182n7

Miller, J. Hillis, "Anachronistic Reading," 39–40

Mímir (giant), 89, 152, 205n10

modernity: borders between humans and the world and, 131; change in goals of, 168; ecological disaster and, 21–22, 124–25, 126, 128, 129–30, 171; golden age of Aesir, analogy to, 133; inability of moderns to conceive of their future in a different way, 156, 176; nuclear weapons and toxic materials compared to gods' treatment of Loki's offspring, 143–44, 163; purification projects, failings of, 174. *See also* Anthropocene; climate change and global warming

Moore, Jason, 27

Morris, Colin, 186n35

Morton, Timothy: on animism, 34; on Anthropocene's correlation with apocalypse, 128, 129; on constant presence of anthropocentric colonization, 81–82; on ecological thought, 69–70; on "ecology without Nature," 36; on effects of living in the Anthropocene, 162; on end of world, 38, 144; on futural threats, 143–44; on Gaia theory, 73–74; on Nature as imaginary thing, 30–32; on nostalgia's dangers, 107; on tree in a nonhierarchical mesh, 87–88

Motz, Lotte, 10, 93, 138
Mueller, Alex, 38
Müllenhoff, Karl, 139
Muspell (Muspellsheimr, in creation of universe), 51, 53–54, 64
mythology: agency and identity of natural world in, 29–30; apocalypticism of, 18, 122–23; both local and universal, 25; deanthropocentrizing tendency of, 29; definition of, 42; ecological concerns in, 17–18; evolving role of, 15, 42–43; fall from state of grace or divinity in, 124; function of, 159; in Norse culture, 15, 37–38; pre-Christian mythology, preservation of, 26–30, 43, 83. *See also* Norse creation myths; Old Norse–Icelandic literature

Nardizzi, Vin, 22, 171
Natura (personification in Latin poetry), 32–33, 187n37
Nature: Christian model of stewardship over, 158; Christian use of *náttúra* in Old Norse–Icelandic literature, 33; collapse of humanity's past way of dealing with, 20, 31; demise of, viewed as emancipatory event, 31; in dualistic worldviews, 21–22, 35, 41; as dwelling place in anthropocentric thinking, 65; as female, 75; Genesis as influence for humanity's disharmony with, 27; golden age of, 177; human domination of, 21; Latour on, 20, 31; Morton on, 30–32; in mythology, 29–30, 60; Nature/Society dichotomy, 56–57, 75, 130, 136, 138, 142, 145, 147, 160, 166–67, 175–76, 178; not a concept in Norse pagan culture, 30–33, 35, 63–83; triumphant in postapocalyptic pastoral world, 154; in twelfth-century thinking, 32
naturecultures, 15, 24, 28, 38, 89, 91, 100, 102, 117, 121–22, 124, 167; decline and collapse in Old Norse

pagan cosmos, 174–75; modernity's failure similar to Æsir's failure to avoid Ragnarǫk, 124; nostalgia of Æsir related to and inability to maintain, 175–77

Navigatio sancti Brendani, 5
Nazis and Third Reich, influence of Old Norse literature on, 173, 208n5
Newfoundland, 108, 114–15, 199n32. *See also* Meadowland
Níðhǫggr (dragon), 148, 157–58, 170, 207n31
Niflheimr (first step in creation of universe), 51, 53–54, 64
Noah and the great flood, 47, 74
Nordvig, Mathias Valentin, 25
Norns (demi-goddesses), 87, 89, 138, 165–66, 194n7
Norse creation myths, 43–56; anthropocentric nature of, 56, 61; brutality of, 55–56; dualism in, 70; fall from state of grace or divinity in, 124; parallel to Judeo-Christian tradition, 48, 49, 50, 53, 61, 82–83, 191n42; reproduction of earliest beings, 54; three creation myths told in *Gylfaginning*, 49–56. *See also* Snorra Edda
Norse heritage of Icelanders, 14–15, 25, 59
Norse pagan culture: animistic character of, 33–35; ash tree's significance in, 9; Christianity's influence on Norse myths depicting, 173; cremation and, 181n6; dependence on connection between Nature and social order, 163; Earth-centered religion of, 172; finite nature of, 158; golden age of, 123, 132–34, 155–56, 174; in Iceland, 14, 25; Nature not concept of, 30–33; Nature/Society dualism in, 178; outside of Greco-Roman sphere, 28; polytheistic religious system of, 33; settled in similar latitudes to Eurasian communities, 93; *Snora Edda*'s explication of, 45–46. *See also* mythology

North Atlantic and North America: ecomyths about, 121–22; emerald ash borer attacking ash trees in, 13, 184n41; environmental memory of, 114; failure of Norse colonies in, 115–21; golden age trope of, 113, 123, 174; Icelandic volcano's effect on, 3, 5; naming of lands in, 122; Norse discovery and settlement of, 107, 109–14; settlement narratives as literary colonization of, 114–15. *See also* Greenland; Newfoundland; Vínland

Norway: conversion to Christianity in, 44; ecological similarity to Iceland, 14, 59; Iceland as colony of, 25–26, 106; Knútr (Cnut the Great) in, 78; migration to Iceland from, 23, 103–7; Surtr (fire-giant) known in pagan culture of, 185n47; trees in, 8, 84–85. *See also* Norse heritage of Icelanders

nostalgia. *See* loss and nostalgia, feelings of

Nótt (Night), 75

nuclear weapons and technology, 128, 143–44, 163, 166

oak trees, 9

Óðinn (god): Alfǫðr (All-father) and, 2, 48, 52, 75, 76, 188n12; consulting vǫlva, 68, 154, 156–57, 162, 191n10; dualism of worldview created by, 61; genealogy of, 52, 189n25; in *Grímnismál,* 45; in *Gylfaginning,* 46–48; horse of (Sleipnir), 142; Jǫrð (female-gendered personification of Earth) as wife of, 74–77; killing of giant Mímir by, 152, 205n10; killing of giant Ymir by, 54–56; mankind's creation by, 94–95, 101; as master of disguise, 188n12; as narrator in *Grímnismál,* 57; as personification of world-soul in Platonic sense, 76; revenging Baldr's death, 145; in *Sonatorrek,* 101; spear of (Gungnir), 137;

stealing mead of poetry from dwarfs, 137; in *Vafþrúðnismál,* 45

oikos, 9, 20, 23, 55–57, 61, 81, 149; heimr as, 64–65; Ragnarǫk as collapse of, 126, 149; Vínland as mythologized oikos, 114–15; of Yggdrasill, 88–89, 91

Óláfr skǫtkonung of Sweden (king), 78

Old Norse–Icelandic literature: Christian use of *náttúra* in, 33; derivation from religious culture of mainland Scandinavia, 25; ecocritical approach to, 22–26; Jǫrð (female-gendered personification of Earth) not speaking figure in, 76; large and varied medieval vernacular literary corpus of, 24; as legacy of ecological imagining, 14, 15; pre-Christian mythology preserved by, 26–30, 43, 83, 171; sagas as precursor of European literary realism, 24, 35–37; ways of interacting with natural world different from ways Christianity introduced, 28; women and gender in, 75–77; "world" concept in, 63

Oppenheimer, Clive, 17

Oppermann, Serpil, 19, 35

Óræfajökull (volcano), 6

Orri Vésteinsson, 106

Oslund, Karen, 103

Others and otherness, 135, 140, 142, 146, 157, 175–78; aboriginal inhabitants of Vínland as, 116–21, 122, 138, 199–200n43, 200n47; gendered Otherness, 80; giants as Other in Norse mythology, 131, 134, 160, 163; homes assigned to, 66; of Icelanders, 13; in-space vs. outside ("the wild"), 59–60, 61, 190n38; Loki or wolf Fenrir treated by Æsir as, 153; modern view of Other as requiring separation, compared to Norse view, 172; nonhuman Other, 68; our homebuilding impinging upon worlds of Others, 69; rejection of concept of Other as way to prevent Ragnarǫk,

167; separatist fantasy of golden age of Norse mythology and, 175; settlement of Iceland lacking presence of Other, 122; Us/Other as fundamental divide, 22, 26, 30, 167; volcanoes belonging to otherworld, 14; women as Other in Norse mythology, 139, 165–66

pagan culture: compared to Christianity, 92; as delusion, 46; integrated natu-recultural worldview of, 27–28, 91. *See also* Norse pagan culture; *Snorra Edda*
pan-Scandinavian traditions, 14
Parham, John, 39
patriarchal society: dualistic worldviews and, 21, 31, 42, 54, 72, 75; end of Anthropocene as rejection of, 166; return after apocalypse, 81, 170
Phelpstead, Carl, 22, 26, 36, 185n9, 187n50
phoenix, story of, 2, 181n4
Physiologus, 181n4
pine trees, 183n31
Plato, *Timaeus,* 75–76, 80
Plumwood, Val, 21, 75–76, 80, 166
Poetic Edda: arbor-reality in, 87–94; Christianity reflected in, 173; Hel (goddess) in, 194n9; *Jǫrð* (female-gendered personification of Earth) in, 74; as most important repository of medieval mythological narratives, 29, 44; narrators of, 55; oral tradition and, 44, 46, 95; pagan cosmology in, 157; skaldic poetry compared to, 95; Yggdrasill in, 10, 152. See also *Vǫluspá*
poetry in Norse culture, 15
poststructuralism, 23
Price, Neil, 151–52
Primavesi, Anne, 27–28
Prose Edda. See Snorra Edda
purification, 130–31, 135, 142, 143, 145, 153, 163, 167, 175

queerness, 54, 56

Ragnarǫk, 149–53; anachronistic discussion of, 39–40; Anthropocene experience linked to, 158–66; apocalypse of, 10, 37–38, 60, 71, 80–81, 123, 153, 175; breakdown of familial and communal bonds as part of, 150; as cultural catastrophe, 159; demise of Æsir (gods) at, 89, 128, 129, 153; as ecological catastrophe, 129, 149, 159; evil persisting in world after, 157; explained in human terms, 37, 159–60; failure of gods to learn from, 175–76, 178; failure of gods to maintain Miðgarðr and, 60, 70, 74; Fimbulvetr (terrible winter) as start of, 150; as gendered phenomenon, 165–66; Great Acceleration and end of the end, 61, 152–58; *jǫrð* (earth) sinking at, 72; Loki and, 144–45, 153, 160; Loki's offspring's role in, 143–47; modernity's ecological disaster likened to, 21–22, 124–25, 126, 128, 129–30, 149; naturecultural decline as narrative of, 174–75; postapocalyptic pastoral and birth of new world, 129, 154–58; prevention of, 166–70; resulting from separatist thinking, 178; return of Æsir after, 81, 154–57, 170; starting point of, 160–61, 165; unavoidability of, 124, 129–30, 145, 162, 164, 175; verǫld ("world" concept) and, 69, 152; in *Vǫluspá,* 68, 129; Yggdrasill and, 85, 89, 93–94, 152–53
realist modes of literature, 24, 35
reforestation of Iceland, 103
Rigby, Kate, 153
Ritchey, Sara, 32
Romanticism, 185n8
Rudd, Gillian, 105, 107, 185n8
Ruddiman, William, 126–27
Rudiak-Gould, Peter, 164–65

sacred marriage, ritual of, 78, 193n35
sagas. *See* Old Norse–Icelandic literature; *specific sagas by title*

Samplonius, Kees, 184–85n47
Sayers, William, 199n33
Schatz, J. L., 37, 125
scientific revolution, 26, 31, 34
Scranton, Roy, 165, 176
seismic activity, 25. *See also* volcanoes
and volcanic activity
separatism. *See* dualistic worldviews;
Others and otherness
Siewers, Alfred, 185n8, 186n24
Sigurður Gylfi Magnússon, 106
Sigurður Þórarinsson, 6, 185n51
skaldic poetry, 95–99, 195n32. *See also*
kennings in skaldic poetry
Skalla-Grímr (father of Egill), 100, 104
skrælingar (aboriginal inhabitants
of Vínland), 116–21, 122, 138,
199–200n43
Sleipnir (Óðinn's horse), 142
Snorra Edda (Snorri Sturluson): Christianity reflected in, 47, 61–62, 173; compared to *Vafþrúðnismál*, 156; creation
of universe explained in, 45, 50–56,
61; events leading up to Ragnarǫk
in, 143, 145; Fimbulvetr (terrible
winter) in, 149–51; Giant Builder
myth in, 140–41, 142; goddess's role
compared to male gods' role in, 169;
Hallfreðr Óttarsson in, 77, 99; *Háttatal*
(conclusion), 96; Loki in, 142–43,
145; mankind's creation explained
in, 94; Miðgarðr's construction in,
57–58; as most important repository
of medieval mythological narratives,
29, 45; Nature/Society dualism in,
56–57; oral tradition and, 46; paganism's origins and demise explained in,
46, 48–49, 67; prologue, 46–48, 67,
188n7; Ragnarǫk in, 151–52, 207n40;
reproduction of earliest beings
in, 54; skaldic poetry and, 95–99;
Skáldskaparmál (Language of poetry),
95–96, 97–99; *verǫld,* use of term, 67;
Yggdrasill collocated with *askr* in, 10.
See also *Gylfaginning; Vǫluspá*

Snorri Sturluson, 2, 45–50, 61–62, 64,
74–75, 78–79, 83, 181n6, 191n3,
193n38; Yggdrasill (world tree) and,
84. See also *Snorra Edda*
soil erosion, 13, 106, 127
Sonatorrek (poem by Egill Skallagríms-
son), 100–102, 194n10, 196n42
Stanbury, Sarah, "Ecochaucer," 185n8
Stearney, Lynn, 80
Stevens, Wallace, 39–40; "The Man on
the Dump," 40
Stewart, Susan, 106
Stoermer, Eugene, 201n5
Ström, Folke, 78
structuralism, 23
sulfur dioxide, 3, 182n13
Sunstein, Cass, 164
supernatural aspects of volcanic
effects, 4
Surtr (fire-giant), 16, 185nn47–48
Surtsey (island), 16, 182n15
Svartálfaheimr (realm of elves), 64
Sweden, 28–29, 78, 85, 151

Taggart, Declan, 25
technocracy, 42
Titans, 74
Tolkien, J. R. R., 57
tools and weapons, 119–20
Torfing, Lisbeth, 184n43
tree of life, 10, 90–91
trees: absent from Icelandic landscape
but symbolic in Icelandic cultural life,
14, 84; arbor-reality in *Poetic Edda,*
87–94; as ecological symbols, 85;
interchangeable with people in skaldic
poetry, 96–97, 102, 196n36, 196n41;
interrelationship and empathy of people with, 85, 92–94, 95; lamenting loss
of, 99–102; *mǫsurr* (perhaps maple
trees) in Vínland, 112, 114, 199n32; in
Norway, 8, 84–85; original settlement
of Iceland and, 103–7; reforestation
of Iceland, 103; role in biome of, 89;
on same ontological plane as humans,

Watt, James, 128
Weber, Gerd Wolfgang, 196n38
Weinstein, Jami, 166
Wellendorf, Jonas, 190–91n41
White, Gilbert, 3–4
White, Hugh, 32
White, Lynn, Jr., 27–28, 29, 41, 61, 83, 186n16
"White-Christ" of Norse Christian parlance, 146, 204–5n59
Whitehead, Alfred North, 20
white separatist movements, 173–74, 207n3
William of Conches, 33
willow trees, 184n32
wine and grapes, 110–11, 112, 114, 197n19
women and gender in Old Norse–Icelandic literature, 75–82, 87, 122; anticipating later colonial discourse, 201n61; gender boundaries, 135, 139; gender equality as possible way to avoid Ragnarǫk, 169; goddesses, 135; Líf (only female human to survive Ragnarǫk), 156; Loki's ability to gender-shift, 135, 142, 146, 163, 166, 207n40; women giants, 75, 133–35. *See also* Freyja
Wood, Gillen D'Arcy, 19, 24
world conception. *See* Earth vs. world
Wulfstan of York, 125
Wyatt, Ian, 185n9

yew trees, 90, 183n30
Yggdrasill (world tree): age and eternal life of, 10, 86–87, 101, 179, 183n30; arbor-reality in *Poetic Edda* and, 87–91; as ash tree, 183n30; creatures in symbiotic relationship with, 89–90; in *Grímnismál,* 88–93; interrelationship and empathy with human life, 85, 92–94, 95, 172; Norse significance becoming part of Icelandic culture, 14; in pagan Norse mythology, 9–10, 71, 84–85, 87, 93, 172; Ragnarǫk and, 85, 89, 93–94, 152–53; resisting all teleologies and myths, 179; symbolism of, 85–87, 93, 179, 196n36; as yew tree, 183n30, 195n13
Ymir (primeval giant and source of all life in the cosmos), 50–52, 76, 122; Brimir and Bláinn as alternative names for, 136; as forebear of giants, 66; gods drowning giants in Ymir's blood, 74; killed and dismembered by Óðinn and his brothers, 54–57, 61, 109, 132
Younger Edda. See Snorra Edda

Zeus, 9
Žižek, Slavoj, 31, 32

Þingvellir (site of parliament and law court), 84
Þingvellir national park, 103
Þórólfr "butter," 105
Þórr (god): hammer of (Mjǫllnir), 137; *Jǫrð* as mother of, 74, 75; killing giant hired as mason by gods, 142; thunder associated with, 25; transgressing gender boundaries, 135
Þorvaldr Eiríksson, 117–18
Þrymskviða (Eddic poem), 74

Recent Books in the Series

Under the Sign of Nature: Explorations in Ecocriticism

Kate Rigby
Topographies of the Sacred: The Poetics of Place in European Romanticism

Alan Williamson
Westernness: A Meditation

John Elder
*Pilgrimage to Vallombrosa: From Vermont to Italy in the Footsteps
    of George Perkins Marsh*

Mary Ellen Bellanca
Daybooks of Discovery: Nature Diaries in Britain, 1770–1870

Rinda West
Out of the Shadow: Ecopsychology, Story, and Encounters with the Land

Bonnie Roos and Alex Hunt, editors
Postcolonial Green: Environmental Politics and World Narratives

Paula Willoquet-Maricondi, editor
Framing the World: Explorations in Ecocriticism and Film

Deborah Bird Rose
Wild Dog Dreaming: Love and Extinction

Axel Goodbody and Kate Rigby, editors
Ecocritical Theory: New European Approaches

Scott Hess
*William Wordsworth and the Ecology of Authorship: The Roots of Environmentalism
    in Nineteenth-Century Culture*

Dan Brayton
Shakespeare's Ocean: An Ecocritical Exploration

Jennifer K. Ladino
Reclaiming Nostalgia: Longing for Nature in American Literature

Byron Caminero-Santangelo
*Different Shades of Green: African Literature, Environmental Justice,
    and Political Ecology*

Kate Rigby
*Dancing with Disaster: Environmental Histories, Narratives,
    and Ethics for Perilous Times*

Adam Trexler
Anthropocene Fictions: The Novel in a Time of Climate Change

Eric Gidal
Ossianic Unconformities: Bardic Poetry in the Industrial Age

Jesse Oak Taylor
*The Sky of Our Manufacture: The London Fog in British Fiction
from Dickens to Woolf*

Michael P. Branch and Clinton Mohs, editors
"The Best Read Naturalist": Nature Writings of Ralph Waldo Emerson

Lynn Keller
Recomposing Ecopoetics: North American Poetry of the Self-Conscious Anthropocene

Serenella Iovino, Enrico Cesaretti, and Elena Past, editors
Italy and the Environmental Humanities: Landscapes, Natures, Ecologies

Christopher Abram
Evergreen Ash: Ecology and Catastrophe in Old Norse Myth and Literature

CPSIA information can be obtained
at www.ICGtesting.com
Printed in the USA
LVHW021715110119
603608LV00006B/94/P